George Adamson: Lord of the Lions

George Adamson: Lord of the Lions

Sandy Gall

GraftonBooks
A Division of HarperCollins*Publishers*

GraftonBooks
A Division of HarperCollins*Publishers*
77–85 Fulham Palace Road,
Hammersmith, London W6 8JB

Published by GraftonBooks 1991

10 9 8 7 6 5 4 3 2 1

A CIP catalogue record for this book
is available from the British Library

ISBN 0-246-13699-5

Phototypeset by Computape (Pickering) Ltd,
North Yorkshire
Printed in Great Britain by
Butler & Tanner Ltd, Frome

Grateful acknowledgement is made to Chatto & Windus
for permission to reprint an extract from *Forks and Hope*
by Elspeth Huxley

CONTENTS

'Who is Lord of this Land? … Who is Lord of this Land? … I AM! … I am! … I am! … I am! …'

> Korokoro saying, often repeated by George Adamson, who enjoyed its deft imitation of the lion's roar, the magnificent opening and the dying refrain

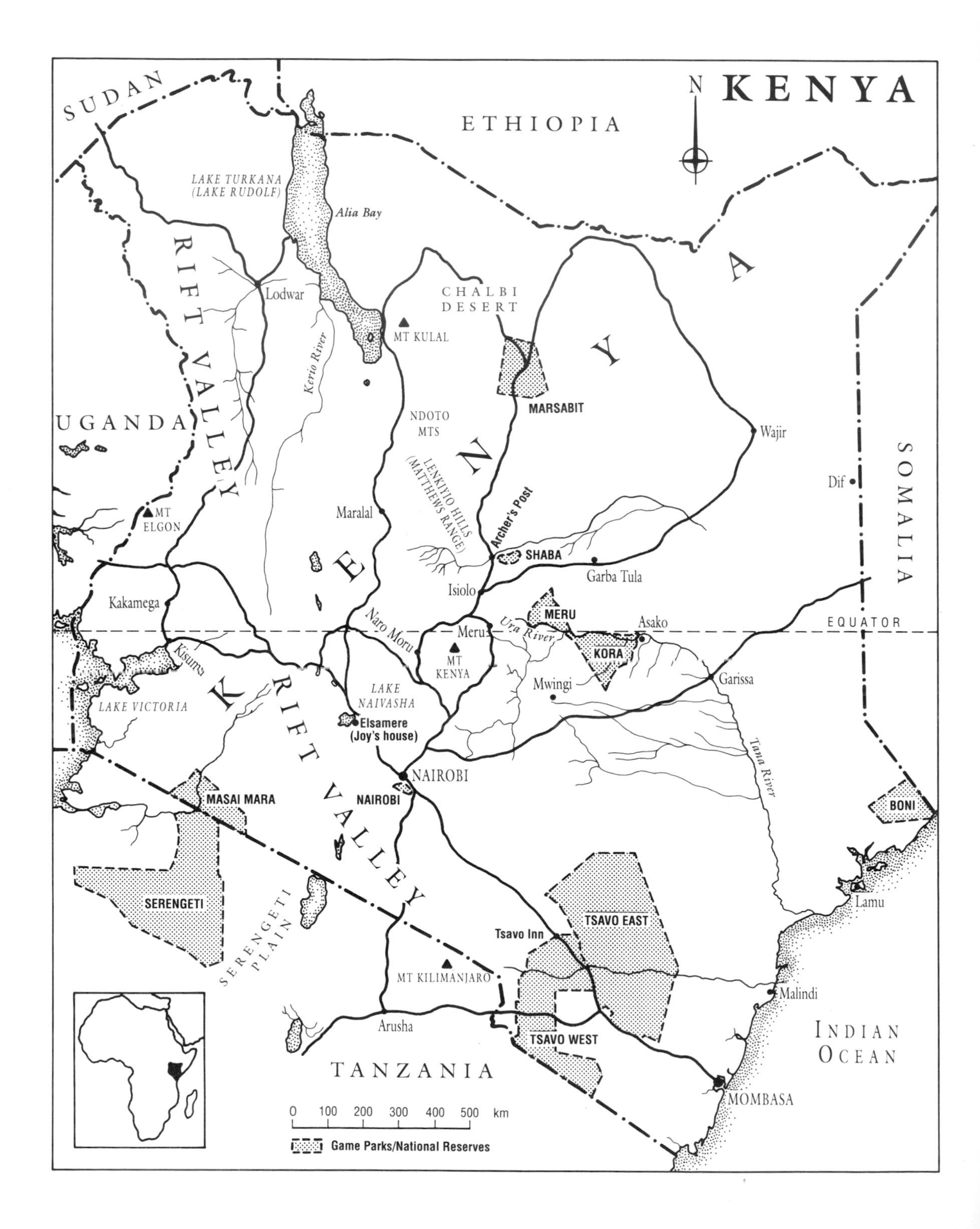
KENYA
N
SUDAN
ETHIOPIA
UGANDA
SOMALIA
TANZANIA
INDIAN OCEAN
LAKE TURKANA (LAKE RUDOLF)
Alia Bay
Lodwar
RIFT VALLEY
Kerio River
MT KULAL
CHALBI DESERT
MARSABIT
NDOTO MTS
LENKIYIO HILLS (MATTHEWS RANGE)
Archer's Post
Wajir
Dif
Maralal
MT ELGON
SHABA
Garba Tula
Isiolo
Kakamega
MERU
Naro Moru
Meru
Ura River
Asako
EQUATOR
MT KENYA
KORA
Kisumu
LAKE VICTORIA
LAKE NAIVASHA
Mwingi
Garissa
Elsamere (Joy's house)
Tana River
NAIROBI
MASAI MARA
BONI
SERENGETI
SERENGETI PLAIN
Lamu
Tsavo Inn
TSAVO EAST
MT KILIMANJARO
Malindi
Arusha
TSAVO WEST
MOMBASA
0 100 200 300 400 500 km
Game Parks/National Reserves

ACKNOWLEDGEMENTS

This book was never meant to be anything like a full-length biography of George Adamson. After all, he had written one account of his life, *Bwana Game*, and later, with help, expanded and added to it in *My Pride and Joy*. I enjoyed both and owe much to them, for which I am grateful to Collins. Add *Born Free* and Joy's other books and it could be argued that everything that needed to be said had already been said about both of them. So I set out to write a book that would be short on text and long on pictures. It still is long on pictures – some of which, notably those of Joy as a young girl, have never been published before – but the text has grown almost despite myself. The main reason for this is that I had an enormous stroke of luck. Through a chance encounter with her daughter, Margaret, I established contact with Joy's sister, Dorle, or Dorothy, who married an Englishman and lives in Lancashire. Dorothy has been enormously helpful and generous, lending me all the family pictures of Joy and her sisters, several from Joy's life in Africa and a number of letters from both her and George. George's letters to Dorothy came as a fascinating revelation, for here was this strong, silent man of action laying bare his soul, often in very moving terms, as he describes his acute unhappiness at Joy's repeated affairs with other men. And yet, despite what can only be described as Joy's callous behaviour, George continued to love her and to be faithful to her.

To me, the great surprise is Joy's character: passionate, selfish, single-minded and, eventually, totally impossible. In some ways she was a monster, George a near saint. This emerges not only from the letters but even more from the conversations I was lucky enough to have with many people who knew them well. I am therefore extremely grateful for their time and valuable assistance in different ways to Jack Barrah; Jonny Baxendale; Osman Bitacha; Carol Byrne; Pam Carson; Dougie Collins (a very special thank-you); David Coulson; Sue Gardner (a most special thank-you); Willie and Morna Hale; Margot Henke; James Hill; Elspeth Huxley; John Jay; Tim Lapage; Mary Leakey; Richard Leakey; Inge Ledertheil; Lois Low; Ray Mayers; Esmond and Chryssee Martin; Julian McKeand; Andrew Meyerhold; John Millard; Naveed Rasul; Giles Remnant; Monty Ruben; Werner Schillinger; Ken Smith; Irene Stirling; Simon Trevor; Matt Turner; Elizabeth de Warenne Waller; and Donald Wise.

Among those who also lent me photographs or helped me in other ways were Siggy Aiken, Bunny and Dave Allen, Mark Collins, Cynthia Downey, Nick Gray, Warwick Johnson, Henry Hughes-Smith, Mike Shrimpton, Bridget Spence, Jason Witney, and Gavin Young.

Finally, I owe thanks for the patient and expert guidance of Richard Johnson and Katherine Everett of Grafton Books; to Janice Robertson who read the MS several times, and above all to my daughter Carlotta, who at all stages of the book was indispensable.

Sandy Gall
Penshurst
January 1991

Chapter One

A PERFECT GENTLE KNIGHT

Sunday, 20 August 1989 dawned as nearly always warm and clear in George Adamson's camp at Kora, in the remote bush country of north-east Kenya. His three lion cubs, now growing fast, woke with the sun in their compound next to George's palm-thatched hut. The old man, who always slept outside in the dry weather, was lying so still that Inge Ledertheil, a German friend who was staying with him at Kampi ya Simba (Lion Camp), thought he had passed away peacefully in the night. 'The bedclothes were so neat and unrumpled that I thought he was dead. Then he stretched his arms above his head and I knew he was okay.'

For a few minutes George delightedly watched the antics of the cubs, the first he had raised at Kampi ya Simba for a decade and which he had named Batian, after a famous Masai *laibon* or chieftain, Rafiki, which means friend in Swahili, and Furaha, Swahili for joy or happiness. Their mother had been reluctantly shot by a farmer, Ian Craig, for killing cattle the year before on his farm at Lewa Downs on the slopes of Mount Kenya. As he watched them grow, George Adamson cannot have failed to draw a parallel with the death thirty-three years before of another lioness, who also left three cubs, one of them destined to become known to millions of people across the world as Elsa, the heroine of *Born Free*. Elsa's mother was shot by mistake in a hunt for a man-eating lion.

At about ten past six George got out of bed and went into his hut to dress. Although quite small and extremely simple, George's hut, a combination of bedroom and study, contained his most treasured possessions: his father's old carriage clock, presented to him when he retired from India in the 1920s; a shelf of books including George's favourite adventure story, Joshua Slocum's *Sailing Alone Around the World*; photographs in silver frames of his mother and his brother Terence as a boy; snapshots of various young women friends who had stayed at Kora and helped him to run the camp over the years; and black and white pictures of two of the most important females in his life, his wife Joy and Elsa the lioness.

Dressing did not take George long. He emerged a few minutes later, wearing only a pair of baggy khaki shorts and an old pair of sandals, and made his way to the mess hut for a cup of tea. There, in the virginal peace of the African morning, facing the great granite triangle of Kora Rock bathed in the golden light of the rising sun, George sipped his tea, surrounded by the birds and animals who were not only his friends but his family as well.

Now eighty-three, but still alert and active, he felt particularly contented this Sunday morning as he looked out over his austere domain, the dry thorn bush country that had hardly changed for a million years. After much anguish and hard work, the future of his beloved Kora seemed assured. In Inge's words, the night before had been one of the most magical she had ever known there. In the late afternoon she had come back from the airstrip, after taking a visiting German family to their plane, and had just had a shower when she heard George calling: 'Inge, come quickly and bring your camera. All the lions are here and it's still light.' Inge had bought a new video camera, especially to take pictures of the lions, but so far had had no luck. Snatching up the camera and hurrying outside, she saw that George was not exaggerating. 'All the lions' really had come to the camp. Inge had never seen the whole pride gathered together before and even for George it was a rare and exciting moment. According to

George and the cubs, with Kora Rock in the background. As with Elsa and her sisters, thirty years before, he loved watching them play, stalking one another and climbing trees

Inge, 'George took his loud-hailer and called all the lions by name and they answered him from every quarter of heaven.' There was fresh camel meat, and with two of his Africans to help him, the old man opened the small wicket gate in the wire and, torch in hand, went out to feed the pride, reciting their names as they came padding towards him out of the bush: the matriarch Growe, the leader of the pride; her daughter One Eye and One Eye's various cubs, Maggie, Denis and Boris, born in 1987 – Denis now a superb young lion with an impressively sprouting mane – and Monty, Sue, Sally and Elke, born in 1988; plus Hoarsy, a wild lion, the father of the cubs, making ten in all. It was a remarkable sight, the handsome old patriarch advancing unarmed as the lions approached, one by one, to take the lumps of meat he tossed them, talking to them in his soft voice as lesser mortals talk to their dogs. A party of game rangers who had run out of petrol and had come to borrow some from George, 'watched, shook their heads and laughed'.

After the lions had been fed and were devouring the remains in the bush beyond the wire, George and Inge had sat in the warm dusk, George with a glass of whisky at his elbow and his beloved pipe in his mouth. Behind them the two Tilley lamps, one in the mess hut, the other hanging in a small thorn tree, both meticulously primed and lit by George each evening, made pools of yellow light in the darkness. With his faded blue eyes and long white hair that made him look like an Old Testament prophet, George Adamson was a happy man, not only because of the appearance of the whole pride, but for a number of other reasons. Kora, at present a Game Reserve, was going to be elevated to the status of a National Park: more money would be forthcoming, plus a new Land-Rover and a lodge for visitors. There was a little joke about the lodge. Inge coyly asked if in future she would have to sleep in the lodge, and George, she said, 'found the question a very silly one.'

'I then told him all the things I would have to get for his Christmas presents: a new stamp saying Kora National Park, new headed paper with National Park on it. He was so pleased about the whole thing, really happy. We sat outside for a long time; the lions were there all night. They roared all night, and ran round the camp.'

All the time he had been at Kora, George Adamson had bought old, decrepit camels, past work or breeding, from the local Somalis to feed his lions. One of his lionesses, Coretta, had been very fond of the head, Inge recalls. 'He always kept the head for Coretta; now Denis gets it. They love the head, probably because of the brain. When he gave Coretta the head, she used to wrinkle up her lips – you could see all her teeth, she actually laughed – then she'd grab the head and take it into the bush. Denis does the same. George got a terrific kick out of that. Growe's just the same as Coretta ... That evening Denis got the head; he spent the whole night in the bush with it.

'George was so happy because Denis had grown into such a fine lion. He spoiled him, you know, that's why he always threw him the biggest pieces of meat. He was the first male lion George had raised from infancy ...

'The week before,' Inge said, 'when the lions suddenly appeared and there was nothing for them to eat, George sent me with some of his people to get camel meat. But we couldn't drive out of the camp because all the lions were standing outside the gate. So we blew the horn and clapped our hands to get them to move, drove out quickly, closed the gate, and as we drove down the road, the lions ran after the Land-Rover.

George in the mess hut, where he entertained a constant stream of visitors, animal as well as human, and from where he could look out at Kora Rock

'We spoke about everything that evening, about Kora becoming a National Park, about a new vehicle, about the camp, that George was the King of the Lions. I always used to compare George with Albert Schweitzer. Albert Schweitzer in the Congo was for people, and George was for animals. We were all alone; the rangers had left and we had a little celebration and a nice supper which the German visitors had brought with them: good bread with butter and proper ham and green salad, you know, one of those long loaves. George only ate half of his, he wanted to keep the other half for Sunday, but it didn't turn out that way. Then he listened to the news, I think at eleven. I went to my hut and he went to his a bit later, with the lamp, and did some writing. He did every evening, he had a lot of writing to do.'

The one unusual thing about this particular weekend was that Inge was the only visitor in camp. Very often, Kora was as busy as any safari lodge. Quite apart from the scientists and wildlife enthusiasts, the journalists and television crews, the odd film star and rock musician, there was nearly always a constant stream of more humble visitors, most of them young, usually female, attracted by George's saintly personality and the beauty and tranquillity that Kora offered. Involuntarily, he had become a sort of nature guru to whom all these often troubled seekers after spiritual peace were irresistibly drawn. Bwana George, as his African staff called him, was extremely hospitable by nature but he also knew the value of keeping open house, and he depended on the more generous guests to leave a donation for the upkeep of Kora, which he had to finance largely from his own modest funds. In the past couple of weeks he had been host to a whole succession of visitors, including John Aspinall and his family. Aspinall had made a fortune out of gambling and now spent his time running two zoos in Kent, where he kept tigers and gorillas. Then there had been an American family, so unused to the bush, according to Inge, that the daughter screamed in terror when she discovered an entirely harmless ground squirrel inspecting her sleeping quarters. Finally, there had been the recently-departed German family.

But Kora on this particular Sunday was utterly peaceful, and after his morning tea George proceeded with the daily ritual of feeding the guinea fowl. There are four different kinds of guinea fowl in East Africa, but the Kora variety, known as vulturine guinea fowl, must be the most infuriating. When demanding to be fed they emitted a fiendish, persistent screech which sounded like a piece of corrugated iron being sawn in half and which would have driven anyone to drink, except perhaps St Francis of Assisi and George Adamson. When the guinea fowl heard the sound of George's millet tin, they came running at top speed from every direction, surrounding the old man as he walked slowly amongst them. It amused him that these odd creatures always ran round him in an anti-clockwise direction. 'I become quite dizzy watching them,' he would say from the middle of a sea of cobalt blue and white striped backs and greedy red eyes. 'Perhaps it's because we're south of the equator at Kora. Maybe if we were north of the equator they'd go the other way.' It was a conundrum George, as far as I know, never solved. Shaking out the last grains of millet, he wandered back inside the wire. With their hunger momentarily assuaged, the guinea fowl's shrieks subsided and the camp resumed its soporific tempo, the sun already too hot for the young lions, who sought the shade and lay quietly dozing.

The feeding of the guinea fowl accomplished, George went back to his hut to resume his letter writing while Hamisi, the old Sudanese cook who had been with him and his brother Terence before him for thirty years, laid the breakfast. Today, there was no home-baked bread but there were plenty of eggs and George knew the hornbills like fried eggs, scooping them up with their huge, curved beaks. Three kinds of hornbill – red-billed, yellow-billed and von der Decken's – were usually in attendance at George's breakfast table.

Having devoured their eggs, the sharp-eyed hornbills were ready for the next course, deftly catching the peanuts as George lobbed them into the air – 'they would make an excellent cricket side' – while the noisy and inquisitive fan-tailed ravens, Good, Bad and Worse, descendants of the original inhabitants, Crikey and Croaky – watched every move from the rafters, ready to swoop on any unattended morsel. The mess hut, which was adorned with a profusion of blow-ups of George's lions, was open on one side and from his place at the table he could look out through the wire at the marabou storks, vultures and an occasional martial eagle, at the long-tailed go-away-birds, the sunbirds, weavers and superb starlings which certainly live up to their name, their exotic plumage a blaze of glossy green, blue and rust. Beyond were the outcrops where the lions liked to lie up during the day with Kora Rock and the smaller Kora Tit rising into the sky behind.

When the hornbills had had their fill, the ground squirrels moved up to the attack, boldly invading the table top, stuffing their little cheeks to bursting point with an impossible quantity of peanuts which George pushed in their direction with a generous finger. There were doves in profusion: namaqua doves, mourning doves, laughing doves and emerald-spotted wood doves, some billing and cooing unashamedly until, with a soft rush of wings, they fluttered down prettily to bear off a nut or crumb of toast. In the small tree in front of the mess hut, other friends were congregating: small, delicately-made vervet monkeys with long tails and cheeky black faces, the males proudly displaying their electric blue testicles – George always had a chuckle about these brightly-coloured private parts – and soon they too would make their assault on his tins of peanuts.

After breakfast, George opened the big box in the corner of the mess hut and took out some papers. While his back was turned the monkeys pounced, snatched some of the papers and tried to make off with them. Inge came to the rescue and, half cursing, half laughing, she and George managed to recover them. Inge then went off to wash her hair while George disappeared into his hut and she soon heard him typing away on the new Adler she had given him to replace his ancient Remington, which was now almost a museum piece.

Inge had made her first visit to Kora in 1984. Uncharacteristically, George turned down her first requests to visit him on the grounds that Kampi ya Simba was too remote and dangerous and there were too few facilities. But Inge was nothing if not persistent and she finally got her way, hiring a car and a driver in Mombasa and making the long journey over bad roads from the coast, eventually arriving in the dark. Her relief at finding Kampi ya Simba, when she and her increasingly nervous driver had become convinced they were lost, was so great that she threw herself into George's arms. Once admitted to the inner sanctum, she became a regular visitor, flying out to Kenya at least once a year. She did not speak much English, and George no German, despite the fact that his late wife Joy had been Austrian. Yet George's friendship clearly meant a great deal to the buxom, black-eyed Bavarian with a fringe. In her early forties and single, a secretary in a practice of acupuncturists in Stuttgart, Inge saved up to indulge her passion for wildlife in general and Kora in particular. She repaid George's hospitality by always arriving laden with presents for him and his staff and with plentiful supplies of food and drink.

At eleven o'clock on the dot, Inge poured George a gin and orange topped up with cold water from the thermos and took it to his hut. This was a habit which George, as a young game warden, had learnt from his first boss in the Game Department, Archie Ritchie. Ritchie had a big clock in his office and punctually when the clock hands reached eleven, he would reach down to a bag beside his desk and produce a bottle of gin. George used to recount with relish how the ritual was observed even on safari.

'Archie Ritchie always believed in travelling in comfort and it didn't matter where he was, at eleven o'clock a table used to come out of the car with a bottle of gin on it and some syphons and angostura, and religiously he had to have a gin at eleven o'clock, didn't matter a damn where it was.'

An hour later, George was still typing away in his hut and Inge was reading next door in what had originally been Terence's hut, when they heard a plane. Since they were not expecting anyone, both of them went outside and looked up into the deep blue of the midday sky to see who it was. 'Look, George,' Inge remembers saying, 'it's the red plane, the one that came over yesterday.' A few seconds later it circled low over Kampi ya Simba – the signal that it was about to land and wanted someone to meet its passengers – and then headed for the airstrip about seven kilometres away. George disconnected the leads from the solar charger to the Land-Rover battery and Inge got in. Although this was the newer of George's two Land-Rovers, the starter motor was not working and they had to give it a push start. 'When I got into the Land-Rover,' Inge recalls, 'I looked at my watch and it was half past twelve. I thought, if we're quick we'll just be back in time for lunch. Bitacha (one of George's staff) got in beside me and we drove off.'

A few minutes later, the sound of five or six shots was carried faintly on the wind to George's camp. The headman, Mohammed Maru, ran to alert him. 'When I heard the sound of the shots, I quickly went to tell George that the plane had landed but the car [Land-Rover] had been shot at and that I myself had heard the shots. George stopped writing his letters and we all got into his car [Land-Rover] and drove off. With George in the car were Hassan, Kiya, Ongesa and myself.'

By some strange twist of fate, the letter that George was writing when the distant, windborne sound of gunfire reached the camp, stops halfway through a sentence at the two words 'Inge Leidersteil [sic]', misspelt as it happens. It was found later, still in his typewriter, and retrieved by Monty Ruben, one of George's trustees and a close friend. It was addressed to Frankie Harwood, an English nurse, then working at Queen Charlotte's Hospital in London.

> Kampi ya Simba 20 August 1989
>
> Dearest Frankie,
>
> Thank you for the interesting postcard, makes one think there must have been more lions than tigers in India at the time of the Moghals?
>
> All goes well apart from the ever-growing pile of letters and muddled accounts awaiting payment and general paperwork.
>
> Now most of my days are spent thumping the typewriter instead of tracking down the lions!! Oh for Doddie!! [Georgina Edmonds, an English girl who worked for George at Kora for about seven years.] Had a letter from her at last! Written from 'The Promise Recovery Centre', near Dover and dated 30th June. Nothing since. No indication whether she had any wish to come back to Kora.
>
> Of course, I long to have her back but only if it would make her happy which is what counts. Anyway I would like to help all I can. I expect by now you are in the land of Skirling Bagpipes? Hope the address on this letter finds you? You are always in my thoughts and I value your friendship greatly and am looking forward to hearing from you.
>
> At the moment there is a German girl staying here Inge Leidersteil ...

About ten or at most fifteen minutes after the shots were fired, as George Adamson rounded a slight bend more than halfway to the airstrip, he and the four Africans with him came on Inge's Land-Rover, halted in the middle of the road. On either side, the grey-green thorn bush with its commiphora trees and frankincense bushes lay like a sea becalmed, flattened into submission by the ferocity of the noonday sun. It is unlikely that George Adamson saw Inge, who was some twenty or thirty yards off the road in the bush to his left, or even Bitacha, the African who had accompanied her. What he would have seen at once were the ominous figures of three Somali Shifta (bandits) armed with automatic weapons, one of them very tall, standing on the road or just beside it. As George drove up, the tall one shouted to his companions in Somali: 'Don't shoot the tyres, shoot the driver!'

It is not clear who opened fire first, but Bitacha says George drew his revolver and, accelerating towards the gunmen like Don Quixote charging a windmill, got off four or five shots at the Somalis, who immediately scattered and took cover. The tall one, however, ran round behind him and aimed several bursts at the Land-Rover, at least three bullets hitting George, the fatal one striking him in the back and making a large hole in his chest. Monty Ruben, who went to the scene next day and saw the body, says: 'George had a very big exit wound in his chest, right beside the heart. That was undoubtedly the bullet that killed him. There was blood everywhere; the floor and the back of the Land-Rover were thick with it.'

George Adamson's death was, some say, the inevitable outcome of his long and almost single-handed struggle to resist Somali encroachment, not only the depredations of the Shifta and the poachers, who in his twenty years at Kora had wiped out all the rhino and most of the elephant there, but the more insidious penetration of their huge herds of camels, cattle, sheep and goats which have turned their own country into a dustbowl and – as they relentlessly push south in their search for new grazing – now threaten Kenya with the same fate. In the days of British colonial rule the Somali herds had not been allowed south of the Tana River, but since Independence in 1963 they had crossed it with impunity and in the dry season, to George's fury, thousands of their stock poured into Kora, devouring the sparse vegetation and driving out the wild animals. Not content with that, the Somali herdsmen cut down or set fire to the riverine forest, believing the tall, stately doum palms which grew along the banks of the Tana harboured the tsetse fly which is fatal to domestic animals but not to game and, adding insult to injury, deliberately poisoned George's lions. The thought of his beloved lions, the most magnificent animals on earth, dying a horribly painful death at the hands of these intruders, was enough to make George's blood boil.

One day, when we were driving from the nearby village of Asako back to camp, we saw thick, black smoke rising from the trees by the river's edge. Swinging the Land-Rover off the road, George crashed his way through the bush in the direction of the fire, eventually coming on a large herd of Somali sheep and goats which scattered at our approach. A few minutes later we were confronted by a terrible sight: a group of magnificent doum palms, a hundred feet and more high, was swallowed up by a column of fire and, as we watched, the thick mass of dry fronds which clothed the top of the trees exploded with a roar and a huge shower of sparks. In the space of a few minutes, what had been a dense and verdant forest sanctuary was transformed into a blackened, smoking ruin. After inspecting it with mounting rage, George spotted two Somali herdsmen and, confronting them, questioned them through his tracker, Abdi. Disdainfully, almost insolently, they denied starting the fire, claimed they had been on their way out of the reserve with their stock when they saw the smoke and had merely walked back to investigate. As I watched them stalk off into the bush, reluctantly admiring the litheness of their stride and the independence of their bearing, prepared to bend the knee to no one, George turned to me and said, 'Bloody Somalis! They probably started the fire in the first place, deliberately, out of sheer destructiveness. They've destroyed their own country through overgrazing and if they're not stopped, they'll do exactly the same thing here!'

Yet he held no personal resentment. When Somali poachers who had come off worst in a battle with local Kamba tribesmen – deadly shots with their bows and poisoned arrows – sent a message to George appealing for medical assistance, he went himself in his Land-Rover and helped to patch up their wounds.

George Adamson died as he had lived, with great gallantry and instinctive courage. 'Completely fearless' is how William Hale, a former Chief Game Warden and George's last boss, described him. Modest and unassuming to a fault, he was, in the words of Chaucer, 'a verray parfit gentil knight' or, as a French medieval chronicler put it, 'un chevalier sans peur et sans reproche', a knight without fear and above reproach.

Monty Ruben, one of his oldest and most loyal friends, summed up his death like this. 'It was the best way for him to go. The last thing George wanted was to die in hospital in Nairobi. He dreaded that more than anything else. It was terrible that he had to die in the way he did, of course, but in a sense, it was the perfect end. After all, it was a hero's death.'

Chapter Two

AN EPIC CROSSING

George Adamson was born in Etawah, in India, on 3 February 1906, at the height of the British Raj. His father was Irish, a self-taught engineer who worked for the Rajah of Dholpur, one of the princely states of Rajasthan, running his army and building a railway. In his autobiography, *Bwana Game*, George Adamson describes his father as both able and adventurous. He joined the Royal Navy in the days of sail and had plenty of exciting stories to tell his sons about rounding the Horn. By nature he was 'extremely placid and even-tempered', and George certainly inherited those qualities in generous measure, whereas his mother, whose family had been in India for generations, was 'highly strung, very tidy, methodical and observant'. Terence, George's younger brother by a year, took after his mother. Dholpur was hot and dry, rather like the semi-desert areas of northern Kenya where George was to spend so much of his life.

Kenya became the Adamsons' home by mistake. On retiring from India, his father intended to settle in South Africa, but on his way there he stopped off in Mombasa and was so taken by Kenya that he decided instead to buy a coffee farm in the White Highlands north of Nairobi. George, who was sent to school in Cheltenham, returned to Kenya at the age of eighteen and was put to work on the farm. Quite apart from the fact that it was not a great success, being too high for coffee, George found the work boring and his father suggested instead that he learn how to plough with a tractor, tractors being comparatively new on the scene. George worked extremely hard, ploughing from dawn to dusk and living rough. The job only paid fifteen pounds a month but, as he says, it certainly toughened him up.

In the months that followed, he turned his hand to a wide variety of jobs: working on a sisal plantation, as a farm bailiff, a milk roundsman in Nairobi, a barman, a bus driver and a livestock trader. Some of these may not seem very exciting occupations, but in pre-war Kenya they were not what they sounded. The milk, for example, had to be delivered in whisky bottles, the only ones available. George admits they had many complaints, but never about the milk tasting of alcohol. Then again, the bus service, linking Arusha in Tanganyika with Nairobi, was unusual in that for much of the way there was no road. In the rainy season the bus would get bogged down and passengers would have to spend the night on board. Not surprisingly, the bus venture, like the road, petered out.

When he had any free time, George and his brother Terence would go hunting, usually accompanied by an old Dorobo tracker called Masondu. Members of the Dorobo tribe traditionally lived scattered among the Masai and Nandi people and hunted for them, and, according to George, Masondu was incredibly good in the bush. He taught the young Adamson boys a lot and could always tell whether an animal had been lightly or mortally wounded; he taught them how to test the wind and read spoor, to check whether leaves or grass had been bruised, whether there was dew on the spoor or insects had made runs over it. He also taught George and Terence to be extremely careful when following a wounded buffalo as they had a nasty habit of circling back and ambushing the hunter. Despite Masondu's teaching, years later George was to be nearly killed by a wounded buffalo.

He also worked for a spell as a government locust officer with about fifty men under him. Half were Suk and half Turkana, neighbouring tribes from the area north of Eldoret, and the only way George could tell them apart was by the fact that the Suk were circumcised and the Turkana not. Since they wore no clothes, he says, recognition was not difficult!

George (left) and his younger brother, Terence, on one of their early hunting safaris

George had a soft spot for the Turkana, admiring their ability to survive in the inhospitable wilderness of sand, lava and thorn bush that was their home. Despite their hard lives they were often fine physical specimens, the men over six feet tall and the women well-endowed. He describes a Turkana family on the move as a fine sight, the men driving their herds along and carrying only a couple of long spears, a stool or head-rest and a container for tobacco, while the women and children followed with the donkeys carrying their few, simple household goods.

Early in 1929, the locust campaign ended and young Adamson was offered a job as a storeman in Nairobi. This was hardly calculated to fire his imagination, so he resigned from government service and, since he was suffering from malaria, went home to the White Highlands. His father had died three years before and his mother and Terence were running the coffee farm. His mother, an expert gardener, had planted plum, peach and other fruit trees round the house, which had staggering views of Mount Kenya and Kilimanjaro. A curious chance brought on a recurrence of the malaria. In order, as George recounts, to celebrate the return of her prodigal son, his mother asked him to fill up a soda syphon. As he did so, it exploded in his face, sending pieces of glass into his eyes. The shock brought on a bout of malaria which laid him low for two months, but at the end of it he set off for Uganda as an assistant to his friend, David Hobden, a man of many parts who was now selling life insurance.

They finally arrived in a small town near the northern border where George made the acquaintance of a young lady geologist he describes only as Miss L. On their last night, the three of them gave a farewell party. George, feeling another bout of malaria coming on, retired early to bed. Hobden and Miss L celebrated until the early hours and next morning informed him that he, George, and Miss L were to be married that very day.

Never having contemplated marriage before, George was not surprisingly somewhat taken aback. Miss L was a very charming girl, he says gallantly, but she was also very determined and of a powerful physique. Had he not seen her knock an insolent African flying? He suggested that Miss L and Hobden should go ahead in their car and he would meet them at the local magistrate's office. As soon as they had gone, George drove south at top speed. Their next meeting, he says, was distinctly chilly.

George now turned to long distance transport, driving a lorry from Mombasa to Kampala, a distance of about eight hundred miles, carrying cargoes of whisky, scent and other luxury items. Even today it is a long and tiring drive, but in the thirties it must have been something of an ordeal, the road little better than a cross-country track, with plenty of obstacles in the shape of stray elephant and rhino, broken bridges and impassable morasses. But since he was his own boss, George was able to indulge his passion for the wild and went on many hunting expeditions. On one of them he fell foul of an angry hippopotamus. He and a friend, Bill Thompson, had been on a long walk after an elephant and arrived on the banks of the Tana River. They had a bathe and were sitting naked on a sandbank, George trying to take a photograph of a big bull hippo which was behaving in an unusual way, rearing up out of the water and plunging back again, only about thirty yards away. Suddenly as he was peering through the view finder, the hippo broke surface a few feet in front of him, looking distinctly unfriendly. George leaped up and started to run along the sandbank with the hippo after him but tripped and fell in the loose sand. With the huge beast almost on top of him, he managed to throw himself to one side as it thundered past. Jumping to his feet again, he sprinted for the river bank across what he thought was shallow water. It turned out to be six feet deep and George went under still clutching his precious camera. Luckily the hippo, after seeing George off his sandbank, abandoned the chase and plunged back into the river. Otherwise, the intrepid hunter says, that would have been the last chapter of his story.

Soon after this, George Adamson, always ready to try his hand at something new, decided to become a gold prospector. Gold had recently been found at Kakamega, near the north-east corner of Lake Victoria, and he decided to join the gold rush with an equally adventurous friend, Nevil Baxendale, rather younger than George and twice his size – whom he describes as 'a tower of strength both physically and psychologically'. They set off late in the year with all the confidence of youth, convinced they were about to make their fortunes. They worked hard, digging and panning, living rough and usually very hard up. If they were lucky they would end up with a 'lump of spongy gold that looked enormous but was actually very light'. This was cashed in at the bank in Kisumu and, armed with the proceeds, they would buy some stores and return to the job. On top of the rigours of prospecting, they had to contend with a plague of poisonous snakes. On one occasion a large cobra came down the sluice box, scattering everyone before it. On another, George almost stepped on a cobra which suddenly reared up at his feet. He did the only thing he could, dropped his gold pannings on top of the snake and fled. Another snake which was common in the Yala River valley was the rhinoceros-horned viper, beautifully marked but extremely poisonous. Anxious to obtain a good specimen for the Coryndon Museum in Nairobi, George and Nevil let it be known they were offering a small reward.

One day a child of about four arrived at their camp dragging an enormous viper by a piece of grass tied round its neck. In spite of this undignified treatment, the snake did not appear to be unduly angry. George wondered if being partly throttled had something to do with its imperturbability. It was three feet long and enormously thick – out of all proportion to its length. They christened it Cuthbert Gandhi, after Mahatma Gandhi, the architect of Indian independence who had a propensity for 'fasting unto death'. Cuthbert was similarly inclined and, after refusing food for a long time, only regained his appetite when they introduced him to a live rat which he dispatched with deadly speed. Poor Cuthbert, he eventually finished up in a glass jar in the Nairobi museum.

Despite their lack of success in the Kakamega gold fields, George and his friend Nevil were determined to try their luck in the Kerio Valley, which runs through the heart of Turkana country to the inhospitable shores of Lake Rudolf (now Lake Turkana) in the far north. It was on this safari, which involved walking for hundreds of miles, that Nevil, George recounts with glee, suffered grievously from chafed testicles, caused by marching for hours in sweaty trousers. It would have been more sensible to have worn a loin-cloth, George opines or, better still, to have marched in shirt-tails. But those were the days when the white man's burden made it impossible, even in the back of beyond, to go about improperly dressed.

They had to abandon the trip when their supplies ran out, but, lured by the legend of the 'Queen of Sheba's mines', which were rumoured to lie somewhere between Lake Rudolf and the Ethiopian border, planned a more ambitious trip for the following year. On 5 February 1934, two days after George's twenty-eighth birthday, Nevil Baxendale, George and Yusuf, their cook, set off in George's old lorry loaded down with provisions and gear. Leaving the lorry at the road end, at the head of the Marich Pass, they proceeded on foot, their equipment now transferred to the backs of a dozen donkeys. It was a three-week march to the 180-mile-long lake known because of its remarkable colour as the Jade Sea. By the time they reached it, their stock of food was almost finished. Luckily the local chief, named Egbert, came to their rescue, and when he discovered they were proposing to walk round the lake's southern shore, suggested some of his tribesmen should accompany them. They chose only two, one rejoicing in the name of Tobosh, and although the men were told there would be no wages and no rations, both accepted in the belief that their employers would keep them well supplied with whatever game they could shoot for the pot.

Tobosh was about twenty, well over six feet tall, perfectly proportioned and, as was the custom among the Turkana then, wore not a stitch of clothing, not even sandals, and carried with him not a single possession, not even a spear.

The march to the south end of the lake was the hardest part of the journey and, alas for the tantalising legend of the Queen of Sheba's mines, disappointment was added to hardship: in the parched, volcanic wastes that surrounded the lake, they found no trace of gold. Lake Turkana, especially the southern part, is notorious for the gales which blow, night and day, from a south-easterly direction. Everyone who has travelled there, including the first Europeans to discover it, L. R. von Höhnel and Count Teleki, have been struck by the ferocity of the wind which can attain speeds of up to eighty miles an hour. George says their food was often blown off their plates before it could reach their mouths, or was so covered in grit as to be inedible. At night, the only way they could get some rest was by sleeping behind a parapet of stones, a trick that Teleki and von Höhnel had also discovered. Even so, by morning, they were covered in sand.

In the afternoons the wind would often drop and then the heat would strike like the breath from a furnace. But there were compensations. On their walks along the lakeshore they saw many different kinds of birdlife, plenty of crocodile and an occasional hippo. In addition, there was always the spice of danger, more real than they realised at the time, of running into armed raiders from across the

Ethiopian border. Eventually, they arrived at Loingalane, an oasis of palm trees and warm springs on the south-east side of the lake. Since it is only about twelve miles from Mount Kulal, which they had come all this way to see, they climbed it, but once again found no gold. Back in Loingalane, the prudent course, George acknowledges, would have been to admit defeat and make their way back. Their food was nearly exhausted and their clothes and footwear were in tatters. But since they were both enjoying themselves, they decided to carry on. For eleven days they followed the lake shore northwards, until their last supplies of sorghum meal ran out and they were forced to turn back.

One night all their donkeys disappeared. Next day, after a long search, Tobosh finally found them being stalked by two lions. Without hesitation and despite being unarmed, he got between them and their prey and drove the donkeys back to camp, closely followed by the lions. Two donkeys were missing and they never saw them again; presumably they had been killed and eaten. But for Tobosh's courage they might have found themselves without any transport at all.

The following night George was dozing off when Nevil suddenly asked why, instead of walking two hundred miles round the end of the lake, didn't they sail across it? Thinking Nevil had gone off his head, George asked, 'Go across the lake, in what?' 'In a boat,' Nevil replied.

George with the home-made boat in which he and Nevil Baxendale crossed Lake Rudolf in 1934. It was an epic feat

When, in September 1988, I accompanied George on his last visit to the shores of Lake Rudolf, this is how he described to me his crossing of the lake, fifty-four years before. He was then eighty-two, but he still revelled in the retelling of his great adventure.

'This friend of mine, Nevil Baxendale, was an accomplished boat builder. He'd built several boats, but when he first made the suggestion of crossing Lake Rudolf I thought he'd gone off his nut. Anyhow he explained what he wanted to do, and so we decided that, rather than go about two hundred miles right round the south end of the lake, it'd be much easier to cross. [The lake at this, its narrowest point, is about twelve miles wide.] So we set to and started building this boat. One of the difficulties was that we had to make a framework from branches of an acacia tree. Now, none of the branches of an acacia is ever straight, so we had a rather difficult job. We had a certain amount of rawhide thong that we'd collected along the way from shooting buck. The frame was bound together with these rawhide thongs. It must have taken us about the best part of the week to build this boat. I did the sewing. We had a canvas tarpaulin, a fairly good one, and we covered the frame with the tarpaulin. Also we made a mast and a sail because we hoped that we'd be able to set sail and just sail across without any trouble. But we made a couple of paddles in case it was that calm, and then when the boat was ready it was taken down towards the lake.

'We sent off the ten donkeys and told the Turkana to make the best way they could round the lake; and if they were really pushed for food they could eat a donkey. So off they went and we were intending to start the same day. Then a terrific gale started up and the weather went really bad. It was either a howling gale or flat calm. The first morning after our donkeys had been sent off, we went down to have a look at the boat that had been parked on the shore of the lake. Much to our dismay we found that the whole thing had collapsed. During the night jackals had come along and eaten all the rawhide thongs. So then it meant rebuilding this wretched boat and we'd got no food, you see, not a thing. Luckily there was a plant, a bush called the Salvadora with berries rather like an English blackcurrant that were ripe. One of us would go and gather berries and the other'd scout around and see if there was anything to shoot.

'We'd got no more rawhide thong so we had to get the inner bark of an acacia tree. It's very strong actually, but it's quite a job to collect it.

One day it was my turn to try and shoot something. Nevil had gone off collecting berries and I found a goose sitting on a nest up in an acacia tree. Obviously it was sitting on eggs. I thought, well, if I shoot this goose from underneath, I'll kill the goose but I'll also smash the eggs. So, with considerable difficulty [acacias are extremely thorny], I climbed up another acacia tree so that I was parallel with the goose. And then I blew its head off and killed it and got three or four fresh eggs which was a change from a diet of only berries and meat.

'The weather was really bad. There'd been a howling gale at night and this boat of ours, you couldn't describe it as very seaworthy. The gale would stop but the sea would still be pretty rough until early afternoon. We decided the only thing was to wait until there was a calm and the gale had stopped and the sea subsided a bit. About three o'clock one afternoon we set off rowing. I had my cook [Yusuf] with me, and his job was to bale while Nevil and myself rowed. So we started off. The boat had a tendency to go round in a circle so it meant that one of us – we had to take it in turns – had to row harder than the other one.

'When it got dark we were right in the middle of the lake and it was a pretty dark night with not much moon, but we could see the outline of the hill on the other side so we made for that. We rowed and rowed and went on rowing until our hands were raw and bleeding and then, finally – we were afraid that the gale would start you see – I heard a noise. And I said to Nevil, "What's that noise?" He said, "I think it's the gale starting." So we redoubled our efforts. And then suddenly we hit the other shore. The noise we'd heard was multitudes of frogs croaking. Once we realised it was frogs we knew we must be fairly near.

'We landed and I thought, well, by Jove, this is an emergency! So we split the half bottle of brandy my mother had given me. She had said, "On no account can you use this unless you're in dire straits." I thought, Well, I think the time has come to celebrate our crossing! As far as I know it was the first recorded crossing.'

It had taken them between six and seven hours. Only half an hour after they landed the gale started and blew furiously for the remainder of the night and till late the next morning. Had it caught them in the middle of the lake, the flimsy boat would not have survived for more than a few minutes.

In the afternoon, the wind having abated, they set sail and ran north before a gentle breeze, eventually landing on a sandbank among a school of hippo. On the way Nevil had tried trolling with a large spoon, but a huge Nile perch struck and snapped the line. They had as little luck trying to find a bird to shoot and had to go supperless to bed. Next morning, desperately hungry, they *had* to find something to eat. They had had only one small cup of milk which Yusuf had managed to get from a poor Turkana. Luckily, just over the sandbank was an isolated pool covered with duck and geese. Nevil managed to bag four duck and a goose. They put the lot in a large pot and boiled them up. They turned out to be very fat and tender and provided their best meal for a very long time.

After a night made uncomfortable by mosquitoes and hippos, they set sail in a moderate gale and, keeping close to shore in case of disaster, flew before the wind to reach Egbert's village by noon, much to the astonishment of the local Turkana who had never seen a boat like theirs before. Egbert was away but his second-in-command produced a fat sheep and plenty of milk in return for the wood in the boat. Both sides were happy with the bargain and next day Tobosh and his fellow Turkana and the donkeys arrived; incredibly they looked little the worse for their hard march.

Three days later, George and Nevil reached the desert outpost of Lodwar, the administrative headquarters for the area. George, wearing his carefully preserved trousers, and Nevil trying to hide the holes in his, called on Morgan, the District Commissioner, and Willie Hale, his District Officer. They were amazed to discover that the intrepid pair had crossed the lake, believing at first that the travellers' tale was just a joke.

More than fifty years later, the same Willie Hale was full of admiration for the epic crossing. 'The trouble with George's book, I told him, was that he underplayed the story. It was a terrific feat.'

Chapter Three

THE URGE TO PROTECT

For the next four years, George Adamson tried his hand at a variety of occupations, becoming in turn professional hunter, hotel manager, mica miner and trader in beeswax, gum and leopardskins, none of which did more than keep the wolf from the door. It was a lonely, rootless existence and, being young and vigorous, George often felt the urge for the pleasures of female company. He was sorely tempted to acquire 'a native girl' and found that the only antidote was to seize his rifle and go off hunting. On one such occasion, in 1938, travelling once more along the Kerio River, he came across a game warden called Tom Oulton. George, who had never seen a camp like Oulton's before, found the warden seated in a bower of freshly-cut branches, with green leaves strewn on the ground all around.

Oulton was undoubtedly an odd bird: for example, he insisted that the head of his bed always pointed to the north, regardless of the shape or location of the room or tent he might be sleeping in. But he did George a good turn, advising him to apply for a job in the Kenya Game Department. 'We got talking one evening and he said, "Why don't you get a job in the Game Department?" and I said, "Well, I'd very much like to." So he said, "Well, I'll talk to the chief" (who was Archie Ritchie), "and suggest that he offer you a job." So I said, "That's fine. If I can get a job in the Game Department, just what I want."'

Meanwhile George continued to make a living by taking parties of tourists on photographic safaris, including one to the Serengeti, in Tanzania, then Tanganyika. This was before Serengeti became a national park, and when you could still shoot wildebeest, zebra, eland and Thomson's gazelle there, but not lion. In *Bwana Game*, his first book, George recaptures one of the more magical moments of that safari and uses it to put forward his already strongly held views that animals have as much right to a place on earth as man.

Seeing a magnificent lioness lying as if sculpted on a rock, gazing out across the plain, he wondered how many lions had lain on the same rock over the centuries while the human race was still in its cradle. This prompted the thought that while man spends a fortune restoring old buildings and other works of art, he is prodigal in his destruction of noble creatures like the lion, which typify the perfection of the natural world, often for no better reason than a shameful desire to show off its skin on the floor of his otherwise graceless home.

At the end of June, the *deus ex machina* which was to change the course of George's life arrived in the shape of a telegram from the Game Department offering him a job: Oulton had been as good as his word. A few days later, in July 1938, at the age of 32, George Adamson was enrolled as a temporary assistant game warden at the salary of thirty pounds a month. His orders were to carry out extensive foot safaris throughout the Northern Game Reserve, as it was then known, with his headquarters at Isiolo, a small, dusty town which was the administrative capital of the Northern Frontier District. A fortnight after being appointed and after hiring several game scouts and a team of donkeys, George set off on his first official safari. It was to take him three and a half months and, although it was more of a reconnaissance of his vast new area than an anti-poaching expedition, he did catch twenty-five poachers, most of them Turkana tribesmen. Poachers then, although a constant nuisance, did not threaten the very existence of big game as they do today, largely because they still used traditional weapons.

When, for example, the Turkana, who used dogs to hunt the oryx, the beautiful desert antelope, had exhausted their prey and brought it to bay, they would run up and kill the animal with a spear. They would stalk and spear big game as well, including giraffe and buffalo, even rhino and elephant. They also employed some extremely cruel traps. One was a device consisting of a rawhide noose and a circular piece of wood like a wheel armed with sharp, pointed stakes. The other end of the noose was attached to a heavy piece of wood about four feet long. The trap was hidden on a game path and when the unsuspecting victim trod on it the spokes fastened round the animal's leg, the noose drew tight and eventually the effort of dragging the heavy piece of wood through the bush exhausted the beast and left it an easy prey. George caught one poacher with several of these traps and shortly afterwards came on a Grevy's zebra with one of the nooses round its forefoot. It was in such a sorry state, its hind legs raw and bleeding from dragging the heavy piece of wood, that George shot it to put it out of its misery. He was so angry that he says he felt like tying one of the nooses round the poacher's neck and dragging him along for a day's march. But however cruel this form of trap, was it any crueller than the 'civilised' steel gin trap? How many hundreds of thousands, perhaps millions, of animals, he asks, have suffered unspeakable agony in the steel jaws of such traps merely to provide furs for fashionable women and civic dignitaries?

At the end of the colonial era, Africa was still largely unchanged physically and its wildlife was almost as rich and varied as it had ever been. The young game warden was lucky enough to come across some magnificent sights, such as no longer exist today. Late one night he camped in an old government post overlooking a broad sandy river-bed with just one small pool of water. Soon after sundown a herd of elephants appeared, filling the river-bed until it was one heaving mass of animals struggling to drink. The noise was deafening and continued until near dawn. George set off early to follow them, finally climbing to the top of a small hill from where he looked down on a huge herd of about three hundred elephants. It was, he says, a stirring spectacle. Many of the bulls carried huge tusks of a hundred pounds and over and he saw two pairs mating, a very rare sight which he had not witnessed before. The act was performed in the normal manner, but the unusual feature was that a number of cows and calves gathered in a circle round the pair and seemed to be very excited. George was fascinated by the herd and watched the elephants all morning through his glasses.

Back in Isiolo, his thoughts turned to romance. For the first time in his life he had a steady job and prospects for the future. He began to think about acquiring a wife, but with little experience in this field, did not know how to go about it. His first attempt, with a delightful French girl who was staying in Isiolo, led to near-heartbreak. One wonders how the usually taciturn and phlegmatic George behaved as a lovelorn swain. He does not say but, philosophical as always, eventually concluded it was all for the best, since for the next few years he would constantly be away on safari.

In 1939, George Adamson had an encounter which could easily have crippled if not killed him: that he not only survived, but survived virtually unscathed is striking proof of his remarkable toughness and good fortune. He was on a foot safari with pack donkeys in Samburu country, in the Ndoto Mountains, south-east of Lake Turkana, when a deputation of local tribesmen came to him complaining bitterly that a pride of three lions was killing their cattle and had even taken to man-eating. The lions had killed and eaten one young man and seriously injured another. George told them to go off and find out where the lions were and report back to him in camp. This was his invariable practice and saved him much aimless tramping through the bush. Describing the incident to me with undimmed animation nearly fifty years later, George said he sat in his camp for two days waiting for news.

On the third morning, while he was having his tea, 'There was a fearful uproar from the donkeys behind and they came racing past the tent with a bad-tempered elephant after them. The donkeys easily out-distanced the elephant and disappeared down a sort of glade in the valley. I continued with my tea but, seeing a lone Samburu coming up this glade, I thought I'd better warn him because the elephant was somewhere there. I got up to shout to him and at that moment the elephant appeared and charged the Samburu and the Samburu took to his heels promptly and managed to get away. Everything was quiet again and I decided to go for a walk by myself. I walked down this *lugga* [dry river-bed] until about eleven o'clock when, since the sun was getting hot, I thought, well, I'll go back. On my way I saw a lioness crossing in front of me, about a hundred yards away, and I thought I suppose this is one of the ones that have been causing trouble. So up with my rifle and I shot it and knocked it over and then almost immediately after it got up again and went into a patch of long grass. I walked round this grass to see if it was dead or whether it had gone out or what had happened, and I couldn't see any sign of it. I threw stones in and I climbed up a tree to try to look into this patch of grass. But I couldn't see anything, and I decided to go back to camp and return with my rangers. Then if the lioness wasn't already dead we'd get her.

'I turned to move away, and I was about thirty or forty yards from this patch of grass when I heard a growl, and I spun round. There was this lioness coming for me. I had a quick shot with apparently no effect, but I thought, well, when she gets really close I'll certainly hit her. I had a magazine rifle and I went to reload it and the empty shell had not extracted and I tried to ram in another one and it jammed! Of course by then she was just about on me. All I could do was to ram the muzzle of the rifle into her mouth and she bit the rifle and wrenched it out of my hand and got me in the right forearm and knocked me over backwards. I got up and I had a hunting knife on my right side, but as I tried to draw it – my arm was quite numb and useless – she came at me again. She grabbed me by the left thigh and shook me like a rat and then she disappeared. I thought maybe she is just behind me, and any movement I make she'll be on me again. So I kept absolutely still: my rifle was lying about three or four feet in front of me. Then the tension became unbearable and I finally edged forward, got the rifle and managed to get it working again. I stood up and there was no sign whatever of the lioness. By then I was losing quite a lot of blood and I thought I'd better try to make my way to the camp; and I started but couldn't go very far because I was losing blood. So I sat down with my back to a tree and I fired off shots and, I suppose an hour later, my men had heard these shots and came to look for me. I was carried to camp because I couldn't walk. The first one to come, funnily enough, was a prisoner, a poacher; he couldn't speak Swahili. Anyhow, he saw that I was injured and I pointed to the camp and motioned, so he went and got the rangers and brought along a camp-bed and I was carted back to camp and put into my tent.

'In those days, of course, you had no radio and they were saying I had to get some sort of help. So I sent a ranger off with a message in a cleft stick to Maralal, which was the headquarters of the district. It took him about three days to get there, and when he got to Maralal the DC [District Commissioner] wasn't there; he'd gone on safari another forty miles. So the ranger had to go the other forty miles and finally he gave this message to the District Commissioner, who then had to telegraph from a place called Archer's Post to Nairobi for help. Luckily the RAF were in Nairobi and they very kindly volunteered to come and pick me up at Maralal and in the meantime the District Commissioner had to get to my camp. There was no road; they actually had to cut a road. So it was six days after I got mauled that he arrived. They carted me back to Maralal and during that time just by luck I happened to have a pillbox of sulphanilamide among the pills which I'd used previously for a poisoned hand. It'd only just come into this country, this drug. Luckily I had some of it left and I took it and I'd instructed my men to bathe the wounds every hour or so with a solution of epsom salts and to do this whether I protested or not. [Because of their habit of eating putrid meat, anyone mauled by a lion runs a serious risk of getting gangrene. Later, George told Jack Barrah, who was one of his trainees and is now a senior wildlife adviser, that he took the new drug, sulphanilamide, known as 693, every six hours and that really saved his life.]

'I remember while the man was off with this note, one night there was a commotion in the camp, again the donkeys all braying, and an elephant trumpeting. I was helped by a man who was sleeping in the tent looking after me. He handed me a rifle which luckily was loaded and I propped myself up against the front pole of the tent with the rifle and there was this dark shape coming down, this elephant charging, the same elephant that I'd seen that morning. I was in no state to dodge away [on top of everything else, George was suffering from a bout of malaria, brought on by the shock] so all I could do was to shoot into this elephant, and he came past the tent and collapsed and the next morning they found him about eighty yards away, dead.

'Eventually the District Commissioner arrived and I was carted to Maralal and there were the two RAF planes waiting, two bombers, Wellesley bombers, complete with a doctor and blood transfusion apparatus and saws and knives and all that sort of thing, because they thought I'd be in a pretty bad way. Anyhow, I wasn't too bad, because I'd had the sulphanilamide pills.'

When it came to getting into the aeroplane, George offered to climb into the cockpit. 'They said, "Oh no, we've got a special drill for casualties." So the doctor put me in a sort of strait jacket and I was pushed through the bomb hatch into the aeroplane, the first time I'd ever been in an aeroplane. And I was able to sit up and see the scenery; it was quite nice, actually.'

After three weeks George was fit enough to leave hospital. His right arm was still stiff but a month's massage put it more or less right and by mid-August he was back on duty again.

Sometimes, the man-eaters were so bold and cunning that even George failed to get the better of them. Just before the Italians invaded Kenya in 1940 he made another safari to Lake Turkana via the Mathews Range, visiting on the way a place called Kitonongop. The local Samburu were being terrorised by a pride of five lions and were so frightened that they were on the point of evacuating the area. His description of the ensuing hunt is extremely exciting, despite being charmingly underplayed, as was always his way. One can see why Willie Hale described him as 'completely fearless'.

Late in the afternoon on the day of George's arrival, while the donkeys were being unloaded, there was a great commotion at a nearby *manyatta* [native camp]. A lion had just taken a sheep and was eating it inside an adjacent thicket. It was a big animal, the Samburu said, and very aggressive; it would attack anyone who approached while it was feeding. With characteristic *sang-froid*, George walked up to the thicket, expecting to hear at least a warning growl, but there was not a sound. Entering the thicket, he found the half-eaten remains of the sheep and the pug marks of a big lion leading away. Taking two of his scouts with him, George followed up the spoor until it was too dark to go any farther, but they did catch a glimpse of a large animal as it disappeared into the thick thorn bush.

All night long the lions roared near the camp, as if to taunt their pursuers, one of them in particular having a deep, gruff roar. This, George was convinced, was the man-eater. At dawn, a Samburu tribesman came running up to say one of his cows had been taken during the night. George set off to investigate and came upon the kill in thick cover with the lion still on it. Unfortunately the Samburu had failed to warn George that they were getting close and, as he was in the direct line of fire, the lion, a big specimen with a dark tawny mane, was able to escape. They followed his trail, which led in a circle, until once more they heard the crunching of bones at the kill. But the lion had heard them and again managed to slip away. They pursued him for another two hours but although they could hear him in the bush just ahead of them, it was so thick they could never get close enough to glimpse him. Eventually they stopped for a rest, and George was having some cold tea when there were yells and shouts from a *manyatta* some distance away: another goat had been taken, this time by a lioness. It was too late to try to follow.

During the night George was woken up by an odd sound which he at first could not identify, until he realised it was made by lions drinking from a small rain pool not more than a hundred yards away. It sounded like a dog lapping, only much louder and with longer pauses between each lap. George got out of bed and went to the door of the tent with his torch and his rifle at the ready. Five pairs of eyes stared back at him, reflected in the beam. He fired, but missed.

In the morning he again visited the remains of the cow but no lions had been there, so after making a wide circle through the bush he and his rangers returned to camp. Late in the afternoon he suddenly heard the terrified braying of a donkey and the growls of lions and raced over to find two young lions on top of one of his donkeys. Breathless from running, his aim unsteady, George missed and the lions made off. With his scouts he tracked them until nearly dusk, when the lions apparently went through a small herd of elephant, causing great alarm and excitement, with loud trumpetings from the cow elephants as they circled in the bush looking for the lions. George and his men had to get out in a hurry. Lions sometimes attack baby elephants and so a herd containing cows and calves will not tolerate their presence, although adult bulls usually take no notice.

The donkey was so badly mauled that George had to shoot it. In desperation he poisoned the carcase with strychnine, the first and only time he deliberately used poison against a lion. During the night he heard them at the carcase and at first light found two hyenas dead near the remains and the tracks of two lions leading off into the bush. He and his men followed and soon came to a place where the lions had vomited. A little farther on his trackers disturbed the lions but in the thick cover George was again unable even to see them. But they had gone straight up a twelve-foot river bank, so it was evident they had fully recovered from the poison. On his return to camp, the African who looked after the donkeys reported that soon after they left another lion had come and dragged the donkey remains away. With exemplary persistence George set off once again, but once again they were outwitted, the lion keeping just ahead and cunningly working round back towards the donkey remains.

This time George hid behind an anthill and told his men to talk loudly and then walk away. He hoped that when the lions heard the men's voices receding, they would be duped into thinking that the hunt was over and return to the kill. This stratagem had often proved successful in the past, but the lions of Kitonongop were possessed of devilish cunning and, he says, no doubt laughed at him as he lay in wait for two hours in vain.

That night, 'as if in derision', the lions came close to the camp and roared. At dawn George and his rangers were off again, the spoor leading westwards along a wide game path for about six miles. They came across a pugnacious bull elephant who would not give way and later were held up by a herd of cow elephants and calves. They had to be given a wide berth, too, as they were already angry at the passing of the lions. Picking up the lion spoor again, they came to a place where the lions had made an unsuccessful attack on a giraffe; then the tracks turned off into particularly thick bush. George was certain the lions had gone to lie up for the day, so with infinite caution the men followed, and soon heard the familiar low growl, followed by the sound of the lions escaping. At this point George broke off the pursuit. He had already spent a week on the hunt and the safari was well behind schedule, so he advised the Samburu to admit defeat and vacate the territory of the Kitonongop lions for the time being. He told them, not quite as confidently as General Douglas MacArthur at Corregidor, that he hoped to return.

Continuing the safari, George proceeded to Loingalane, the oasis of warm springs and nodding palms, and then turned east towards Mount Kulal, which he had climbed five years before with Nevil Baxendale in their fruitless quest for gold. This time he chose the southernmost of the three peaks, which was covered by thick forest and was the home of that most regal of antelopes, the greater kudu. George had never shot one but it had been his ambition to do so for a long while. One morning when he was out alone, he saw a magnificent bull standing alone on the summit of the ridge. He stalked it and paused when he was only sixty yards away. Slowly the kudu grazed towards him and he watched entranced until it was only thirty feet away. George thought how easy it would be to shoot it and perhaps bag a record head. But he immediately rejected the idea: it would be despicable to take the life of such a noble creature. Finally, the kudu passed only fifteen feet from where he was sitting, still unaware of his presence, and went on its majestic way. For George Adamson, for whom hunting had always been a passion, this was a dramatic turning point. He had lost the urge to kill and, instead, found in himself the urge to protect. It was a feeling which would become steadily stronger during the course of his long life.

Chapter Four

A CHRISTMAS PARTY

Mussolini declared war on Britain on 10 June 1940, but his armies were already in Italian Somaliland and Eritrea, from where they had invaded Abyssinia (now Ethiopia) four years before. Il Duce's announcement posed an immediate threat to neighbouring Kenya, and the colony's slender defences were immediately mobilised. George Adamson only learned the news on his arrival in Marsabit, in the far north, after nearly being arrested by a suspicious police patrol which thought he and his men were an Italian raiding party. When that misunderstanding had been cleared up, he hurried south to Maralal – it was a twelve-day march – impatient to join up. To his disgust he was told to stay in Samburu country with his six game scouts and eight policemen and patrol the northern borders of the district, an area of four thousand square miles. His task was to prevent panic among the tribesmen and stop them fleeing south into the European farming area. Later he joined military intelligence and was sent to Wajir, another desert outpost, this time in the east near the Somali border. Wajir boasts a royal yacht club, said to be the only yacht club in the world in the middle of a desert. As patron, Prince Philip is entitled to wear the club tie, a silver yacht and palm tree on a dark blue background, undoubtedly one of the more exclusive relics of colonial English life. The club's *raison d'être*, according to an old member, Major Douglas Collins, was simple: it had nothing to do with yachting but a great deal to do with gin.

In Wajir, George Adamson's job was to recruit Somali agents to spy on Italian troop movements. Although they did not always know the difference between a tractor and a tank, the Somalis were very accurate when it came to enemy locations and numbers. This training in basic intelligence techniques was to stand George in good stead later when, as a game warden, he ran his own extensive and efficient anti-poaching networks. After several comic-opera raids against irregular Italian native forces, called Banda, a friend of George's suggested he should join him in raising a counter-force drawn from local Somali and Boran tribesmen. George was happy to do so and enthusiastically began to recruit volunteers on the principle of 'the wilder and woollier they were, the better we liked them.'

At one point he and his irregulars were attached to a South African force which had established a perimeter base at Dif on the Kenya–Somali border. Shortly after their arrival, they were bombed by the

Italian air force. The bombs fell close and machine-gun bullets whistled all around but luckily no one was hit. Just as the Italian aircraft – five Caproni bombers and four Fiat fighters – were turning away, a single Hurricane fighter came skimming over the bush. It was the first they had seen, and it went straight for the Italian formation and, in a few minutes, had brought down three bombers and a fighter. This victory did wonders for British morale as, until then, the Italians had enjoyed almost complete air supremacy, the British having nothing to challenge them apart from some ancient biplanes.

Soon afterwards, the British and South African advance into Somaliland began, and so feeble was the Italian resistance that George and his men quickly found themselves at the Somali port of Kismayu on the Indian Ocean, about one hundred miles north of the Kenya border. The fighting over, George Adamson found himself assigned to the less dashing role of colonial administrator. Most of the Italian farms in the Juba River area were deserted – their owners having left in a hurry – and the local Somalis had helped themselves to the contents. Having found a fine new house in a large banana plantation, the new administrator was not pleased to discover that it had been completely cleared and used by the local tribespeople as a lavatory. George sent for the local headman and when, predictably, he denied all knowledge, led him to the front of the house, pointed to a large tree with many spreading branches, and told him he would hang at dawn unless the new occupier slept on a comfortable bed in a clean house that night. Shortly afterwards a long line of villagers appeared, carrying most of the looted furniture on their heads. George set them to work to scrub out the house, making sure the headman got his hands dirty too. Although it was clear that the plantation had been run with farm machinery, the tractors had all entirely disappeared. George summoned the headman again and told him he was seriously thinking of using the tree after all, as his orders had been disobeyed. Where was the farm machinery?

Swallowing hard, the headman quavered that he had been so frightened by George's threats that the tractors had completely slipped his memory. Protesting he had hidden them to keep them safe, the headman disappeared and shortly afterwards came the roar of heavy engines and two caterpillar tractors appeared. But there was nearly a last-minute upset. One of George's irregulars thought they were enemy tanks and, diving into a ditch, opened fire. Fortunately, he did not shoot very well.

In 1941, after nearly eleven months of active service, Adamson was due for leave. Since there was no transport in the interior, he returned to Kismayu on the coast, hoping to get a boat to Mombasa and then a train to Nairobi. But there were no boats and he decided to hitch a lift with an Arab trader who offered him a seat in one of his ramshackle lorries in return for George's help in getting him a permit to enter Kenya. The intrepid warrior nearly came to grief before he started. During the night he was woken by a loud bang but, thinking it was merely another unexploded Italian bomb or shell going off, turned over and went back to sleep. In the morning, to his consternation, he found that a huge chandelier had come loose from the ceiling and crashed in smithereens on the bedside table. A few inches closer and it would have fallen on George's head. It would, as he put it, have been an odd way of ending his career as a soldier.

The journey itself was almost as hazardous. It started fairly normally, until suddenly the lorry in which he was travelling with his Arab friend shot off the road and ran up against a tree, shattering the best headlamp. The driver staggered out and lay on the ground groaning while everyone gathered around to commiserate. After a quick examination George was able to assure him that he was not fatally injured and insisted they continue on their journey. Eventually he reached Nairobi where, after a long talk, his mentor, Archie Ritchie, applied for George's release from the army on the grounds that he had joined the forces to fight, not to act as an administrator-cum-policeman in occupied territory. The request was granted and he was soon back at work as a game warden in the Northern Frontier District.

There was plenty to do. Poaching was rife; the illegal trade in ivory, rhino horn and leopardskins had thrived in his absence, and there were numerous complaints of marauding lion and elephant. But he was unable to do anything about the vastly destructive legalised slaughter of game occurring on the European ranches, where great numbers of animals were being killed to provide meat for the Italian prisoners of war. This massacre was not carried out by Game Department employees but by private contractors who shot the animals with no regard to whether they were pregnant females or with young, and sold the carcases at a handsome profit to the prison camps. The whole thing was anathema to George, who believed the wholesale slaughter of eland, oryx and zebra was causing irreparable damage to wildlife, not only in those areas but to the whole migratory cycle. Indeed, he said in the late 1960s that almost thirty years later some of the species, particularly the oryx, had still not recovered. To make matters worse, there was no truth in the claim that this was the only means of feeding the prisoners: many native areas were grossly over-stocked with domestic animals. It was simply, George felt, an easy way out for the Government. It fed the prisoners on cheap meat and mollified the European farmers, who constantly complained about the depredations caused by game on their grazing, while avoiding the awkward issue of de-stocking the native reserves.

Typically, George Adamson's first thought was for the wild animals, which he always saw as being, in a sense, the wards of man. He certainly considered himself their guardian and came to feel that mankind as a whole must share that responsibility. His concern for the animals in his care was well demonstrated when at the end of 1942 he was ordered to take over the Garissa District on the Tana River as well as his own. This involved a lot of elephant control, or culling, which he found distasteful. In the dry season herds of elephant had to cross cultivated land to reach the Tana River and there was constant trouble about damage to crops. George's sympathies were almost entirely with the elephant. How were they to differentiate between unprotected cultivation and their natural food? The tribesmen were too lazy to build fences or to guard their crops at night, but it was his duty to protect them, however much it went against the grain to kill 'these noble creatures'. The noble creatures, of course, could turn nasty and give the hunter a bad fright. One day, George went after an old bull which, having raided a banana plantation, was sleeping it off in some dense riverine forest. After a long, difficult stalk through the undergrowth to get a clear shot to the head, George fired and the elephant fell like a log. Then, just as one of his scouts was cutting off its tail, the beast hauled itself up. The scout, who was carrying George's heavy rifle, promptly took to his heels and George had to run after him. He managed to get off two more shots, but the angle was awkward and they had to track the old bull for six hours before they finally came up to him – lying on the ground. This time he was really dead!

The District Commissioner in charge of Garissa was Willie Hale, whom George Adamson had first met on the Kerio River eight years before while prospecting for gold. Hale and his wife Morna invited George to spend Christmas 1942 with them. The festivities began with a Christmas Eve party, and among the guests were a couple called Peter and Joy Bally. Peter, a member of the famous Swiss shoe family, was a botanist, and Joy had just started painting flowers. (Her collection is now in the National Museum in Nairobi.) In the first of his two autobiographies, *Bwana Game*, George says his recollections of the evening are vague, but he does remember waking up in the morning fully dressed with his feet on the pillow. In his second, *My Pride and Joy*, he goes into more detail. There he says that, although Peter Bally, with his monocle, retained a certain formality, 'his wife, whom he introduced as Joy, and who turned out to be Austrian, was quite uninhibited. Fair-haired and slim, she wore a slinky, silver dress and seemed entirely unaware that her growing animation accentuated the distortions of her curious English.' No wonder Joy was animated. Willie Hale, whom George describes as an amusing and relentless host, had laid in a stock of very potent drink.

Talking to me nearly fifty years later, Willie Hale recalled, 'It was still the wartime. We got only a ration of beer but the Italians down in Somalia had manufactured a lot of booze from sugar alcohol which they flavoured with various things like millefiori, rum and whisky. It all tasted the same but it had a kick in it. The policeman and myself used to go down to Kismayu to discuss various matters with the European district officer and bring it back, and as the policeman and I were also the customs officers these things came in duty free! Well, we had a consignment of this stuff, which was fairly strong if you hadn't drunk it before. We sat up on top and we had an *ngoma*, that is a dance, of all the locals down below, and to be honest I was so full of good cheer that I can't remember very much of what happened.'

It was clearly a very convivial evening. As the *ngoma* got going, the singing and the dancing began to infect the European party. Some of them went down to dance in the moonlight, while George and Joy started to sing on the roof. From the moment they began to compete with the rising shouts of the tribesmen, however, George's memories grow dim. Joy admitted the next morning, however, that on the way to her tent she ripped her seductive dress on the few strands of wire which the Ballys had put round their tent to ward off wild animals.

In her autobiography, *The Searching Spirit*, published in 1978, Joy says the two things which struck her most were George's romantic arrival and his capacity for alcohol. She remembers that a crowd of Somali and riverine tribesmen had gathered round the house all set for a big *ngoma* when, suddenly, they scattered and a line of camels appeared with George Adamson riding at their head. After a quick bath he joined the other guests on the roof. Willie Hale offered him a stiff whisky, then a second, then a third. By now, Joy says, she and Morna Hale were showing some concern, but George said defiantly: 'I never get tight.' That was all the ladies needed to try to prove him wrong. They poured brandy into his soup, into his gravy, into everything he ate. Joy watched him anxiously, attracted by his large blue eyes, his sun-tanned face framed by blond hair and his carefully trimmed goatee beard.

Whatever the details of the evening, Willie Hale says he is quite certain about one thing. 'As soon as Joy set her eyes on George, I think she'd made up her mind. George – he was not unwilling if you know what I mean – he'd been wandering about without a woman for some time and he was quite willing to make friends with Joy and I'm pretty certain that Peter Bally was anxious to … he just gave George a little poke in the back and pushed him down the hill. Archie Ritchie said that George was like a sitting rabbit.'

In the euphoria engendered by the Hales' party, George had apparently extended an invitation to the Ballys to join him on a forthcoming camel safari. Next day, to George's horror, Peter Bally announced that they would be delighted to accept. He could remember nothing at all about it. He was off to the Boni Forest which was believed to be very tough going, and a frivolous young woman from Vienna seemed a most unsuitable travel companion. But the Ballys were keen, and also Willie's guests. George felt he was not in a position to turn them down.

The next few days seem to have been spent in preparing for the safari and indulging in a quaint old colonial custom. Morna Hale, whose memory is still sharp, says, 'I can remember we went out and had what was known as a "Baldwin in the bush". There was nothing to do up there so we picked up our drinks and went out and we went to the nearest tree and sat down. We had a drink and then we came back again. I can remember them doing that and laughing at it.' The 'Baldwin in the bush' was apparently named after Stanley Baldwin, who was Conservative Prime Minister in the twenties and again from 1935–37 at the time of the abdication of King Edward VIII. Perhaps it appealed to the colonial sense of humour to contrast the imagined sophistication of life at Number Ten with the extremely primitive conditions that existed in a place like Garissa.

Leaving the Hales behind, George and the Ballys departed. As soon as they set off on their camels Joy started to talk, very fast, in her guttural Austrian accent. Among the things she told George were that her real Christian names were Friederike Victoria and her nickname Fifi. But Peter had found the first two such a mouthful and the last so frivolous that he called her Joy. George soon discovered that there was nothing frivolous about her stamina. Her mental and physical energy were astonishing and her clothes, from sun helmet to canvas boots, impeccable. She had never ridden a camel before, and was soon chafed and bleeding, but she never complained. From being impressed, George became infatuated. Within a few days he sensed a growing attraction between them, which Joy seemed to encourage. To respond, he says, would have been out of the question: Peter Bally was his guest and George liked him. He therefore arranged to strike off on his own and let the Ballys join Willie Hale, who would soon be coming that way on his own safari.

This did not please Joy, who, according to Morna Hale, 'said she was very cross at having to go down to the coast without him.' She was clearly intrigued by this strong, silent 'he-man'. He was a puzzle to her, she confessed, attributing his silent nature to his lonely life. Morna had told Joy only half-jokingly that George never listened to what people said and had only three answers which covered all possible situations. 'Oh', 'Really', and 'How extraordinary'. They were clearly falling in love but did it go any farther? George says he did not respond but both Major Dougie Collins and another old friend, Ray Mayers, believe the contrary. Dougie Collins told me, 'By this time in their marriage Bally wanted out and I don't blame the fellow. She knew exactly what she wanted. She, by this time, had obviously set her cap at George. Dear old George, he hadn't a chance. She went into his tent and George seduced her, or rather, she seduced him. Then Bally – it must have been arranged between them – came into the tent as the Frogs would say at the *moment critique* and dear old George, being a gentleman, shot out of bed in his kikoi, saluted and said – I don't know whether he was puffing his pipe or not – "Of course, we are in love and intend to get married."'

'That's the story that went round,' says Ray Mayers. 'George was too much of a gent to say no and when he was caught by Bally, he said, "I'm going to marry the girl." That's what everybody believed. Joy made the proposal and took him, more or less.' Of Joy, Mayers says, 'She was man hungry. All those Austrian and Danish women – they're all man hungry.' Whether George was the perfect gentleman as he insists, or was swept off his feet and seduced by Joy, as Dougie Collins and Ray Mayers insist, we may never know. Given Joy's personality, and her determination to get what she wanted at all times, it is very possible that they are right, but George would never admit it. One thing does seem beyond doubt. As surely as George Adamson ever had a man-eating lion in his sights, Joy Bally had him in hers. All she had to do was to wait for the right moment and pull the trigger.

The right moment took a little time to arrive. George Adamson tried to put the Ballys and the disturbing personality of Joy out of his mind and concentrated on catching poachers. It was six months before he next visited Nairobi, summoned to a conference by Archie Ritchie. Stepping out of the Norfolk Hotel he was amazed to be 'seized' by Joy Bally, who immediately invited him to tea the next day. George tried to put her off, but that evening he bumped into Peter Bally, who repeated the invitation. So the next afternoon, he arrived to be greeted warmly, even affectionately, by Joy and her grey cairn terrier, Pippin; but there was no sign of Peter, nor of any servants. That was strange enough, but the real surprise was to follow.

Joy said she was very unhappy and that she and Peter were getting divorced. Just before George had arrived at the Hales' at Christmas, she said, they had all been talking about his narrow escape from the lioness and the elephant and she had decided that he was just the man for her. Their few days on safari together had confirmed it. She then fixed George with her blue eyes and smiled an unspoken question. George says that it took him several days to absorb this extraordinary state of affairs and he hesitated even after Peter had corroborated it all. It was only later, when the divorce had been planned in some detail, he says, that he surrendered to Joy's attractions and fell madly in love.

It was during this period, in 1943, that a curious incident took place which does not appear in either of George's autobiographies, nor, needless to say, in Joy's strait-laced story of her life. It is not only, to the onlooker at least, an extremely funny story, but it does show, even at that early stage in their relationship, just how spectacularly bad-tempered Joy could be. It was told to me by Ray Mayers, the son of a wealthy Australian sugar baron who made one fortune in Australia and another in Kenya, where he finally settled. Ray had been a close friend of George and his brother Terence from the early thirties when the young Adamsons were making their living collecting wild honey in the bush. Sitting on the verandah of his ranch overlooking the Tsavo National Park, a bottle of gin in front of him, Ray Mayers recalled how he met George one day in Nairobi and went on a pub crawl with him. George, partly because he never liked being in a city and partly to save money, was camping with Joy at Lone Tree in what is now Nairobi National Park. 'It was already late in the evening,' Mayers told me, 'when George announced, "We'll take some girls [mutual friends] and go up to the camp for dinner." He said nothing about having got engaged to Joy or anything. We took two cars. I had a pick-up at the time. George and Helen [Ray's wife] were in front, and we went up over what is now the [National] Park and drove across the plain and saw a hell of a lot of spring hare. They jumped up in front of the car. They're easy to catch if you get them in your lights; you just walk round in the shadow behind them and grab them by the leg.

'As we drove up to the camp, George still said nothing, and I saw a woman come out of the tent. I thought, Bloody funny, George isn't inclined toward women very much. Then George said, "We've come to have dinner." At this the woman went back into the tent and came out with George's suitcase and all his clothes, walked about thirty yards to the gorge that runs up to Hippo Pool, and threw all his things into the ravine – it's very steep there! Then she came back into the kitchen, took all the pots and pans and threw them over the edge too.

'All George could say was, "Good Lord, good Lord." I said, "George, what the hell's this?" and he said, "I didn't tell you. I'm engaged to Joy Bally!" Anyhow, George said, "We'd better go back and have dinner in town." And so we left Joy there. She didn't offer to get in the car or anything, and on the way back we tried to catch a spring hare, and one of the girls fell off the back of the pick-up and broke her neck … luckily she was all right.'

Ray Mayers says he expected George 'got hell' from Joy afterwards, because 'he always did'.

In the late forties, after the war, when Mayers was buying cattle for his farm, he lived near the Adamsons at Isiolo. George, despite being a man of few words, enjoyed company and would often call in on Ray and be offered a drink. Sometimes, one drink would lead to another.

'George used to have to come past my camp to go into Isiolo,' Mayers recalled. 'One day he had a very important letter from Joy to post. But for two days he never got past my camp! After I'd had him in my house for a couple of days, I went up to say good morning to Joy and she slammed the door in my face.'

Opinions vary greatly as to how attractive Joy was then, when she was in her early thirties. Willie Hale says: 'Joy was not an attractive woman. She was very talented; she was a good painter, a botanist, a sculptor, and I believe she was a musician too. She was not attractive. She lacked the one thing a woman must have and that is charm. She was only out for herself, she talked at the rate of knots, she was a very bad linguist. She spoke English badly, with a strong Austrian accent. Her Swahili was appalling and she was a terrible car driver and that was a tragedy because I've forgotten how many accidents she had.

'Eventually she broke her right arm, and she had a claw hand and found it difficult to paint. She had a small body and strong legs. How do I know this? When I went on safari with Joy and George to Marsabit I walked up a hill in the forest behind Joy and I could see those two legs of hers, pounding away. She had a little body and she was indefatigable, she didn't know what fear was. She was not attractive, not for me anyhow. But she was a very strong character.' Other men clearly did find her attractive.

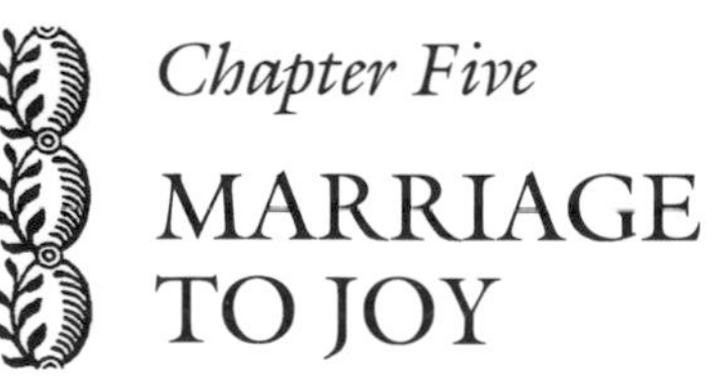

Chapter Five

MARRIAGE TO JOY

Despite his personal happiness George Adamson found 1943 the 'most anxious and difficult' of his life. Divorce was still a dirty word in the colonial Establishment – whatever went on in Happy Valley, the home of the hard-drinking, fast-living rich white settlers – and he was seriously worried that he might be asked to resign from the Game Department for running off with another man's wife. His boss, the ever resourceful Archie Ritchie, had to assure the Chief Secretary, the most important man in the colony after the Governor, that George Adamson had not caused the break-up of the Ballys' marriage. Official approval was eventually given for a discreet divorce and an equally quiet wedding in due course, but George and Joy's troubles were far from over. During the year it would take for the divorce to come through, Joy wanted to camp near George's house at Isiolo, collecting and painting wild flowers. But the idea was officially vetoed as 'highly improper'. As a way out, George reluctantly agreed to install Joy on Mount Kenya, about fifty miles to the south-west, where she would paint the mountain flora. She camped at eleven thousand feet in a lovely forest glade, from where she could look up at the snow-covered peaks six thousand feet above; and if her camp was invaded by a wandering elephant or buffalo, a convenient tree with a sloping trunk would make an ideal escape route. After fixing up the camp, Joy and George set off with two mules and a small tent to climb to the foot of the main peaks and then go round them. George was quietly pleased that, although he had never been so high before, the altitude of about fifteen thousand feet did not make him ill. But even more impressive was his fiancée's stamina: Joy proved once again that she was a tireless walker and they completed the circuit in about eight hours.

For company on the mountain, Joy had only a cook, her gun-bearer and her cairn terrier Pippin. It sounds idyllic, but it must also have been very lonely. George would visit her whenever he could and they would go for long walks across the moorland searching for plants which Joy would later draw and sit talking for long hours beside the camp fire.

George's last foot safari as a bachelor nearly proved to be the last of his life. He was called out to deal with a rogue elephant which had been chasing local tribesmen and killing cattle near Maralal, in the Samburu country. Moving through dense bush, George was surprised to see the four Samburu who were accompanying him and his scout,

Lembirdan, race past him on his right. He was caught off guard when the elephant then materialised, without any warning, almost on top of him but to the left. He had no time to aim, fired blindly into its face and then, as he sprang to get out of its way, tripped and fell in front of it. Just as he expected to feel an enormous trunk gripping him or a huge foot descending, Lembirdan, who had stood his ground unflinchingly, fired and forced the elephant to change direction. It was a close escape and taught George a lesson: never turn your back, however close an animal may be.

A little later, when George had recovered, they tracked the elephant down in even thicker bush. He was killed by two more shots from the heavy double-barrelled rifle, a very big bull with tusks weighing together about 140 pounds.

Whenever he could, George would spend the weekend at Mount Kenya. Once, he had to change his plans at the last minute to deal with man-eating lions. Camping out by a stream near a Boran village on the Kinna River, he listened to lions roaring continuously some distance away most of the night. In the dark and quiet their voices expressed, for George, the very spirit of the wild and the free. In poetic mood, he listened to their chorus and thought what a splendid theme it would make for some great composer. He also imagined some long-dead ancestor crouching in his smoky cave, putting another log on the fire and perhaps praying silently for the safety of himself and his sleeping family as the roars came closer. Finally George went to sleep hoping that this link with the past would never be silenced.

So, with Joy in her alpine refuge on Mount Kenya, and George pursuing his adventurous but often dangerous life as a game warden, the weeks slipped by. Separation and hardship only increased their love for one another but Joy's courage and determination, in particular, were remarkable. How many women would have lived in the bush in Kenya, halfway up a mountain, alone except for a few servants, and taken it all in their stride? But perhaps in the end it was too much even for Joy. At the last minute, she said she wanted to call the whole thing off.

George reacted with, as he says in *My Pride and Joy*, 'a combination of anguish and anger'. He was extremely upset at Joy's sudden change of heart and, frightened that it would scandalise the stuffier members of Kenyan society, thought his livelihood might be threatened as well. Typically, he drew a parallel with the courtship of lions: 'The message had gone out from the female [he says] and had produced a response from the male, which was being treated in turn by rebuff. There was only one thing to do [he decided], to put down my foot and mobilise the full support of our friends.' George's perhaps unexpected show of spirit carried the day. Just over a year after they first met, Joy Bally, née Gessner, and George Adamson were married in Nairobi. In George's words, 'it was a simple wedding, on African soil, of an Irishman born in India to an Austrian who was leaving a Swiss.' They were penniless.

Joy brought to her third marriage a fairly complicated and colourful past. Born in 1910 in the Sudetenland, the German-speaking part of Czechoslovakia, Joy and her two sisters, Traute and Dorle (Dorothy), grew up in comfortable surroundings. Her mother's family owned large estates and her happiest childhood memories were of large family parties in the country. But the smooth tenor of her childhood was shattered when her mother left her father to marry someone else. She was only twelve. Much later George Adamson was to say he did not think she ever really got over the shock and unhappiness, and he felt there must have been something cruel, or at least unusually cold, about Joy's mother. However, by the time she was twenty-five and living in Vienna, Joy had developed into a sparkling, attractive young woman. At a party in 1935, she met a rich aristocrat, Victor von Klarwill, who fell in love with her at first sight and vowed to marry her. He did the same year and they had an exciting life together for a time, ski-ing in

Below left: Family portrait taken before Joy's parents divorced when she was twelve. (From left to right) Joy, her father, her mother with baby Dorle on her lap and her elder sister, Traute

Below right: Joy and Traute, in best bib and tucker

the Alps and travelling the world; but von Klarwill was Jewish and felt threatened by Hitler's increasingly strident demands that Austria should become part of the Third Reich. He and Joy, who was now pregnant, decided they should settle somewhere else and were thinking about Kenya when she had a miscarriage. Von Klarwill put her on a boat to Mombasa to convalesce but during the voyage she fell for the charms of a fellow passenger. His name was Peter Bally. By the time they docked in Mombasa, she had decided to marry him. Joy returned to Austria to break the news to von Klarwill and arrange a divorce, and then, in March 1938, sailed again for Africa. It was the day of the Anschluss, when Hitler and his Stormtroopers marched into Austria.

Safely installed in Kenya, Joy took to her new life with enthusiasm. Peter Bally was a Swiss botanist working at the (then) Coryndon Museum in Nairobi, travelling all over the country in search of plants. As befitted the scion of a shoe magnate, his safaris were on the grand scale, with one hundred and fifty porters carrying all the necessities for civilised living through the forests and highlands of Kenya. But physically it was strenuous and Joy had a second miscarriage.

Dr Mary Leakey, whose husband, Dr Louis Leakey, the distinguished anthropologist, also worked for the museum, met Joy soon after she arrived in Kenya. The Ballys used to go and stay with the Leakeys at their camp in Nakuru, about one hundred miles north-west of Nairobi. 'We were friends,' Mary Leakey told me, 'and later on

Left: 1920. Joy (right) and Traute, in period costume, going to a fancy-dress ball. Joy was ten

Right: Joy in elaborate fancy dress, as a 'Russian candlestick' wooden doll. She wrote to her sister Dorle: 'I hope you like it. Love, Fifi.'

when we moved to Nairobi they lived in the guest house. That was at the outbreak of war. Louis thought she was a spy. He was convinced. He hated her. He really did. He tried to convince himself that she was a spy but really on no grounds at all. He wanted to believe it.' So much so that when Joy and two friends visited the Congo, Louis Leakey, who was in Intelligence, sent a message to the Ugandan border post at Jinja suggesting that Joy, as an Austrian, should be stopped and investigated. They were strip searched and held up for several hours. Joy was furious, although she says the thought did occur to her that this might be one of Louis Leakey's 'jokes'.

Mary Leakey says: 'From his [Louis'] point of view it wasn't a joke. He really would have been delighted to catch her out in something. I think we parted company at that point.' Mary Leakey, a small, soft-spoken woman now in her seventies, said neither she nor her husband liked Joy. 'Very few people did, to be quite honest. In a way she was quite attractive, lively, but not a likeable personality.' Asked if Joy was difficult then, Mary Leakey says, 'Difficult? Not as she became later on, wanting to run the show so to speak. But irritating I would say, more than difficult, she talked too much and didn't really listen to what anybody else had to say, or didn't pay much attention to anyone else. Very irritating personality, that's all there was to it.

'She talked so fast, so much rubbish, one tended not to listen. She wasn't dumb stupid, but on the other hand she wasn't intellectual, and she had a knack of putting people's backs up. She never had any staying power, much. She would take up one thing and get very excited about it for a bit and then, before she'd really seen it through, she'd be off on another tangent. She was pretty nasty to Peter Bally, too. She was very selfish. That was apparent to everybody, I think. It was really only Joy that mattered, although the animals mattered to her; that she was quite genuine about. And the money she made, she certainly put into animal welfare, not like some of the other ladies who've done that sort of thing and put money into their pockets. In that way you can respect her.'

Like many others, Mary Leakey sees Joy as quite ruthless, someone who knew what she wanted and 'went straight for it, regardless'. Peter Bally, on the other hand, was a nice, quiet, well-educated German-Swiss. 'I think at first he genuinely fell for her and wanted to marry her but it soon wore off, that's the impression we got. And although they weren't officially separated or divorced, they led fairly separate lives. They worked together on botanical things, her flower paintings and so on, but that was very early on in the marriage.'

By the time Joy met George Adamson at the end of 1942, the marriage was virtually over. 'I think she found it wasn't such fun as she thought it was going to be and Peter Bally was just tired of her. George was a heaven-sent gift at that time, because it meant that she could go into the bush and do all the things she'd been wanting to do.' Mary Leakey shares the view held by Willie Hale, Dougie Collins and Ray Mayers, that from the moment she saw him, George had no chance at all. 'He was,' she says with a chuckle, 'compromised immediately.

'When Joy was killed [at her camp in Shaba, northern Kenya, in 1980],' Mary Leakey continued, 'Peter Bally's comment was, "All the

Joy on board ship on her way to Mombasa in 1939

world mourns Joy, except her three husbands." That's just about right.'

Joy's own explanation of the break-up of her second marriage is, understandably, much blander and less unflattering to herself. Although their minds were in harmony, she says, their characters and energies were not compatible. Soon after she had reached this conclusion, George Adamson appeared in her life. It was too good an opportunity to miss.

Soon after their marriage in January 1944, the ever practical George persuaded the Game Department to give him £1,500 to build a house at Isiolo and got his brother Terence to design it with a sitting room large enough to take Joy's piano and easels. Joy tried to adapt herself to the life of a game warden's wife, but she did not find it easy, while George admits she was not always easy to live with either, being restless in body, mind and spirit. At the end of a hot day or after a long, exhausting safari, George was content to relax with his pipe and a glass of whisky. His was not the kind of life to encourage intellectual pursuits. He took little interest in art or music and this irritated Joy, her frustration sometimes erupting in a 'torrent of reproach'. George was afraid that the black moods that had preceded their marriage

George in the living room of their house at Isiolo, the headquarters of the vast, semi-desert Northern Frontier District of which he was game warden

would return. Although she loved going on safari and was probably at her happiest then, she also hankered for the bright lights and the stimulus of city life. If crossed she would sometimes stalk off into the hinterland alone and unarmed, and walk there for hours. She hated both George's pipe and his glass of whisky, believing both a waste of money and George's drinking 'excessive'. To avoid continual rows, George kept a bottle of whisky and water, ready mixed, among a row of other bottles containing turpentine, methylated spirits and so on, on a shelf in his workshop. Lois Low, a neighbour and friend, says the bottle was marked 'strychnine'. Her husband, George Low, remonstrated. 'Look here, George, you shouldn't be leaving a bottle of strychnine open like this.'

'Oh,' Adamson replied. 'That's not strychnine, that's whisky!' While planing away or sawing a piece of wood, George told me many years later, 'I'd reach up and get this bottle and have a swig. On one occasion I reached up and pulled the bottle down and had a swig and it happened to be rust remover! Thank God I didn't swallow it! The inside of my mouth was sore for days. I rang up a friend of mine, Gerry Dalton, who was a park warden, and told him the story, and he said, "Well, it's probably just what you needed after all the water Joy's made you drink!"'

Later, Joy became so obsessive about his whisky drinking that George and Gerry Dalton hit on what seemed to be a foolproof plan. The local Asian *duka wallah* or shopkeeper was instructed not to put

On safari: the Adamsons in the early days of their marriage. On the back of this photograph, Joy wrote in English, 'George, myself and two game scouts', then in German, 'The mountains in the background are about 3000 metres (10,000 feet).'

any whisky on George's account. It would all go down on Dalton's bill and George would square up with him later. At that time, George had a young trainee called Jack Barrah working under him. Jack recalls George saying to Joy, '"I'm taking Jack out to sit up for a lion." So off we go and we weren't going after a lion at all, we were going for a sundowner. We stayed up there until about eight o'clock, and George would stoke up on his whiskies and then come back. After I left, Joy found out what was going on with the Dalton account, this Asian let the cat out of the bag. She was really furious. Anyway, she waited till George came back and ambushed him with a dining-room chair, actually broke his ribs for deceiving her. Gave him a hell of a whack

May, 1946. Joy loved the safari life, and George was the ideal companion. This was undoubtedly when they were happiest

and cracked his ribs. That was typical of Joy. "How dare you deceive me, putting whiskies on Gerry Dalton's account!"'

George had an impish sense of humour and got his own back by playing an elaborate practical joke on Joy. It involved drinking at this period a considerable amount of White Horse whisky, which in turn gave rise to the myth that nothing else would do. When I first went to visit him at Kora in 1988 to get his agreement for a documentary film about his life, I was advised to take a bottle of whisky, 'but it must be White Horse'. George quickly disabused me, 'Oh no!' he said. 'Any kind of whisky will do,' and gave one of his famous chuckles. It was George's godson, Jonny Baxendale, who supplied the real story behind the White Horse myth.

'The only reason he drank White Horse whisky was that on every single bottle there was a tag with a white horse on it. He would take great pleasure in removing this tag and hanging it up on a wire – he put a wire up on his *banda* [hut] in Meru. He would hang up each new white horse with great glee, and every time Joy came in she would look at this line of white horses – the look on her face! – and he would smile and puff on his pipe. It was the only thing I know of that he ever did just to irritate Joy!'

Jonny Baxendale and his twin brother Michael, sons of Nevil Baxendale with whom George crossed Lake Rudolf, used to stay at Isiolo with the Adamsons in the school holidays. 'We were cubs with Elsa if you know what I mean.' The two boys were part of the family, but for Jonny Baxendale, 'George was always the great guiding light as far as I was concerned.' He remembers Joy's tantrums with a small boy's wonder. 'I know of at least three occasions when she actually ran away. I remember my father saying, "Why on earth does he ever go and get her back? Let her run away." I can distinctly remember being rather horrified as a child at this extraordinary performance of Joy running away.' But, Jonny Baxendale says, George never shouted back.

'George of course would listen very nicely and puff on his pipe and basically had the most amazing ability to switch off completely and leave Joy jumping up and down screaming at him, but in actual fact he was just thinking; he was probably a thousand miles away thinking of something else completely. He was the only person who could have taken that sort of treatment. This went on all through the years [at Isiolo], and through Meru too.'

Jack Barrah says: 'Occasionally George would take his pipe out of his mouth and say "Oh, shut up, Joy."'

'Or,' Jonny Baxendale adds, 'something like "mumble, mumble, absolute rubbish." He never said anything stronger than that. Never swore, never said anything against Joy, that was the most amazing thing. I never heard him say a thing against her. He just had the most amazing ability to accept Joy for what she was. Very few other people had that ability, that's for sure. I for one. I was very young at the time but I just remember, the only way to survive with Joy was really to stand your ground. But George had this amazing ability and that's the only reason they remained together in any way at all, because George could cope with Joy. They always got together for birthdays, Christmases. Joy had no one else to spend Christmas with.'

Later Jonny worked as the old man's assistant. 'He was held in the highest regard by professional hunters,' he told me. 'By God, they didn't break any rules because he always found out. He used to put informers actually in with the camps and hunting parties. If someone was a bit dodgy, he would line up a guide to show them where to go and hunt and he [the guide] would report straight back and George would be there next morning. He had a fantastic reputation, a great intelligence network.'

Baxendale says George was 'quite fussy' as to who went with him on safari. 'He used to love going off on his own and Joy invariably wanted to go on many trips and he wouldn't take her. He just didn't want the hassle, the extra hassle.'

Although most of George Adamson's time was spent in hunting down African ivory poachers, many of whom he later enrolled as game scouts, he had also to keep a sharp eye on European hunting parties. Most of the safaris organised by professional white hunters, men like Bunny Allen and Syd Downey, many of them honorary game wardens, were well run and usually stuck to the rules. But some of the private hunting parties were not so strict. George had little time for people whose one ambition was to kill all their licences allowed and then go home with what he called a bone-yard of indifferent trophies. Although normally very easy-going, he was extremely strict when it came to the game laws. Joy used to say that George would have locked up his own grandmother if he had caught her breaking the rules.

'He didn't like these Afrikaner hunters who used to come up hunting,' Jack Barrah told me. 'They'd have permits for one or two animals but they'd put them all on. On one occasion he found a lorry full of meat. They got very stroppy with George and he wanted to arrest them. They said, "Arrest us if you dare." So he just got his rifle out and flattened all four tyres on their lorry and put a bullet through the radiator. Then he went back with police reinforcements and arrested them all. It was the sort of thing over which George did get irate, but he did it in a very quiet way, just bang out your tyres to make sure you didn't move.'

Jack Barrah says George Adamson's knowledge of the Northern Frontier District, an area the size of Britain, was unique. 'He knew every single river crossing; he never went on roads and he knew exactly where everything was. "Would you like to see some greater kudu? I'll show you where the greater kudu live," and he'd hack across country about ten miles and there they were! He was totally at home in the bush; whether he was on a donkey or his own flat feet, he was master of the situation. A remarkable naturalist, absolutely at peace with the world. He had a very good rapport with his rangers and he had a fantastic informer system. Nothing went on that George didn't know. If anything was killed, the information came straight back.'

On 7 August 1952 George Adamson wrote to his sister-in-law, Dorothy, known to the family as Dorle. It was one of many letters to her in which he spoke of his life on safari, his hopes and his disappointments, especially in his marriage to Joy. But whatever his own troubles, he was always immensely caring about his sister-in-law.

Acknowledging Dorothy's rather short letter to Joy and himself he says he is glad that her life has taken a turn for the better, as she had had her share of bad luck. He wishes he could be of more practical assistance to her but Africa and England are far apart, although he and Joy hoped they might be in England the following year. It was more than twenty-seven years since he first arrived in Africa as a young man of eighteen. Since then most of his uncles and aunts in England, Scotland and Ireland had died and he was no longer in contact with his cousins. So he felt less of a reason to go back and since they would have to stay in hotels the expense was a bit of a worry. But he had accumulated three years' holiday and his bosses had told him he must take six months of it the following year. The one good thing about it all, says the ever-gallant George, was that he would finally have the chance of meeting Dorothy, something he had always wanted to do. Joy had disappeared once more on one of her painting trips and he would be on his own for nearly five months, until Christmas.

He was a poor letter-writer and should have been in touch much sooner but his silence did not mean that she was not in his thoughts: she was, frequently. As to posting the letter, it might not be very soon because he was on safari far upcountry and he might not come across anyone who could post it for him. He was on the trail of a group of Somali elephant poachers who had come down from Ethiopia with their camels and when they had made a sufficient haul of ivory would head north again for the border. He would try and stop them but since they were housed and looked after by the local villagers he had to send informers ahead to find them and then try to surprise them and round them up. Despite the Northern Frontier District being a virtual desert, it was extremely hard to keep his plans secret. Two years before, he had been involved in a very similar sort of mission. The people he was after got wind of his coming and made a dash for the border, 250 miles away. On that occasion, luck was not on their side. Two of their camels were found dead near the border and the poachers had disappeared, quite possibly having died of thirst. He half admired the hardiness of these nomads, until he saw the gruesome remains of the elephants, rhinos and other animals they had killed for gain.

The local tribesmen, the Boran, still indulged in the tribal custom of blooding their spears. Young men making the transition to the status of warrior had to blood their spears to prove themselves and make a hit with the young women of the tribe. To qualify, the candidate had to kill a member of another tribe, preferably an adult male, with less kudos for a male child and less still if the victim was female. But even babies were allowed. This murderous habit persisted until the British arrived, imposed Pax Britannica and started stringing up the guilty parties. Nowadays it was only the hard core who still indulged in these nasty practices; most aspirant warriors did their spear-blooding on big game animals such as elephant, rhino, buffalo and lion. The killing of game was of course forbidden, so it was George's job to stop it. He had to admit, of course, that it took a lot of guts to attack an elephant or a lion with nothing more than a spear in your hand and very often the young men involved got badly hurt. But what in one sense was a piece

George and small furry friend (a ground squirrel) at Kampi ya Simba, Kora

Two cubs from Emperor Haile Selassie's private zoo in Addis Ababa, lent for the filming of Born Free

Boy and Girl of Born Free *fame, the first lions George released in Meru. It was there that Boy clawed four-year-old Mark Jenkins, which led to bitter criticism of George's work*

Henrietta, the playful one. When she arrived on the set of Born Free *from Entebbe Zoo she was skin and bone, but George fed her up and turned her into a star*

Boy with a bottle of White Horse. Giles Remnant, George's assistant on Born Free *and at Meru afterwards, teased Joy by showing her this photograph and telling her even the lions had developed a taste for whisky!*

Above: *George with one of his Kora prides. Shade, which attacked and mauled George's brother, Terence, is on the right*

Above: *Terence's grave, in a* lugga *near Kampi ya Simba. George is buried next to him and a lion called Supercub*

Right: *Elsa's grave on the Ura River, in Meru. George was visibly upset when he discovered it had been broken into for the second time*

Opposite: *George and Abdi, his tracker, look on while Batian, Rafiki and Furaha cool off in a rain pool at the foot of Kora Rock*

Above: *The art of preparing cubs for return to the wild. Almost every day, George took Batian, Rafiki and Furaha for a walk to get them used to the sights and smell of the bush*

Left: *Batian, the only male among the cubs, named by George after a famous Masai* laibon *or chief*

Below: *In the heat of the day, the cubs would seek the shade and play games while George looked on like an indulgent father*

What George liked doing best: an early morning stroll through the bush, looking for the pride. He could read the bush like a book.

of admirable sportsmanship became less so when the victim turned out to be a female with young or even a baby. Still, although George arrested the culprits and locked them up, they never seemed to bear him a grudge. They were a fine-looking lot, the Boran, many of the girls stunningly good-looking, pale-skinned and with delicate features, with no sign of the thick lips and noses of the negroid tribes.

George completed the letter after his return to headquarters in Isiolo, having been unable to find anyone to post it en route. He found waiting for him a registered letter containing a £10 Postal Order which he had sent to Dorothy, marked 'insufficiently addressed'. He was very sorry this should have happened but it was entirely Joy's fault. It was she who had given him the address. He hoped Dorothy would get it this time. George signs off in characteristically charming fashion, sending Dorothy his best wishes and his hopes for her future happiness.

In 1953, the Adamsons decided to drive to Europe across the Sahara, a journey much more formidable then than now. But, as one would expect, George took it all in his stride, saying that it was just like the north of Kenya and that there was no danger of becoming lost, provided they were careful. Finally, after travelling through Uganda, the Belgian Congo, French Equatorial Africa, Nigeria and Algeria, they arrived in Paris. Joy knew the city fairly well, but George had never been there before.

'I'd always heard a lot about the Folies Bergère,' George told me many years later, 'and thought it a good idea to go and have a look at it. So we went to the Follies. Most entertaining! Among other things I remember there was a completely nude girl, painted in gold. Fascinating! When it finished, some time in the early hours of the morning, we set off back to a small hotel we were staying in. We started off and then I got into an argument with Joy. I can't remember what it was about. Anyhow, she said, "Stop the car!" and I stopped the car. Next thing, she'd just gone. She had the money, I didn't have any money with me. I didn't know where the hell the hotel was although I had a vague idea of the direction. So then I had one of the worst experiences in my life, driving round trying to remember where this wretched hotel was and, at that time of the night, you know, early morning, there were very few people on the street. There was the odd woman wandering about and if I stopped to ask them they were all very friendly and that, but I couldn't get them to understand my predicament. So I thought, now what the hell do I do? Eventually, I suppose, I'll find a policeman and I can't talk French. He'll take me somewhere to interpret, and probably put me on to the local British Consul or something. And the first thing the Consul is going to ask me is, "Where are you staying?" and I'll say, "I don't know," and probably be stuck in the loony bin. Anyhow, I went on driving and just as dawn was breaking I recognised the street this wretched hotel was in. So I got back and Joy, of course, had been snoring away for a couple of hours!'

Chapter Six
ELSA

As the Game Department's expert on lions, George Adamson was often asked to give new recruits the benefit of his vast experience. They would be posted to Isiolo where he would initiate them into the secrets of lion control, which, essentially, meant learning how to hunt and shoot man-eaters. One of his first trainees was a young Scot from Edinburgh, Ken Smith. He remembers the Game Department in 1955 as being the worst paid and poorest of all government departments, 'sucking the hind tit', as he puts it. Although lowly in one sense, its staff considered themselves an elite and boasted among their number men with distinguished war records: they had several MCs and a DSO. 'It was a privilege to get in,' Smith admits. 'Jack Barrah and I were on a short list of thirty out of two hundred, then we were whittled down. We were lucky, there was a lot of competition.'

Having bought a new Land-Rover, Ken Smith set off for Isiolo, arriving just as it was getting dark. 'I stopped my car and walked up to where I could just see a roof. I heard pianoforte music. I can't remember what, but classical, maybe Chopin, beautifully played. I remember hesitating, stopping, listening entranced. Then I approached the house and there Joy was playing the piano. That was my first meeting with Joy.'

He was installed in a guest house and made very welcome. George mapped out a programme, explaining that the area was notorious for man-eating lions which attacked the local Africans and their domestic animals indiscriminately. Part of a game warden's job was to deal with these man-eaters and Ken Smith was now given instruction at first hand. 'Joy always went on these safaris – she was charming,' he recalls, although he was later to revise that opinion. Leaving Joy at the camp, the two men would set off in 'a very old truck' at about six in the evening for a prearranged place where George had left a kill, a zebra perhaps, as bait.

'We went into the back of this open truck and there was a safari chair for George and a safari chair for me. We got ourselves in position after working out where the wind would be, stationed ourselves in the truck with the driver underneath and, when we heard something, he would switch the lights on and we would bang away. Well, it wasn't what I expected. Here we were, sitting in the back of a truck and George was smoking his pipe! As far as I was concerned, everything that you could do wrong was being done wrong. We sat there. I was very tense. Then George would bring out a whisky and he'd puff his pipe, and we'd sit there and sit there. The idea was that if we saw something we'd tap the hood, and if the driver and the scout in the truck heard or saw something they'd tap and switch on the lights. We had one or two false alarms, a hyena or a jackal. I thought, what with the whisky and puffing away on his pipe, I wonder if he knows what he's doing. George did of course. Along came a lion in due course, down went the whisky on the floor, out went the pipe, on went the flashlamp attached to his rifle. Bang!' They shot three lions, George getting two and Ken Smith one.

'You seriously sat up from about eight until three in the morning,' Ken Smith went on. 'And at that time, invariably, you could almost set your watch to it, the wind would drop. Then you rather gave up because the wind was all over the place. It worked extraordinarily well. After a night or two of that we got a report about an actual man-eater – these were lions that were killing stock.

'George had another excellent system which we naturally adopted. Any of these lion or elephant reports can be over a very wide area. George used to just sit down in his camp instead of dashing all round the country looking for tracks and information. He used to go on the principle that, if these chaps want any assistance, I'm ready. But I cannot be everywhere at once. So he said to the chiefs, the assistant chiefs and headmen everywhere, "I am here. If you've got any information about anything that's causing damage, come hot foot and you'll find me in my camp." Invariably this is what he did. He might be having breakfast or a cup of coffee, a call came in, off he went.'

One day in January 1956, Ken Smith and George set off after a man-eating lion but, tragically, came to shoot a lioness which had just given birth instead. 'A runner came in at about eight o'clock, just after breakfast. He brought with him a report of a man-eater easily identifiable because he had a splayed pug. I was still very much the lamb. There was George, a very experienced sergeant, a local tracker who knew the area backwards and another scout and myself. The tracker and sergeant went ahead, George, myself and the scout behind. Once we got on to the spoor, we knew that the lion was in this area because the spoor was fresh. We'd seen it going into this *kopje* [small hill]. It was a big area rather like Kora, full of little rocks and gullies and tracks. We followed the tracks and we were pretty sure it was that particular lion.

'It was at about nine-thirty, ten o'clock and we were plodding around, lagging a bit, not going hell for leather, and as I remember we came to a largish cleft, a largish rock. We were slightly spread out, not single file, and as I went forward, George on the left, this lion or lioness – when confronted you can't say, but it looked like a lioness – she came on, very very fierce, snarling, and very very near. She was obviously very threatening, ready to charge. I happened to be more in alignment to fire than anyone else so George said, "Shoot". I had a double-barrelled 470 and so I up and shot. Obviously a 470, wherever you get it, is a terrible shocking heavy weapon and she stumbled and went off. I took a general aim because she started to move. I imagine I got her in the shoulder. I don't know. She went off immediately and down over a very big rock. So we had to follow her, naturally. The ethics are that the chap who shoots, follows up, so I followed up. As I remember, the sergeant was slightly ahead of me. There was a very heavy blood trail went down round the edge of a big boulder, and he pointed to it and I went round and came to a rather big cave. I looked in, and out of this [cave], staggering, very very staggering, came the lioness. I gave another shot; she wilted and then the sergeant or the other scout from up top gave another shot, but by that time she was finished.

'In actual fact, I killed her; she was finished. So that was that. We looked at the various wounds. We saw the first one had gone in towards the lungs and virtually finished her. We pulled her on to a rock slab. We were all very sorry because it obviously wasn't our quarry. We were after a big lion with a splayed pug. The scout who was behind had a haversack and a thermos of tea so we squatted in some shade, it was getting hot, and did a bit of a post mortem. George milked her and there she was, heavily in milk. So she had cubs, and very obviously young cubs. So we started to mill around and very near us we started to hear squeaks and squalls. In this cleft of two big boulders, right in, you could barely put your hand in, there was this squeaking and squalling. Obviously that was why she had become so enraged and fierce, scared stiff for her young. We couldn't get our hands in so the sergeant got a bit of a cleft stick and slowly but surely we pulled out these tiny little cubs. Tiny little things cussing, spitting and swearing. A week, ten days old perhaps. Of course, we were so remorseful, you know. The obvious thing was to get them back as quickly as possible, away from that area and get someone to tend them. So we just cupped them in our hands, I had one and George had two. Off we went, down to the truck, straight off to the camp. That's where the saga started. Joy was in absolute raptures and took them over completely. She looked after them tremendously. But she was such an odd person. When we went off to do another job of work, she spat and cursed us for not staying and helping with the poor orphaned cubs whose mother's death we had been responsible for. On the other hand, if we were hanging around, we couldn't do anything right. Joy was a magnificent person, but so difficult. George and I carried on looking for the man-eater which we never got.'

Joy's account in *Born Free* of the cubs' arrival is predictably dramatic. When George got back much earlier than expected, she heard him shout: 'Joy, where are you? Quick, I have something for you!' Joy rushed out with Pati Pati (her pet rock hyrax) on her shoulder and saw the skin of a lion lying in the truck. But before she could ask about the hunt, George pointed at the three tiny balls of spotted fur, each trying

Joy feeding Elsa on tinned Ideal Milk outside their house at Isiolo in 1956

to hide its face from the outside world. They could barely crawl, were only a few days old and their eyes were still covered with a bluish film. Joy held them on her lap to comfort them, while George, who was very upset at having had to shoot the mother, told Joy the whole story.

George's account is typically self-effacing, but almost certainly more accurate. Joy was waiting for them back at camp and the first question she asked was, 'Did you get him?' (the man-eater). George pointed to the back of the truck and said: 'Look what we've brought you!' As soon as she saw the cubs, Joy completely took over. One of George's men, Ibrahim, was sent fifty miles in the Land-Rover to Garba Tula, the nearest trading centre, to buy a case of evaporated milk and a feeding bottle. George, meanwhile, fashioned a teat out of sparking plug lead with the wire core removed.

How could the Adamsons ever have dreamt that the story of the smallest of the three cubs, and the cubs she herself would have one day, would be translated into thirty-three languages, sell several million copies, be made into a film and have a lasting impact on the way the world thought of wild animals? They were all females and Joy named them Big One, Lustica, after the German for jolly, and Elsa because she reminded her of someone of that name. Elsa was the runt of the litter, but the pluckiest and the most inquisitive, and was always sent by the others to investigate anything suspicious. In the wild, Elsa

George playing with Elsa, the runt of the litter, who was the most inquisitive of the three sisters

would probably not have survived. The average litter contains four cubs, but one usually dies soon after birth and very often a second is so weak that it also dies. Usually, only two survive.

But with plentiful supplies of cod-liver oil, milk and glucose, all three cubs flourished and were soon bounding about the camp, wreaking havoc. Two luckless visitors who pitched their tent at the bottom of the garden at Isiolo had a rude awakening. Within five minutes it was a wreck and the Adamsons were wakened by the cries of their guests as they vainly tried to rescue their belongings, while the cubs, wild with excitement, dived into the wreckage and reappeared with a variety of trophies – slippers, pyjamas and shreds of mosquito netting. Discipline had to be restored on that occasion with the aid of a small stick. Putting the cubs to bed also took some doing. Joy compared them to three very naughty little girls, who like all children hated bedtime, but who could run twice as fast as their elders and betters and had the added advantage of being able to see in the dark.

For Joy, who had a third miscarriage after her marriage to George, the cubs soon became a substitute for the children she seemed destined not to have. (When she was still married to von Klarwill, an Austrian fortune-teller had prophesied that she would live in the tropics and have no children.) Looking after three boisterous young lion cubs was not only a full-time occupation, even for Joy, but there were outside

Joy with Elsa and her two sisters

pressures on George to get rid of some of the cubs, not least from his boss, the Chief Game Warden, Willie Hale. 'I said to George, "You can't keep three cubs, I think it would be a good idea if you got rid of, anyhow, two of them." I think we came to an agreement that he could keep one. I did not give any strong orders, but I said, "I think it's advisable."' Reluctantly, when they were about six months old, the Adamsons decided that the two bigger ones should go to Rotterdam Zoo. Later, when he fully understood what intensely social animals lions are, George Adamson bitterly regretted having separated them. Quite apart from their strong sense of family, a lion, especially a young lion like Elsa, finds it almost impossible to survive on its own.

When Joy and the two cubs left Isiolo on the long drive to Nairobi and the aeroplane to Europe, Elsa ran a short way down the drive and then stood with a very sad expression in her eyes as she saw the car containing her two sisters disappearing. While Joy was away, George told her later, Elsa was extremely upset, and never left his side; she followed him everywhere during the day, and slept on his bed at night. Each evening George took Elsa for a walk, but on the day of Joy's return, she refused to accompany him and sat down in the middle of the drive. Nothing could move her. Joy wondered if Elsa could have known, somehow, that she was coming back, but found the idea hard, if not impossible to explain.

Years later, when he had had experience of many lions, George Adamson was to say that, although he could not offer a scientific explanation for such behaviour, he was convinced that lions possessed a sense that humans had lost. Was it a kind of sixth sense? 'Well,' he told me, 'it's happened so often that I think it must be so. Again and again, when I've been away for a long time – when I went to hospital, for instance, and was away several weeks and the lions hadn't been seen around for some time – I came back to Kora and that evening they turned up. I can't explain it, all I know is that it happened, and it has happened so many times that it is not just a coincidence. The lions appear.' Recalling that they tried to re-enact the Elsa incident in *Born Free*, George added: 'That sort of thing happens so often that one is forced to conclude that telepathy, or something like it, is involved. They obviously have a sense that we have lost.'

Elsa got her early education around Isiolo, a dusty little town on the edge of the desert, on walks with Joy and George. Since elephants would often come right up to the house, and had a particular liking for the shrub of which the garden hedge was composed, she did not have to go very far to make their acquaintance. Poor Joy seems to have been alternately delighted and horrified by her protégée's daring playfulness. Elsa's first encounter with an elephant was both exciting and worrying. As Joy pointed out, Elsa had no mother to warn her against elephant, which regard lion as the only enemies of their young and therefore sometimes kill them. One day Nuru [Elsa's keeper] came running to the house from Elsa's morning walk to say that she was playing with an elephant. George took his rifle and followed Nuru through the bush to where a huge old elephant, his head buried in a bush, was enjoying his breakfast. Suddenly Elsa, who had crept up from behind, took a playful swipe at one of his hind legs. A scream of shocked surprise and injured dignity followed this piece of impertinence. Then the elephant backed from the bush and charged. Elsa hopped nimbly out of his way and, quite unimpressed, began to stalk him.

Joy found it very funny although alarming and hoped fervently that George would not have to use his rifle. Luckily, after a time, both

George and Elsa at Malindi. Elsa, then nine months old, loved games on the beach and swimming in the sea

parties tired of the game; the old elephant went back to his meal and Elsa lay down and went to sleep. Rhinos and giraffe, also abundant around Isiolo in those days, provided the next stage of Elsa's education and finally, she was ready to go on safari, something she eventually enjoyed as much as the Adamsons. When she was nine months old and already a sleek, powerful young lioness, they took her to the Indian Ocean. After a tentative start, Elsa became water-crazy, in Joy's words, swimming effortlessly far out of her depth, ducking George and Joy and splashing the water with her tail. Joy said she usually stayed behind when the others went fishing; otherwise Elsa would have swum out after the boat.

She loved going for walks on the beach and, most of all, like children of all ages, she loved chasing the sand crabs. As anyone who knows the superb and almost endless succession of beaches which stretch the length of the Kenya coast, every evening as the sun sets, the crabs come out of their holes to disport themselves by the water's edge, feeding off the scraps of edible flotsam cast up by the warm blue waters of this most beautiful of oceans. At the approach of danger the crabs rise up on their hind legs and scuttle for their boltholes, holding aloft their pincers to warn off the intruder. As Elsa discovered, they can impart a healthy nip.

Elsa was still young enough to enjoy the game, rushing from one racing crab to the other, invariably getting nipped on the nose; but undeterred she would pounce again, only to be nipped once more. To their credit, of all Elsa's opponents the sand crabs were the only ones, not excluding elephants, buffaloes and rhinos, brave enough to stand their ground. As she charged towards them, they waited in front of their holes, one pink claw erect and, however cunningly Elsa tried to outwit them, they were always quicker and nipped her on the nose again.

Then George fell desperately ill with malaria, running a high temperature and becoming so delirious that he threatened to shoot himself. A friend stood by with a stick to club him senseless should he become violent, but George obligingly collapsed and was put to bed unconscious and icy cold. Joy tried to comfort him, talking to him in a low voice, but suddenly, he clutched her to him with desperate strength, as though hanging on to dear life itself. For once Joy overcame her distaste for George's drinking – she says she poured brandy between his dry lips – and told him about his birthday cake which she had carefully brought all the way from Isiolo. Poor man, he had been poisoned by an overdose of mepacrine, then the recognised treatment for malaria. Luckily he had an iron constitution and survived, although he continued to have recurrent bouts of malaria for the rest of his life.

George's younger brother Terence, who was in the Public Works Department, had a house at Malindi, at that time a charming fishing village on the coast north of Mombasa. One evening, Dougie Collins recalls, Terence and George were driving there from the Mombasa Club, a distance of about eighty miles. 'Both of them had had a couple of gins – George never really drank to excess – they were motoring along, the light was going and they saw an African and a bicycle in a ditch. So being kind, both of them, they stopped the car and went to see if the African was all right. As they got out of the car they could smell *chang'a*, the sort of methylated spirits they drink. He was absolutely smashed out of his mind. Then they noticed a python – our pythons here can go up to about twenty feet. The python had tried to swallow him but all it could get was up to the thigh. Obviously it hadn't suffocated him, as the African was still breathing. So they pulled the python off and shot it. They couldn't do much more as they'd got the little car loaded up with everything, so they left the dead python, the African and the bike still in the ditch!'

Elsa loved going on safari too. Here she takes a tentative step into the waters of Lake Rudolf – Porr Hill is in the background. Joy wrote, 'Are there any crocodiles?'

Soon after their return to Isiolo, George was back hunting man-eating lions, but nine months later, in 1957, when Elsa was a year and a half old, they planned a much more ambitious safari, this time to Lake Rudolf [Turkana], the scene of George's famous expedition with Nevil Baxendale. Julian McKeand, another of George's trainees, went with them. He recalls that right from the start the intention was to return Elsa to the wild. 'He even had that idea when he first had Elsa as a cub, that he shouldn't keep her as a pet but should try and return her. "Joy and I are going to do this safari and you should come along and help," George told me. "You can look after the baggage and donkey section while we walk ahead." You couldn't mix them up; the lioness would disturb the donkeys. So that's the way we did it. We drove up to the southern end of the lake; we'd already sent the donkeys up. I think we had something like thirty donkeys and I can't remember how many game scouts as they were called in those days.

'It didn't look too good to have game wardens blasting their way through the country feeding their wretched lion, so we took the precaution of buying a whole load of goats which we fed to Elsa. Of course the whole thing became quite absurd because Elsa controlled the whole safari. George and Joy got up early in the morning and set off walking when it was still cool, but Elsa determined where the camp was going to be. When she was fed up she lay down under a tree and that was it, you couldn't move her. I came along with the donkeys and the rest of the staff. We just tracked them up and sometimes they'd only gone an hour, or an hour and a half. The whole safari came to a grinding halt and sometimes it was in the most hopeless place to camp, the only shade the one tree that Elsa was lying under. There we stayed and if we'd accomplished only a short distance in the morning we'd have another try in the evening and sometimes we'd get going and sometimes we wouldn't. I can't remember how long it took us to get to Alia Bay, about eighty miles up the lake. In those days there was absolutely no one there at all. We started off from Loingalane but from the El Molo [a small tribe that lives on the shores of the lake] north there was no one until you got beyond Alia Bay, and then you got bands of Merille who were always raiding into Kenya coming down from Ethiopia. So we travelled through this country; it was beautiful, absolutely no one there and only a limited number of animals.

'I think it was along the lake that she jumped on one of George's donkeys. She clawed it so badly that the donkey took off. Elsa was riding on it and slipped off the back of it and got her claws right into the kidney area. There was a real trauma in the camp because George, who was very fond of his donkeys, had to go and shoot it. So then we realised that we must never let Elsa and the donkeys meet. She actually ambushed it: they were in some rocks and I came along with the donkeys – no one was worrying about the risk – and Elsa suddenly decided to have a go. She was big enough to kill it; she almost did; she would have killed it on her own if we'd let her. I never saw her killing [wild] animals; I don't think a lioness on her own was capable of running down one of those Grant's gazelles up there.'

At night, Joy would chain Elsa to her bed. 'She wore a dog collar and she [Joy] would put a chain on it, quite a long chain, and tie her to her bed. She kept you awake all night long because you'd hear this wretched chain jangling and think, Oh my God, Elsa's got loose. And of course one night she did. It was a bright, moonlit night, I remember that well. The donkeys and the men and all these goats were camped together – they'd made a little thorn enclosure for them – and I

Joy always fed Elsa by hand. Here she gets her daily ration of water and cod-liver oil

suddenly heard Joy shout to George to wake him up. I sat up and Elsa was stalking the donkeys, and I thought, My God, she's going to leap on one of those donkeys or goats; she's going to be right in amongst all those armed game scouts! The scouts will panic and there will be shooting. I've never seen George move so fast in my life. He shot straight out of bed, ran after Elsa and did a rugger tackle on her. Stopped her. I took my hat off to him. He obviously saw the same as I did, that there was going to be a fiasco, and grabbed her. That was a bit of luck, a bit of luck that Joy realised she'd got loose.

'We eventually got to Alia Bay and made a camp there. There was a lot of game. It's since been made a National Park. It was the ideal place to release this lioness. There were other lions there and there were no humans for her to tangle with. I suppose we were there for a week, maybe ten days looking around and trying to see if it was possible to free her. Then Joy decided she could not let Elsa go. She burst into tears and got into one of her terrible moods and said to George: "I won't let Elsa go." George was all set to release her, they both were when we set off from Isiolo. But it never came about. She said, "I don't think Elsa will survive," and maybe she wouldn't have done. So we returned. We didn't come back along the lake, we cut inshore, skirted along the southern part of the Chalbi Desert and went to Mount Marsabit. There we had a lovely camp on the southern end of Mount Marsabit and of course again there was nothing there in those days. Then from Mount Kulal we walked on down and back to the lake, in a big circle, got into the vehicles – put Elsa in the back of Joy's, which had a big wire cage – and motored back to Isiolo. It was a very nice safari, but completely useless.'

An Austrian friend of Joy's called Herbert Tichy joined them on this safari. Tichy was a man of parts, a writer and climber, and Joy had apparently invited him to Kenya to discuss possible collaboration on the book that was to become *Born Free*. But, Julian McKeand says, 'It didn't work out; they didn't get along very well. So that broke down. She was quite impossible.' He remembers an occasion on the safari when there had been a blazing row, with Joy screaming at the top of her voice at George. He could not recall the reason. 'Quite possibly it was over George's pipe. She was always saying things like, "I can't stand the smell of that filthy old pipe any longer," and picking it up and hurling it into the bushes. Usually George would just get up, grumbling, and go and search about in the bushes until he found it. What it was on this occasion I don't remember. What I do remember is that suddenly George struck her. He had a stick in his hand. He struck her across the face and she gave a terrific howl, and with her hand to her face, rushed out of camp in a flood of tears.

'"Let her go," George said, and we did. But three or four hours later, with still no sign of Joy, we began to get worried. It would be dark soon and God knows what might happen to her. So we got all the camp staff together and started to track her up and after a while we found her, lying under a bush, still crying. A bit later, Herbert Tichy sent me a photograph of Joy, lying on the ground, her head on Elsa's flank, still looking pretty tearful. I think Herbert took it that day when she got back to camp.'

Joy seeking comfort from Elsa during the safari to Lake Rudolf. Herbert Tichy, an Austrian friend of Joy's who gave the photograph to Julian McKeand, said he took it after a violent row between her and George

Julian McKeand says that the only time he ever saw George lose his temper was with Joy. 'To give you an example of her temper, George and I were going off on a safari with the Land-Rover and a lorry to look at some problem: in those days there was quite a lot of lion control, or an elephant had stepped on someone. We had all the game scouts and the pets and things. Normally you went off into these areas and you camped. Then these people would come in and say there's this problem and that problem and you'd just slowly work through the various difficulties they had, liaising with the local District Commissioner. We decided we'd go off on our own and we wouldn't take Joy. Joy threw a tantrum and said, "George, if you go on your own I'm going to shoot myself." George said something like, "Well, go ahead and shoot yourself, Joy." So George and I got the Land-Rover – there's an island outside that house in Isiolo – we drove round it and as we got to the other side, "Bang!" George jammed on the brakes and said: "My God, she's done it!" We leaped out of the Land-Rover and rushed across, into the house; it was a big sort of open, verandah-type house. Joy was standing in the middle of the living room and she'd bounced a bullet off the cement floor. She said: "George, if I can't go I'll shoot myself." So we gave in and took her. That was her kind of fiery temperament. The only time I ever saw George lose his temper; he was very annoyed.

'They had constant battles but George was a very peaceful guy. It took a lot to rouse him. He had that ability not to get worked up. I don't know how he did it with Joy. She was very tense all the time, very difficult to be around. I used to get along with her reasonably well but it was always difficult. She was full of ideas, vitality, always off doing things. You never saw her relaxing, ever, she was either painting or writing something. For Joy to have a siesta was quite unthinkable, whereas George after lunch liked to flake out for a couple of hours. She'd go traipsing off up some mountain, somewhere along the shores of Lake Turkana at the hottest time of day with a shovel over her shoulder looking for graves, fossils, plants. She was always terribly interested in everything. She took me to see the rock paintings in a gorge called Sirima at the southern end of the lake. [Joy had discovered these on a previous visit; they depicted various animals including a string of giraffe apparently led by a man.] She actually painted them. They had big sliding doors in the old house in Isiolo – it's been burnt down now – and on the back of the sliding doors, which went right across the verandah, she reproduced the whole rock engraving.'

Joy's rapport with Elsa was astonishingly close. Elsa would lie on Joy's bed, eat out of her hand, and in general behave more like a pet than a wild lioness. George's explanation to me was simple. 'Some you can trust completely like Elsa. Others you can't trust. Elsa happened to be one that you could trust.' That is possibly the understatement of understatements, even for George Adamson. That Elsa was exceptionally trustworthy was proved in Julian McKeand's presence one day in rather frightening fashion.

Joy and Elsa: they could not have been closer – until the day Elsa attacked Joy

'There was only one time I ever saw Joy panic with that lioness. It was an extraordinary thing. The lioness came up behind her when Joy was sitting on a rock, painting, and Elsa came up and took her complete skull in her mouth. Everyone froze. I just didn't breathe, and Joy, it was the only time I ever saw her panic. She suddenly felt the jaws of this lioness on the back of her skull. Then Elsa spat her out; she didn't do anything, thank God. Joy screamed "Elsa!" or something; it was quite alarming. George was somewhere, I don't think he was too close. There was nothing you could do, if you made a quick movement it might just have triggered her off to bite.'

'Did it change Joy's feelings towards Elsa?'

'No. I think Joy trusted her even more, that she'd had her in her mouth and dropped her.'

Chapter Seven

COMMAND PERFORMANCES

One day, Joy's idyllic relationship with Elsa turned sour. Although Joy never makes any mention of it in *Born Free*, she suddenly became frightened of Elsa. This must have been a shattering blow, since she looked on the young lioness almost as her own child. Possibly the only person she confided in was her close friend at the time, Lois Low. Lois, the wife of George Low, the veterinary officer at Isiolo in the fifties, when George Adamson was the senior game warden, was a neighbour of the Adamsons and helped Joy with the typing of her first books. She and her husband were present one evening when Elsa attacked Joy without warning and, but for George Adamson's extremely fast reaction, might well have injured her extremely seriously, or even killed her. If that had happened, George would have had little option but to shoot Elsa, which would have been a sensational and tragic end to what the whole world had been led to believe was a unique, natural idyll.

Lois Low had raised a young lion herself a few years before, when she and her husband were stationed at Garissa, and from that experience, she told me in the course of a long interview, she learned one thing. 'You must never walk in front of a lion. We used to take Patrick [her cub] with us when we went out for a drink to the police or the DC. I always made him walk in front.'

On the night in question, the Lows were going round to have a drink with George and Joy. 'We arrived at the foot of their drive and there was a Land-Rover with George and Joy, not in it but standing there. George had a *kiboko* [rhinoceros hide whip] in his hand and Joy was almost in hysterics because Elsa had gone out with some of the game boys [scouts] for the day and she hadn't come home. They'd sent the game lorry out to look for her, and it was then dark. Joy was very worried. Suddenly in the moonlight we saw this figure coming for us at the rate of I don't know how many miles an hour. This was Elsa and I was standing directly in her path, and my George said, "Stand still, don't move." Joy was standing a little bit away. Elsa came straight for me like that and George [Adamson] got in front of her and gave her a thrashing with this *kiboko* and beat her off. They all thought she would have jumped at me. But I had to stand still because I was too petrified with fright to move anyway!

'Then Joy said, "Come on, we'll go to the house." So Joy started walking to the house – it was only twenty or thirty yards, I suppose –

with Elsa following her, then George [Adamson] in his Land-Rover and us in our car; and I said to my George, "Joy's asking for trouble, walking in front of Elsa like that." As I said it, Elsa gave one bound and knocked Joy flat on the ground! So George [Adamson] had to come out [of the Land-Rover] and beat her off her. She dug her claws into Joy's head at the back and all over her back. By this time Joy was almost hysterical and weeping, so I got her into the bathroom, undressed her and put her into the bath and tried to clean all these deep wounds. They were deep, you know! I cleaned them up as much as I could and put on some disinfectant and said to Joy, "You'd better go and see a doctor."

'All the time she was weeping and saying it was George's fault, George's fault. She went up to Nanyuki and got treatment and was all right again. But it was an awful moment, one of the few moments I'll always remember with George and Joy. I thought she'd had it by then. I was still shaking as a result of my own fright. George Adamson was very quick. He was out of his Land-Rover in a minute with this *kiboko*. I don't know what Elsa would have done to Joy. I didn't know Elsa very well. She was a difficult lion to come to terms with. I had an instinct about Elsa. I thought, she doesn't like me, and I kept away from her.

'Joy told me one day she was frightened of Elsa. She told me that. I didn't tell anyone else, not at that time. People were making enough nasty remarks about Elsa and Joy. You see, you've got to make a contract with an animal, and fondle them or talk to them and then they'll always reciprocate. I never saw Joy showing Elsa any affection.'

Lois Low's remark that she never saw Joy demonstrate any affection for Elsa comes as a surprise and one is tempted to imagine she is mistaken, forgetful or malicious. But she knew Joy extremely well over a period of several years when Elsa was growing up at Isiolo and demonstrated, in the course of our conversation, that her memory was very precise. She also went out of her way to say nothing unkind about Joy; indeed she was noticeably protective.

It would be hardly surprising, indeed it would be entirely natural if, after the attack witnessed by Lois Low, Joy's relationship with Elsa had undergone a drastic change. Whatever her faults, Joy was unquestionably a brave and resilient person. Later on, she had to wear arm guards to protect her from the claws of her leopards, but she never complained and was certainly not frightened of them. For Joy to be frightened of Elsa, with whom she had this extraordinary bond, celebrated in word and picture, not only destroys the myth, but raises very serious questions about her own relationship with the largest of the African predators.

None of this would come as a surprise to Jonny Baxendale, who told me that Joy, far from having George's natural affinity with lions, was 'frightened of our lions. Here's the great lion lady ...' He did not finish the sentence but the meaning is clear. Some sceptics, like Ray Mayers, think that Joy came to value Elsa more for the publicity she brought her than for any other reason. What is indisputable is that after Elsa's death and the release of the cubs in the Serengeti, Joy seemed to lose all interest in lions and devoted herself to raising cheetahs and leopards. But this was still some way off.

In her book *Forks and Hope*, Elspeth Huxley saw only the idyllic side of the relationship:

'Her [Elsa's] charm and grace were undeniable, and even more remarkable the love, care and patience devoted to her by both her foster-parents in their different ways; Joy with the intensity, passion and taut-nerved concentration of a highly strung, single-minded woman of exceptional talent (she is also a first-rate botanist and skilful painter) without children, George with the unruffled calm, keen observation, quiet humour and aloof and yet companionable reserve of the born naturalist, sportsman and nomad.

'Joy herself became more and more leonine as she and Elsa developed their extraordinary relationship. Her colouring is tawny, her figure sinewy and her eyes, although pure blue instead of agate, harbour that pin-pointed, hard-packed intensity you can also see in those of a lion. Perhaps it was only in the beholder's imagination that these qualities seemed to grow more pronounced.

'Often Joy would withdraw at about six o'clock into Elsa's apartment – you couldn't use the word cage, for she was never confined – and sit with her for the rest of the evening, oblivious of a meal, talking, sketching and sometimes just sitting and watching her companion. They understood each other better than many human pairs do. Joy, as we know from photographs, had complete trust in Elsa and would put a hand in her mouth or roll and wrestle with her on the floor. But Joy was terrified of elephants, and sometimes in the

Land-Rover would shout to George to go no closer to a herd, or to turn quickly and drive away. George would pay no attention. Joy feared the elephants might injure Elsa, who sometimes teased them, leaping off her seat on the Land-Rover's roof to gallop up to them and practise stalking. The elephants paid no attention. Elsa was an obsession. You cannot rear and tame an animal unless you allow it to possess you.

'As guests, we saw more of Pati Pati the rock hyrax, than of Elsa; she was always around, whereas Elsa was normally excluded from the bungalow when visitors occupied it, in case they did not like a lioness inviting them to rough games at all hours or jumping on their beds. Pati Pati, with her thick furry pelt, her purposeful actions, strong will and beady eye, had great charm; also a marked ruthlessness of character. She knew exactly what she wanted and allowed nothing to stand in her way.

'One of the things she wanted was to curl herself round the neck of anyone who occupied Joy's bed. Generously, Joy would surrender her own room to her guest and retreat to a camp bed in the office. Pati Pati went with the room. My mother, deeply flattered by this mark of trust from Pati Pati, struggled through her first night with the furry hyrax encircling her neck; but Isiolo can be very hot and, during the second night, she attempted gently to disengage Pati Pati and persuade her to sleep at the foot of the bed.

'This move was ill-received. After a good deal of argument, Pati Pati turned and bit, quite savagely. An unfortunate scene ended with Pati Pati chattering furiously on the veranda, and Tilly [Elspeth Huxley's mother] dabbing iodine on her neck.

'In the morning, both felt ashamed. Tilly apologised to Joy, but Pati Pati did better; she apologised to Tilly. With the early morning tea she entered the room, approached the bed and rolled over on her back with all her feet in the air. Her meaning could not have been plainer. All the same, Isiolo was not getting any cooler and it was fortunate for both parties that we left later in the day.'

A guest of the Adamsons must have been hard put to know whom it was more dangerous to offend, Joy or Pati Pati.

Ken Smith, who knew the Adamsons much better than Elspeth Huxley did and who was very fond of Elsa, would hardly have been surprised by Lois Low's story. 'When she became much bigger,

George had much more control over Elsa than Joy, not that they needed to, but sometimes she would get a bit robust. Joy was always slightly cagey about Elsa when she became too robust, slightly wary …'

Many of George Adamson's friends and colleagues think Joy depended heavily on her husband's knowledge and expertise, and in particular his habit of meticulously keeping a diary every day, when she came to write *Born Free*. Jonny Baxendale, for example, has no doubts about the key role played by his godfather. 'Joy's original books all came from George's diaries and then she herself, after a while, decided it was a good thing to do, so she started keeping diaries of her own. All the original books, *Born Free* and all that, were basically from George's diaries,' he says.

Julian McKeand vividly recalls George's discipline with the diary. 'After tea everything stopped and George wrote his diary. Religiously. He never missed.' According to Julian, Joy had already roughed out the Elsa story when she asked Herbert Tichy to come out to Kenya and help her to finish the book.

'I think it really started by keeping pages of a diary every day about Elsa and how she grew and what happened. And she suddenly realised that she'd almost got a book already written. And she wanted the final chapter to be the releasing of Elsa at Alia Bay.'

After Joy's cantankerousness put paid to the joint venture with Herbert Tichy, she approached Elspeth Huxley, whose best-known book, *The Flame Trees of Thika*, tells the story of her childhood in Kenya. According to Joy's autobiography, *The Searching Spirit*, Elspeth Huxley turned the idea down on the grounds that the book 'must be written in the first person. I therefore began to write,' says Joy.

Julian McKeand recalls: 'Elspeth came out and I remember driving her around at the time, and they were trying to work something out. It all fell apart; I don't know why. I was told – but I hardly think it's credible – that Elspeth wanted it "*Elsa* by Elspeth Huxley with Joy Adamson" and Joy the other way round. Neither would give way. Whether that's true or not I don't know. She was trying to work something out with Joy, and of course no one could; it was quite impossible.'

In 1958, when Elsa was just over two and beginning to take too great an interest in the local cattle, the Adamsons decided she would have to leave Isiolo and find another home. Since neither of them could contemplate the prospect of her spending the rest of her life in captivity, they started looking for a suitable environment where she could be released to the wild. Even in a country as big and wild as Kenya, this was not an easy task. First they tried the great plains of the Masai Mara, on the Tanzanian border, but Elsa fell ill and this delayed the release attempt. By the time she had recovered the Game Department in Nairobi had decided that it was too risky to have a tame and possibly too playful lioness wandering about among the tourists who would soon be flocking there – the season was about to begin – and the Adamsons were told to remove her. George went to see Willie

Joy and Elsa would spend hours together, Joy writing, painting or, as here, engaging in more humdrum tasks

Hale 'in despair' and got his permission to move Elsa to the Ura River, a small tributary of the Tana near the Meru Game Reserve, not far from where she was born. This turned out to be a perfect spot and George put up a camp in a grassy clearing near the river. Not far away, rising out of the surrounding bush, was a great smooth rock from the top of which Elsa loved to survey the world: in a cleft at the bottom she would later have her cubs.

For Joy, life with Elsa on the banks of the Ura was one of the happiest periods of her life. She used to spend much of her time painting and writing in her open-air 'studio' at the edge of the water, with Elsa stretched out at her feet. George still had his headquarters in Isiolo, but during his frequent visits to the Ura River camp, he would take Elsa out hunting and, since she still could not kill for herself, would often shoot the animal she was stalking in an attempt to replace the mother who would have shown her cubs how to kill. Elsa really came of age as an adult lioness when she trapped an old bull buffalo in

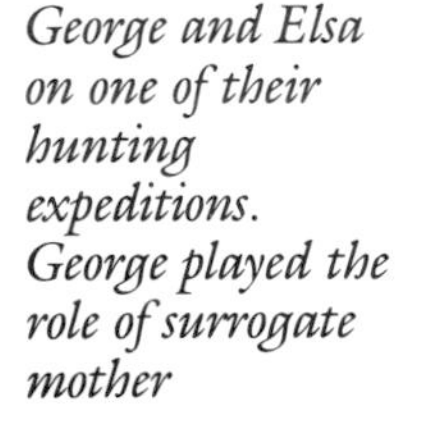

George and Elsa on one of their hunting expeditions. George played the role of surrogate mother

the river one day. Trying to escape, it slipped on the rocks and Elsa was on it like a flash, half drowning the enormous beast by holding it under water until George arrived to deliver the *coup de grâce*. Then Nuru, who had looked after Elsa since she was a cub, waded into the water to cut the buffalo's throat before it expired. Otherwise, being a good Moslem, he would not have been able to enjoy his share of the meat, since the animal had not been bled to death as Islamic law requires. Elsa sat on top of the buffalo, growling furiously as he advanced, but Nuru persisted, wagging his finger and telling Elsa 'No, no.' To everyone's surprise, she let him do it.

At the end of the 1950s, Lord Beaverbrook hired Godfrey Winn, known as the darling of the women's magazines, to visit Kenya and write a series of articles for the *Daily Express* about the antics of the white settlers in Happy Valley. Donald Wise, the local correspondent of the *Express*, who was much more at home covering wars than nannying VIPs from London, was instructed to show him round. Apart from the settlers, Godfrey Winn insisted on seeing George and Joy Adamson as well.

'By the time we got around to the Adamsons, some two weeks after Godfrey arrived in Kenya,' Donald Wise recalls, 'he had shown me what a charmer he was. The toughest and most reactionary settlers ate out of his hand wherever he appeared; and so did the army general in charge of all troops in East Africa. When I had told him that Lord Beaverbrook hoped he would talk to Godfrey, he merely growled: "I hear he's limp-wristed. I'll give him ten minutes before lunch." On a Saturday. Godfrey's comment was unprintable.

'But I had to wait one hour and thirty-five minutes before the pair came out of HQ with the General pumping Godfrey's hand and booming: "Now look here, Winn, if you don't come to supper tomorrow night my wife will leave me."

'So it was with every confidence that I popped Godfrey and myself into a small plane for the seventy-minute flight to the nearest airstrip to the Adamsons where George and his Land-Rover would be waiting for us.

'But George looked downcast. "Joy is being difficult," he told us, "and refuses to see either of you."

'"Well, we've come all this effing way and I'm not going back," snapped Godfrey; so we clambered aboard George's Land-Rover and set off through the bush. After some fifty minutes or so I actually *saw* a man running towards us down the dusty track with a *cleft stick* in his hand. A note from Joy was wedged in the cleft.

'"Get rid of them straight away," Joy had written. Godfrey looked on the edge of a flood of tears and, with the wind whipping his halo of grey hair, we came to Joy's camp in another twenty minutes. Joy's face set in a rictus of fury as Godfrey approached her; on George's advice, he and I hung back, carrying stores into his main tent.

'Some four minutes later Joy was calling to George that she and Godfrey were going to see Elsa playing with her cubs. We should follow if we felt like it. We did and came upon a scene that I can only describe as a sort of Lesbian romp with the cubs watching in some astonishment as their mother and Joy, embracing each other fiercely lips to lips, rolled about in the heart of Africa, watched by a delighted Godfrey and watchful George. "Can I go and play with them?" Godfrey asked.

'"No," said George gently. "Elsa does not know you well enough yet." Indeed, it was only a few minutes away from feeding time when every evening Elsa taught her brood how to eat dead goat.

'At 9 P.M., after a real bush supper of antelope meat, fish from Lake Victoria and some apples, we sat in canvas chairs at the entrance of our tents and waited for Elsa to come and say goodnight. "Don't make any

George and Elsa camping out in 1959, when Elsa was three

sudden move when she comes to see who you are," George warned us, and for about half an hour we talked of Elsa until Joy said in her very Germanic accent: "Perhaps Elsa is shy tonight?"

'Almost immediately there was a rush through the bush and with a great crash Elsa landed on the bonnet of the Land-Rover a few feet away and turned her big yellow eyes on us. "Oh," said Godfrey, rising slowly to his feet, "what a lovely effing lioness," and put his arms round her neck.

'George, who had been tying fishing flies the other side of the bonnet, said very quietly: "Godfrey, don't do that. You really do not know her well enough." Rooted to my canvas chair in terror I caught Elsa's look in Godfrey's arms, which seemed to say, "I've got a right one here."'

In February 1959, when Elsa was three, Joy went to England to try to sell the story of *Born Free*. How she found a publisher, on the very last day of her stay in London, is a classic tale of its kind. Julian McKeand remembers her setting off for London. 'It sounds incredible now. She had this huge great lionskin coat, which of course no one would dare

Joy wore a lionskin coat when she came to London to try to sell the story of Born Free. *Even after it became a world best-seller, she saw nothing incongruous in wearing a leopardskin coat and hat while posing with a leopard cub*

wear now, let alone Joy Adamson, a full-length lionskin coat, shot by George. Off she went to London and she stomped round London in this lionskin coat going in to various publishers and eventually it was some elderly lady [Margery Villiers] in Collins who picked it up. And away it went. Of course they had to rewrite it and everything. Joy's English was appalling. But she seemed to go along with that, I don't know why. I think she got along very well with Billy Collins when he was alive.'

Lois Low does not mention the lionskin coat but she does remember Joy being depressed by her failure to interest a publisher. The Lows had just arrived in London on leave. 'We had just got into our room and were unpacking when who should walk in but Joy. We had no idea she had come to England, and she said, "Oh, I'm in a terrible state." She nearly wept on George's shoulder again. She said, "I've been everywhere and nobody wants to take *Born Free*. What am I to do? I must sell it." She said, "I'm desperately tired. I've been walking all over London, to all the publishers and everything."'

Joy's own account, in *The Searching Spirit*, describes how on a cold and rainy day she happened to pass the office of the Harvill Press, so she rang the bell and asked to see Mrs Villiers (with whom she had corresponded about a book on the tribes of Kenya). Joy reminded her of that but then told her that the manuscript she was now offering was something quite different. Margery Villiers asked Joy to tell her the story, which she did, and was obviously impressed. Joy added that she had hundreds of photographs of Elsa and Margery Villiers arranged for her colleague, Manya Harari, to go to the flat where Joy was staying to look at them. By that evening both had expressed great interest in the book but neither had made an offer, so next day Joy went to see an agent. In fact, Margery Villiers had cabled Billy Collins, the chairman of William Collins, who was abroad at the time, telling him that *Born Free* sounded like a best-seller and that it was essential to make a good offer for it since Joy was in touch with other publishers. It was only later that Joy learned that the Harvill Press was a subsidiary of Collins.

Joy rather grandly talks of a 'manuscript', but Irene Stirling, who worked with Margery Villiers at Harvill, remembers distinctly there was no manuscript. 'The first time I came in contact with Joy, she had very little in manuscript form, in fact only notes and wonderful photographs, and she was just going round all the publishers in turn. She'd been turned down because she had nothing, no manuscript, nothing to see. She was told by all of them, "no manuscript, no book". My boss, Margery Villiers, was, I should think, the best editor in London in the way in which she totally abnegated anything of herself from the book. She actually saw what the other person wanted to say but couldn't – which is a tremendous gift. When Joy eventually landed up at Harvill – how she found it I don't know because it was up a rickety flight of stairs – she had nothing written down on that particular visit. She just had these wonderful photographs and told Margery the story in her rather fractured English. Billy Collins had tremendous confidence in Margery's judgement and she sent him a cable saying, "Wonderful book, no script. She's doing the round of the publishers. I think we ought to buy immediately, give her an advance and stop her wandering around London."

'Billy cabled back, "Yes". I can't remember what the advance was. Margery suggested it should be a big one which in those days was about ten thousand. It was at least five thousand and I should think it was more. It was considered quite a big advance from Collins' point of view. Margery then set to, really extracting the story from Joy, who by that time had got her notes together. But it was really a dragging out – or rather more stemming the flow – making a really readable whole. She was very emotional, Joy, so there were things that sounded much more credible and real if they were toned down a bit. Margery's role was to help her to write the book and they wrote it between them. I think she really put herself into Joy's head. There was nothing that Joy didn't feel in that book but it was written in very lucid English. One of the funny things about this which Margery told me, because it got very good reviews, and the writing was admired, she [Joy] then became totally impossible to edit because she thought: It's quite unnecessary to have an editor, look how wonderfully I write! Margery admired her and liked her, could see the point of her. When she was being difficult, could say, "This won't do!" She was quite firm and was accepted by Joy who was very fond of her, respected and admired her a lot.'

Irene Stirling says that Margery Villiers had less to do with the sequels to *Born Free*: *Living Free* and *Forever Free*, 'But she certainly always had a hand and Joy always wanted her approval. Margery just found her more and more difficult to deal with. However she remained fond of her and excused her occasional bouts of rage, not really rage, but sort of irritation. I think she used her emotions absolutely usefully, consciously, when she wanted to make a point. She wasn't stupid at all. She was a bit of a bully, although she'd never have shown it to Margery who was a very strong character. But there was something very forgiveable about her, however she behaved, because she minded so passionately; and it's rather nice in life minding passionately about anything and that was a hundred per cent real. She would have done anything to further the cause she believed in, so one had to respect her. I always felt very sorry for George. He must have had a very tricky life.'

Joy also wrote *The Peoples of Kenya*, published in 1967, an account of her painting safaris which took her the length and breadth of the country, beautifully illustrated with her own remarkable portraits of warriors, young women, chiefs, witchdoctors and elders of the main tribes in all their finery – a record of a tradition which has effectively disappeared but which now hangs in the National Museum in Nairobi. Irene Stirling says while she was painting these portraits, Joy took 'a lover among the Africans. It was a very happy time of her life. She was a total African in that she didn't care at all what she looked like. She'd wear a bush shirt and those horrible long shorts, a nut-brown face with wonderfully piercing blue eyes, quite a dumpy figure; she wasn't tall. She didn't listen to a word anybody said. One rather forgot what she looked like because she was so busy talking. There were very few people she really listened to. Her ideas would come tumbling out.' There was a huge contrast between Joy's appearance when she wasn't bothering about what she looked like and when she was. 'Going to a party she suddenly became quite the *grande dame*. She could wear clothes; you saw this coming out when she was dressed and going to a dinner party, or the premiere of her film. It was a remarkable metamorphosis.'

The Royal Command performance of *Born Free*, which took place in London in 1966 in the presence of the Queen, was potentially embarrassing for both the monarch and the author, for both women wore the same dress. Jack Barrah's wife, Pat, says, 'This dress was made for the Queen and apparently didn't fit her. Whoever made the dress [Norman Hartnell] must have sold it to Joy, not knowing that Joy was going to the premiere of *Born Free* and would certainly be presented. There's a picture of Joy talking to the Queen wearing an identical dress. Gloves as well.' Did the Queen make any comment? 'I asked Joy that very question,' Jack Barrah says, 'and she replied "Both being ladies, neither of us said anything." It was typical Joy. She was so impetuous. She'd probably only arrived in London the day before. Rushed in to someone, crying, "Where's a dress, where do I get a dress?" "Well we've got a dress here." Didn't say where or what it was for.

'She was very glamorous. In Isiolo in 1956, there were very few women and Joy really was quite outstanding, a very beautiful girl. She never tried to be glamorous but she could be if she had to do it. If you walked up a mountain behind her, she'd be wearing khaki shorts, army boots, a khaki brassiere and a Bombay bowler, and she'd stomp up with all the Turkana gasping for breath behind her. They used to hate going for walks with her; she'd walk them off their feet.'

Joy being presented to the Queen at the premiere of Born Free *in London, 1966. By some amazing oversight, both women wore the same dress (by Norman Hartnell), even down to the long gloves. Virginia McKenna and Bill Travers are in the background*

Irene Stirling says, 'She must have been very pretty as a girl. She had good bones to her face, high cheekbones. She suddenly decided she'd have all her teeth out for no reason, except that they were a bother, and being in Africa it was more convenient. She was very, very unvain, too absorbed, too interested to bother about her appearance.'

Most women resented Joy's habit of making a beeline for any man who interested her and ignoring their womenfolk. Lois Low was an exception: she seemed to be quite unruffled by the fact that when they first became neighbours in Isiolo, Joy behaved as if she did not exist.

'She was very fond of my George [Low]. She used to walk round and see him and complain about her George. She'd put her arms round him and weep like anything – George would say: "I'll have to get a new shirt" – but she ignored me completely for a long time.

'For years I took no notice. It wasn't her rudeness so much as her total ignoring of all other women. All the other women in Isiolo didn't like her. But I wasn't going to interfere or start up anything because I knew George Adamson and my George were very good friends.'

Lois Low's friendship with Joy started when Joy was given a baby elephant which had lost its mother. 'She used to take it for walks every evening and she usually walked over to us and spoke to George [Low] – I mightn't have been there. One night she walked along with little Pampo. George was out, so I said, "Come in, Joy, George'll be in later."

'"Oh," she said, "I wanted George to see my little Pampo." I said, "He looks a dear little thing," so I went up to him and touched him and he took up his trunk and put it round my waist, and I thought, That's rather nice. Then he took his trunk away and put it up here and blew, not only air but everything else that you do blow out of a nose. I had to go and wash my face and Joy said, "Oh, I forgot to tell you, you should wear dark glasses when you speak to Pampo." But anyway Pampo just took to me like that and I think that's the first thing that Joy noticed about me, because she'd known me for years before and I don't think she could remember what I looked like. She had no time for women at all.

'Then after this little Pampo incident she started writing [about] Elsa. She used to ring me up and say would I come round and see her, so I'd go round. I had a typewriter [Joy did not] so I typed quite a lot of that book. I didn't write it. People say, "Oh, you must have helped

Joy with the book." But I didn't, I didn't help to write it – I'm talking about *Born Free* and *Living Free*. She was such an extraordinary woman, Joy; we'd sit at the table and she'd read out to me. I typed it straight out and then as soon as I'd finished a sheet, she took it out and put it into a big envelope, to take foolscap size, and when it reached a certain weight, gummed it and sent it to Harvill Press.

'Then we'd start on the next sheet, pull that out; she never even read it. She didn't take copies. I said to her, "Joy, don't you want me to make a copy?" "Oh, no, no, we haven't got time." It wasn't bad English; it was a little bit Teutonic; she could have put her sentences in a clearer way. I think I might have made the odd alteration like that while I was typing but it wasn't a studied thing, I hadn't checked it through. So I keep on telling people I did not help her to write the book. It was good enough English for somebody to edit it.'

According to Lois Low, Joy Adamson did not write her manuscripts in longhand first; she simply had 'odd bits of paper and books and she dictated from that. She hadn't drafted that even; it was just straight on to the typewriter. And when she was dictating and there was an obvious grammatical mistake or something like that, I automatically typed in the correct one. But when it came to a long sentence or almost

Joy with Pampo, the orphaned baby elephant which she looked after in Isiolo

a whole paragraph, if I suggested editing it, then Joy would say, "No, there's no time!" She was in a hurry to get this home. I had something to do with *Born Free* but it wasn't anything very vitally important. But *Living Free* [the sequel to *Born Free*] was the one I did a lot of typing for.

'And then she used to get press cuttings and I filled up three books that size with all of them. She used to take hundreds of photographs of the cubs [Elsa and her sisters], and she'd hand me these photographs and I had to sort them out. You know, it would take a whole page for these three [cubs] just to be doing one little exercise. I had to study these photographs to get them in the right sequence – that sort of thing. Well, I did that for her.

'She was tough. She used to go on walking safaris that would have killed me and I thought I was tough enough, in that climate. When we left Isiolo she came to me and said, "I want to give you a present," and I said, "What for, Joy?" "Oh," she said, "you've been so good; you've helped me so much. I'd like you to have something for your house at Vipingo [near Mombasa]," because we'd just bought this house. So she said, "I don't know what you want and I can't go to Nairobi. If I give you a cheque will you buy something you would really like?" I said, "Yes, all right." It took me three months in Lamu [an old Arab town on the coast north of Mombasa] to find the sort of chest I wanted, an Arab chest. I got a beauty and after about three weeks' bargaining I managed to get it down to the amount of Joy's cheque.'

One evening, Lois remembers, Joy rang the Lows while they were having a drink before dinner. '"George, you must come at once, Elsa's ill!" George said, "What's wrong with Elsa?" "Oh, she's constipated. You've got to bring an enema." So George said, "I don't possess an enema and it's a bit late to do that now." "Oh no, it's got to be done immediately, and she's up on the top of the hill, just behind our house." Joy had taken her for a walk up there and Elsa had just sat down. Joy said, "What am I to do?" So George said, "Go down to the little medical clinic in Isiolo and ask them if they've got an enema." I don't know what she did, but the rest of the story was that Elsa was just playing up; she didn't want to walk back to the house. Joy went back to her house, got some game scouts and a camp bed, a stretcher thing, and got the boys up there and they manhandled Elsa on to this stretcher and carried her home. "What next?" George [Low] said, "giving an enema to a lion; that's not my work." Everybody had to jump. It was "You will come!" not "Do you mind coming and helping me out?" That was Joy. I don't think she meant to be like that, she was naturally like that. She had a Teutonic attitude; you can't blame her.'

Joy did not bother much about her appearance in Isiolo. 'She used to wear little khaki shorts and a little khaki bra, that's all she wore. The only time I saw her in a dress was in Nairobi.' Lois Low remembers an occasion when Armand and Michaela Denis, who pioneered television documentaries about Africa and its wildlife in the fifties, came to stay with them in Isiolo on one of their expeditions. Michaela Denis had just published, very successfully, *A Leopard in my Lap* [in 1955]. Joy was keen to meet them and insisted they came round for a drink. The Denises, who had just arrived, were reluctant but finally gave in. 'Michaela came down in a beautiful yellow chiffon dress, diamonds in her ears, diamonds round her neck, diamonds on her wrists and fingers. She looked absolutely superb and she said, "I'm going to show Joy how women ought to dress." George and I didn't go of course; she didn't want to see us anyway. Joy was just writing Elsa [*Born Free*], that's why she wanted to see Michaela. Michaela came back and said, "What do you think? Joy Adamson's trying to write a book! She was asking me about it. I told her, 'Look, don't you worry about writing books, leave it to the people who know how to do it,'" meaning herself of course.

'Joy got that success by sheer determination. She was not to be deviated from what she was going to do. I thought *Living Free* was quite good. I was very interested in what she was writing and I couldn't criticise what she had done with the cubs and how she was doing it because I didn't know anything about it. She had that goal in her life about animals and it took precedence over everything.'

Joy was well ahead of her time in her concern for the environment, Lois Low remembers. 'She was the one who opened my eyes to it – that you mustn't kill off your wild animals, because that's part of nature and they can live quite well together with [domestic] stock. That sort of thing Joy was very good at. She was very interesting about environmental things. She didn't know about it in a scientific way, but she knew from observation.'

Chapter Eight

A HOME FOR THE CUBS

Born Free was an instant success when it was published in 1960, becoming a runaway best-seller all over the world; in Britain, the Commonwealth, Europe, America, Japan and even the Soviet Union. It was soon making Joy large sums of money – half a million pounds in the first ten years, according to George Adamson's own estimate. Whether out of stinginess or spite, Joy refused to share any of the royalties with George, who in a sense could be called the real author. He was a much better writer than Joy: his reports were justifiably famous in the Game Department for being always well-written and often amusing. Willie Hale says he looked forward to them with real pleasure and took them home to show to his wife, Morna: there cannot be many civil servants' reports which inspire that sort of enthusiasm.

Yet it was Joy, with her 'appalling' English but her determination and sense of the dramatic, who against all the odds although with a great deal of help from Margery Villiers, produced the best-seller and became a millionairess. George used to say, 'I got all the fame, but none of the fortune.' In fact, the man who in a practical, day-to-day way knew more about lions than anyone else, without whom *Born Free*, both the book and the film, would hardly have been possible, was so hard up that he had to go cap in hand to ask for the price of a bottle of whisky or a gallon of petrol. A proud spirit underneath the easy-going exterior, he must have hated the indignity of it all. Giles Remnant, who was George's young assistant first on the film set of *Born Free*, helping to handle the lions, and later at Meru, where George began his programme to release some of the *Born Free* lions to the wild, recalls his resentment very clearly.

'That was a big gripe of George's. He always said the Elsa Trust [the Elsa Wild Animal Appeal, set up by Joy in the early sixties to channel her royalties back into wildlife conservation] had all the money and not him. I can remember there was a man from the Elsa Trust who used to spoon-feed him the money, in dribs and drabs. George used to have to go in begging for money, saying I need this to repair the Elsa Trust lorry [at Meru], and he used to have to give a written account of where it was all going to go. Pathetic really, because the Elsa Trust is an extremely wealthy trust. But they used to hang on to the purse strings, whether on the command of Joy or the Trust, I don't know. There again it was the whisky, you see. Joy always said, "He's going to spend it on his visky and tobacco. Tsat man! His visky!"'

'Maybe,' Julian McKeand says, 'she enjoyed having control over him.' Jonny Baxendale certainly thinks so. Even much later, in the early seventies, when George was establishing himself at Kora, he was still hard up. He had a small pension from the Game Department, and a little money from his first autobiography, *Bwana Game*, published in 1968. 'Most of the money he got was from the little movie that Bill Travers made, *The Lions are Free* [a television documentary which sold successfully in America. It was produced by Bill Travers, who co-starred with his wife Virginia McKenna in *Born Free*]. This was really interesting because it infuriated Joy more than anything I know, having George financially independent of her. Up to this point he always had to ask her for help with money on the [lion] project. And that was why she hated Bill. No other reason. She felt Bill had taken sides with George and made a film and basically made him financially independent of her, which was the only hold she really had on him. Which was a delight. I was there when all this happened because every time we needed something, another drum of fuel or whatever it was, we would have to go and ask Joy if we could have the money to buy it. We were really running the whole thing on a shoestring at Meru. So then the funds started coming and George had his own money to run it himself without having to ask Joy. We were able to buy another Land-Rover and exciting things like that. And this Joy didn't like at all, it really irritated her. I remember being quite amused by the whole thing.'

Although Elsa was like a child to the Adamsons, and Joy certainly lavished all her maternal love on her, to most people she remained a very large and rather terrifying wild animal. Billy Collins, Joy's publisher, came back from one visit to the Adamsons with his body covered in long, deep scratches. He went straight to Greece for a holiday with his wife. When he undressed that night to go to bed she looked at him in horror and said, 'What on earth have you been doing, Billy?' He then explained that one night in Kenya, after George had gone to bed, Elsa had visited his tent and insisted on getting into bed with him. It may have been a bit of fun as far as Elsa was concerned, but it was rough fun and the distinguished publisher had one of the worst nights of his life. Desperately trying to restrain Elsa, he kept shouting to George for help, but unusually got no response. George had apparently retired to bed with one of his recurrent bouts of malaria and some suitable medicine in the shape of a bottle of whisky. History does not relate where Joy was, so Billy Collins had to cope with an over-friendly Elsa as best he could. Julian McKeand remembers Herbert Tichy having a similarly unpleasant experience during the Lake Rudolf safari:

'He was lying in bed. We were all just sleeping on the shores of the lake in the open. Elsa had somehow got loose again or maybe Joy had even let her off because it was light when it happened. We were all having a day off and an easy morning and Elsa jumped on his bed. I heard a loud scream from Tichy and I looked across. There was Elsa, and he was under the blankets shouting his head off. George [who] always of course ran to the rescue, pulled Elsa off and I went over to see what was going on. The pillow was absolutely covered in blood. He stuck his head out and all his face was covered in blood. We thought, my God, she's really hurt him.' In fact she had just nicked a small vein above the hairline which bled profusely.

Few visitors would have been as brave, or foolhardy with Elsa as a professional hunter called Reggie Destro. Reggie had called in to see George, who was out, with two clients as protocol demanded, to tell him where they were going to hunt. 'There's Elsa draped out on the floor,' Jack Barrah, who was having tea with Joy, recalls. 'She had this habit of coming up and grabbing you and licking you. Reggie went out for a pee and as he walked past Elsa, she came and grabbed him and bowled him over. She would do that: trip you up and roll you over. Reggie was not at all amused getting rolled over and over by this lion. Meanwhile, Joy had left the room. So Reggie came back from the loo and as he walked past, he said "bloody lion" and gave Elsa the most almighty boot in the guts as she was lying there. I've never seen a lion take off like that, it was just like a scalded cat. Shot out of the door with an enormous grunt and muffled roar and went off into the bush. Joy came running back – she'd heard this sound – and said, "What's happened to Elsa?" We all said, "We don't know, she just took off." He [Reggie] was lucky she didn't turn on him.'

Willie Hale raises the much more serious question of Elsa's effect on the life of the Adamsons, and particularly on George's career. As Chief Game Warden, he says: 'It was my policy to leave my game wardens very much alone, to get on with their job, and I interfered as little as possible with what they did. Somehow George managed to get his work done after Elsa came on the scene. But George's safaris from then onwards went where Joy wanted to go.' Elsa dominated Joy's life, and since Joy dominated George, Elsa's needs became paramount.

Willie Hale was another visitor who was wary of Elsa. 'Elsa was not the dear little thing you could pat on the head unless you knew her. She could turn quite nasty, so whenever I went up on safari to visit him [George], I always made them shut her up. Well, what happened was that George used his African rangers as kennelmen and one of them got knocked down. I don't think he was badly hurt and when we were sitting down at dinner that night – I was sitting next to Joy – Joy said, "George tells me I'm not allowed to use the game scouts to look after Elsa." And George said, "Yes, that is so." And I said, "That is perfectly true, Joy. I gave orders to George that he was not to use Government servants to look after his private property. Anyhow," I said, "some of them are frightened of Elsa." Joy then got up and said, "Willie, you're no friend of mine!" and stumped out. And she didn't speak to me again for fifteen years. So any safaris I did with George after that were minus Joy. She never forgave me, because, you see, she didn't get her way. I didn't kow-tow to her.'

The idea that Willie Hale was her husband's boss and therefore someone to whom she should be polite never occurred to Joy, or if it did she immediately rejected it. 'She wouldn't come on safari. If she heard I was coming she would clear out. But it was a little bit sad in a way, because when I retired – there's a picture of all the Game Department there – George is not in it. Why? George telephoned me and said he wasn't feeling well. Joy would not let him come down, and the result was, we had a tremendous beat-up of a farewell party at Muthaiga Club in Nairobi. It's the last time, I think, it was really beaten up: they had thunderflashes and all sorts of things like that – but George wasn't there and I'm absolutely certain that was because Joy told him not to go.'

There can be little doubt that Joy's artistic spirit found British colonial life unbearably restricting. Willie Hale remembers a time when the Adamsons and he were on safari at a place called Kipini, at the mouth of the Tana River. They camped in the District Commissioner's garden. 'Joy was in fact painting one of the District Commissioner's tribal policemen, who was a very good specimen. It was an eerie place because there are several district commissioners buried there and very, very full of mosquitoes. The District Commissioner was a bachelor and I don't think he was particularly taken with the other sex.' They arranged to have drinks in the Adamson and Hale camp, and dinner in the DC's house. But the Adamsons never arrived.

'After dinner I went back down to George and asked him, "What happened to you people, why didn't you come up and have dinner?" "Oh," said George, "Marmalade" – the District Commissioner was known as Marmalade Brown – "Marmalade is no gentleman." "Oh," I said, "tell me what happened."

'Well, what happened was this. Joy got skittish after a drink or two, got out her perfume spray, went round and sprayed Marmalade Brown, a little whiff, a little feminine whiff, and Marmalade said, "Don't do that, please." And Joy gave him another one, whereat Marmalade Brown gave her a backhander [smacking his hand], wooh, gave her a backhander and walked off. George meantime had not left his chair and was sitting there with a drink beside him, puffing away at his pipe. I never ever in the whole of my life saw George lose his temper.'

Willie Hale has no doubt at all that Joy spoiled George's career as a game warden and caused him to retire early, in September 1961. But he is equally certain that he did the right thing by being tolerant of their activities. 'She undoubtedly did interfere with his job as a game warden and George understood that and he retired, I think, two years after I went. He realised that the two did not go together. He could only go on safari when Joy wanted to. Definitely, Elsa and Joy were number one, and I know now that my happy-go-lucky and easy way with my game wardens saved the day. Supposing I had been a hard master, made them get rid of Elsa, and said to George, "It's work or Joy," and sacked him, the whole of George's greatness would never have come to pass. Had I been a martinet, George would have been out.'

He is sure also that Joy was the driving force in the partnership. 'If it hadn't been for Joy, there's no doubt that George would have just gone on with his quiet life, messing about with lions. What actually we've got to thank George for is not the fact that he rehabilitated a few lions – I told him this. "George, we're not going to remember you for the fact that you've saved a few lions from captivity. What you've done,

I'll tell you, is that first of all you have taught us a lot about the habits of lions, and, thanks to your wife, you have raised an enormously great interest in wildlife." All the characteristics which made her an uncharming person, with her push, her ability, any obstacle she met she was going to overcome; that was what did the trick. And she was lucky to have in George an exceptional person to provide the background. George was a very romantic character. That's what they said, that Joy saw him and thought he was a great big he-man. She married him. He wouldn't have done anything if she hadn't kicked him in the backside. He was a simple old chap with a beard who was able to fit in with a genius.'

Elsa's release to the wild, a long-drawn-out and fraught affair, culminated in her mating with a wild lion and the birth of her cubs at the end of 1959. Elsa chose a cleft in the big rock behind the camp on the Ura River as her lair. 'At first, she wouldn't let anyone come near but afterwards she didn't mind,' George Adamson told me in 1988. 'In fact, it was she who really showed me where the cubs were. I was searching that hill and after a bit she'd look round and growl at me so I knew I was getting somewhere near the cubs. So then I came back to camp and waited until Elsa came here for her food. I sneaked up there and went and had a look and found the cubs in the cleft.'

Wasn't this risky, despite their very special relationship?

'Well, if she'd found me it probably would have been.' George gave a little laugh. 'After that, when the cubs became more active, she brought them down here. Joy was down at the river and Elsa was on the other side with the cubs and she brought them across. By then they were starting to swim and you could see them coming across.' It was yet another touching proof of Elsa's affection for and trust in George and Joy: she was bringing her cubs across the river specially to show them to the Adamsons.

A year later, George was told by the Meru District Council that Elsa and her cubs, as a potential danger to the public, would have to move out of the area. So George and Ken Smith embarked on another safari to Lake Turkana to look once more at the possibility of releasing Elsa and her family there. The trip was inconclusive, and shortly after George's return, Elsa fell ill. She had a high fever, and her condition deteriorated rapidly. George sent a driver to Isiolo with an urgent message for Ken Smith, asking him to send a vet as quickly as possible and also to telephone Joy who was in Nairobi.

This is how George described her final moments to me. 'I found her on the other side of the river, about four or five hundred yards downstream. I at once recognised she was feeling pretty sick. Anyway, I managed to get her across the river and brought her back to camp. You could see that she was ill. The next day, I remember she came down here and went into the river. She stood in the river and was

Elsa bringing her cubs across the River Ura, in Meru, to show them to George and Joy

panting away the whole time. Then she came out and was sitting with me and suddenly, she started to have fits and the next thing was, she died.' George was almost in tears as he recalled the scene twenty-seven years later.

Elsa died of tick fever. The drugs existed which could have saved her but the vet was unable to reach her in time. With Joy away in Nairobi, George had to bury her on his own. To commemorate the world's most famous lioness, he and his rangers placed on the grave, a large mound of stones, a simple plaque with the inscription: Elsa, January 1956 to January 1961. She was exactly five.

Joy arrived a couple of days later, accompanied by Ken Smith.

'I went down overnight to the Norfolk [Hotel],' Ken Smith recalled, 'and told Joy about Elsa's being extremely ill. We leapt into this plane, came up to Garba Tula, hired a clapped-out old Land-Rover and went down to Elsa's camp. I was in the back, she was in the front with the Somali driver, and we just went down to the camp over a rough track. Joy, somehow or other, I don't know what she sensed or anything, but before we got there she said, "Just stop." We stopped. She got out and walked down and I walked behind her, and there was George hunched, forlorn, motionless, looking into space as he can do. Joy stopped and I stopped; she went on, stopped, then George looked up and it was the only time I saw a real clasp of affection, or loss, because they went straight to each other and George sobbed. They both sobbed. I stood well back. It was the most moving thing that I have seen in their relationship; it was a very moving scene. I left them to it for quite a while. We all spent that night together: it was a very sorrowful night and I left at the crack of dawn the next morning.'

After Elsa's death, her three cubs, Jespah, Gopa and Little Elsa, were chased away by wild lions and only discovered six weeks later raiding local tribesmen's stock sixteen miles away. During this escapade, Jespah collected an arrow head in his rump. Julian McKeand says George gave him a graphic description of how it happened.

'The cub went into a *boma* [camp] where the Meru were living, the usual thorn fence with the hut in the middle. They keep the very tiny goats sometimes under the beds, very flimsy wickerwork structures, with maybe a skin on top of that. They sleep on that, with a blanket. This cub which was about half grown, I think all three of them, went into this *boma*, sniffed around, went into the hut, saw the baby goats and all rushed under the bed. The guy woke up, his bed going like this, with three lion cubs underneath trying to catch the goats. All hell broke loose and I think that was the time when they shot a poisoned arrow into one.'

Finding a new home for the cubs now became as urgent as it was difficult. Dr John Owen, then Director of National Parks in Tanzania, says he was rung up and asked for help by Ian Grimwood, the Chief Game Warden in Kenya. 'I'm in the hell of a spot at the moment,' Grimwood said, 'because Elsa has died and the cubs are now big enough to go and chase the goats and so on but not really big enough to hunt. It's become a political issue and I've been told either to get them out to somewhere where they can chase things and nobody comes to harm and there's no fuss or else to shoot them.' Owen then asked him, 'Well, how about the Kenya Parks?' 'Oh, the Kenya Parks won't touch them, they won't have them,' Grimwood said. 'What about the Kenya Game Department?' 'Well, honestly and truly we haven't got an area where I could guarantee what would happen, that they wouldn't become a danger. Of course, the ideal place would be the Serengeti.'

'I'll let you know. I'll write to you,' Owen said. 'It would be a disaster if Elsa's cubs were shot,' John Owen felt, 'not merely embarrassing but a disaster because Joy has done so much to put Elsa and the cubs on the map with enormous advantage to conservation. I had to say "yes" to this.'

After considerable difficulty, George managed to round up the cubs and drive them seven hundred miles to the Serengeti. The actual release took place on 4 May 1961, but there was a strict condition. The Adamsons had only just over a month – until 8 June – to camp out in the Serengeti and help the cubs to establish themselves. This was a very tight schedule. The cubs were only seventeen months and normally young lions stay with their mother in the pride until they are at least two years old.

John Owen recalls that when he first met Joy on her way with George and the cubs to the Serengeti, she kissed him and said, 'Our saviour. It was all over.' But the warmth of their first meeting did not last long. 'Joy was distressed, distraught, bloody rude generally,' Owen said. 'I told the chaps there not to have anything to do with them. If

Joy wanted to do anything she could come into Arusha [Owen's headquarters] and I'd see her there. And she did come in and she departed in a fit of fury because I couldn't allow her to stay on any longer.' Owen was in a difficult position because he was comparatively new in the job and could not go against the wishes of his National Park trustees, who normally restricted all camping to the official tourist sites and were unwilling to make the Adamsons too much a special case. When the time limit expired, Joy pulled every string she could. 'Prince Philip, Peter Scott, Billy Collins, I saw them all off. Full marks to Billy, he and I became great friends afterwards, but the pressure was on.' He did agree, however, to one concession: for a week in July, the Adamsons could sleep out in their cars where they had last seen the cubs: otherwise they had to stay in one of the recognised camp sites and drive backwards and forwards to the release area. Even George found the conditions onerous.

Joy made a last desperate attempt to get John Owen to change his mind. 'She hired an aeroplane to come and see me in Arusha and we gave her lunch. Before lunch I said what I was going to say and we had lunch and she couldn't keep off the subject. The reason Joy wanted me to let them stay on was that one of the cubs, she noticed, had a hot nose instead of a nice, healthy, moist, cold nose and she reckoned that he had some disease, a fever. This was two or three days before the chopper came down. I was absolutely firm on it. I said, "All right Joy, a fortnight more, and at the end of that time for God's sake don't come and see me again, because you'll be wasting your time." She was possessed by a single *idée fixe* to the nth degree. Everything was centred on the cubs.' After lunch Joy flew back to the Serengeti. 'We heard from Myles [Turner, the local warden] that she behaved like a child, lay down on the aerodrome, banged her head on the ground and kicked her heels in frustration because she couldn't do what she wanted.'

Inevitably, Joy took out her anger and frustration on her luckless husband. John Owen says that although he tried to distance himself from Joy as much as possible and never had a row with her, he was conscious that George was feeling the brunt of her wrath. 'The rains were very heavy that year and moving about in the Serengeti was extremely difficult, vehicles kept getting stuck in the mud. Shortly after their arrival, George and Joy went to stay with the Turners. Myles

Turner noticed George's body was covered in weals and said to him, "What the hell's wrong with you?" "Well," George said, "we got stuck really badly in a deep gully and there were no trees so Joy put me out in front [with a rope round his shoulders] and winched." I presume that there were small bushes or small trees or something that he could hold on to to give him a grip. She would then winch the Land-Rover out. Another thing, she was incredibly hard on George from the point of view of money. He was pushed for money. For example, he used to smoke the cheapest of pipe tobacco but all the same Joy grudged him every penny of the money that he got.'

It was therefore all the more remarkable and proof if any were needed of his determination that George Adamson spent most of the next two years searching for Elsa's cubs, sometimes accompanied by Joy but often alone. As before, he was 'relegated' to the status of a mere tourist, camping at one of the official sites and driving out every day. Only someone with George's immense patience and concern would have carried it through. The final stages of the search were made easier by his resignation from the Game Department, which left him free to spend as much time as he wanted in the Seregenti. After twenty-three years as a game warden, he left with some regret, since he felt he still had a few more good years left in him. When he finally finished he was owed two and half years' back leave.

After many disappointments, George finally found Little Elsa. Each time he went back to the little valley in the Nyaraboro Hills and she heard his Land-Rover she would come to meet him and drink the water and cod liver oil he put out for her. He saw her in all seven times and was convinced it really was her. He also thought he saw Jespah once – the lion had a wound in the haunch exactly where Jespah had received the arrow head – but he could not be absolutely sure.

George's description of his last attempt to find the cubs is evocative and rather sad. He called each of them by name – Jespah, Gopa, Little Elsa. Three times his calls went ringing across the valley but the only answer was the echo from the cliffs. Yet he was not despondent. He had seen Little Elsa in good health and so there was a chance that her two brothers had also survived and were happily leading their lives in some hidden valley of the five thousand square miles of the Serengeti.

Chapter Nine

NIGHT MANOEUVRES

It is not clear at what point Joy started being unfaithful to George, but it cannot have been all that long after their wedding in 1944. By about 1950 he was beginning to unburden himself to Joy's younger sister, Dorothy – known as Dorle to the family. In one letter he wrote that Joy's infidelities had caused him numerous 'heartbreaks'. In another letter, now lost, Dorothy recalls George writing that Joy had had passionate affairs with two married men and in each case had wanted to divorce George and marry the lover. But neither had been prepared to leave his wife and family, and eventually Joy went back to George. In this letter, Dorothy wrote to me on 22 April 1991, George described how, each year, Joy was away 'more and more till she stayed away one or two years to live with another man, and that she came back so heartbroken and emotionally destroyed that he hadn't the heart to file a divorce against her.' He admitted that his first impulse had been to refuse to take Joy back but, on seeing her distress, he relented and forgave her.

George's letters to his sister-in-law, which were always uncomplaining and charmingly considerate of her, show just how unhappy he was at this period of his life.

On 24 November 1950, George wrote that 'Fifi' – short for Friederike Victoria, Joy's real names – had always been very honest with him, telling him everything about her past and the various men she had been involved with. But he had always felt that there was something which she was holding back – something which had made a deep and lasting impression on her. (Dorothy's comment to me in August 1990 was: 'Perhaps it was the abortion she once had.')

'I know that Fifi is very fond of me and has ALMOST made up her mind that I *am* her man and to settle down with me – but yet she still hopes unconsciously for her "ideal" man to come along in spite of being disillusioned so many times.'

A few days later, on 5 December, George wrote again, saying he thought the coming year would solve the problem one way or the other. They had often discussed the possibility of divorce, but in the final analysis, in George's view, Joy was difficult and less than fair. He was willing to shoulder the blame and let her go her own way, but she was determined to exercise her right to claim alimony. George simply did not have the money to pay alimony, he told his sister-in-law, and in any case it was he who had the moral right to divorce Joy, especially after the way she had behaved with the two men he had told her about. He had all the evidence he needed if he had wanted to use it. Towards the end of this letter, George Adamson uncharacteristically abandons his usual reticence and speaks from the heart.

'During the seven years we have been married, our sexual life has been practically nil, compared to a normal couple, in spite of the fact that the main reason why Fifi left Peter Bally in the first place was because he was incapable of satisfying her sexually, whereas I could, while she wanted me. As I am a normal healthy man it has at times been hell for me. But nevertheless I have never slept with another woman since we were married.'

On many occasions, George went on, Joy told him that he had carte blanche to sleep with any woman he cared to but, in fact, if he as much as looked at anyone else, Joy immediately became insanely jealous and would do almost anything to harm the imagined rival.

Twenty years later, Chryssee Martin, a young American wildlife enthusiast who worked as George's part-time secretary at Kora in the early seventies, discovered to her cost that although Joy was now sixty she was still 'wildly jealous' of other women. Chryssee told me that when she started working for George, going up to Kora for a week at a time, she always tried to telephone Joy in Naivasha and ask her, '"Are there any messages; is there anything I can do?" Usually there was but sometimes not. One time – this is the embarrassing bit – I went up to George's [camp at Kora] and I could not get a hold of Joy – you know what the telephones are like here – and I had suddenly got someone to fly me up and it was just one time that I didn't get a hold of Joy. So I went up anyway and when I came back I went into Perez Olindo's office [then the Director of Wildlife]. He was the first person I met in this country and Perez was the one who made me an honorary warden. George had some message for me to give to Perez; I think it was about a lion. Joy was in Perez' waiting room which was very small; there were always crowds of people waiting to see Perez, you didn't make appointments. Anyone, whoever you were, could see him if you'd just go in and wait.'

To Chryssee Martin's amazement, Joy cut her dead. 'Joy immediately pulled her compact out of her handbag and started putting on her lipstick. It was very strange! I said, "But Joy, I've just come back from George, don't you want to hear ...?" And she threw a tantrum, you know, that I had not gotten hold of her, and she got very angry with me and said all kinds of awful things. I was absolutely nonplussed, shocked about the whole situation. I think I just left it and decided I could see Perez later. I went back to the house practically in tears and said to Esmond [Chryssee's husband], "What the hell is all this about?" and Esmond said, "Don't worry. I'll talk to Joy." So he did and Joy said, "Oh, don't mind, some time I'll get over it but that was not the time." Whatever all that meant!'

'She was jealous?'

'Which is totally inexcusable, and she knew a hell of a lot better than to be jealous in any way at all. But she got sometimes rather possessive about the situation. Maybe she did think I was spending too much time up there.'

'What did Joy actually say?'

'That I was having an affair with George, which was totally unbelievable. It was just very nasty, it really was. It was months later before Joy invited me to come up with Esmond to Elsamere [Joy's house on Lake Naivasha] again. And then everything was smoothed over.'

Eight months later, on 14 August 1951, George wrote again to Dorothy complaining about Joy's constant absences.

They had just had six weeks together, and that had made George happy, but their reunion followed a separation of five months. Now Joy had gone off again in pursuit of her ambition to portray all the major tribes of Kenya in their traditional regalia and George did not expect to see her again until the end of the year. He was proud of her talent but sometimes wished she was not quite so dedicated since her painting kept them hundreds of miles apart and, as far as George was concerned, made a mockery of their marriage.

He was so fed up at always being on his own that he finally sent Joy an ultimatum, insisting that she choose between her painting and her marriage and that if it was her painting then she need not bother to come back and he would find himself another wife! The threat worked. He had discovered, he tells Dorothy, that you had to take a very firm line with Fifi. There was something else which disturbed George as much as Joy's prolonged absences: her absolute refusal to have children. They argued at length about it, but Joy refused to budge, claiming that the child might inherit George's mother's mental illness.

According to one friend, old Mrs Adamson was 'a bit off her rocker' at the end of her life and was referred to jokingly as the 'Duchess of Kildare'. George went to the length of consulting a specialist who assured him that there was no such risk and he even offered to get a second opinion from a doctor of Joy's choice, but she refused. It also irritated George intensely to watch Joy pouring out all her frustrated maternal love on animals instead of giving it, as he would have wished, to their own child.

He goes on to describe at length the now famous story of his first mauling by a lion, ending up with an account of his stay in hospital in Nairobi. Once he was well enough to have visitors everybody wanted to meet him and interview him, spreading his fame far and wide. Fan mail came pouring in, a lot of it from schoolgirls in South Africa

Joy with a sitter for one of the portraits in her 'Tribes of Kenya' series, now in the National Museum in Nairobi. John Jay is on the left

clamouring for signed photographs. George had become a star. He says he had had other adventures since, but nothing quite so dangerous, possibly because he had learned to be a little more careful. He then throws an interesting light on his state of mind at the time of the mauling. He had just been jilted by a French girl and in his dejection, he suggests, he did not particularly care what happened to him.

Joy had caused him many heartaches since, but he had come through them all without too much damage and, he claims rather defiantly, was now rather hardened. But clearly it gave him solace, as he sat alone in his camp in the evening with only a handful of African servants to keep him company, to unburden his heart to Dorothy. She was, he reminded her, the only one of Joy's family who kept in contact with him, and the letter ends with a touching reminder that he was her brother-in-law and always ready to help her.

In his next letter, dated 10 December 1951, George returned to the theme of Joy's absence and the fact that he had not seen her for four months. He was pinning his hopes on being able to take a fortnight's holiday at Christmas and meet her in Lamu, then an enchanting island on the coast north of Mombasa full of beautiful old Arab houses. He goes on to complain that, the Government having run out of money, Joy had little hope of ever being paid for her portraits. But she was determined to finish the job and, George says ruefully, would probably end up by giving the paintings free to the Kenya Government. A handsome and generous gesture – for which George would have to pay, of course, out of his own slender resources – which he could ill afford. The only good thing about it all, he concludes, was that once Joy had run out of money she would be forced to return to live at home. If only she were more practical, George writes wistfully, they would be very comfortably off.

Towards the end of his letter, George says how strange it is that after nearly eight years of marriage Joy has come round to the view that he is as good a husband as she is going to get, although she still doesn't think very much of him. He adds – and here we get a glimpse of how remarkably tolerant a man he was – that despite all the anguish Joy's love affairs have caused him, he has no regrets and he confesses to being happy that he still loves her.

Then, as if feeling guilty for talking so much about himself, George starts to worry about his sister-in-law's happiness and wonders why she has never married. She must be an attractive person, he tells her, and then launches into a lecture about there being no point in waiting for the ideal man to appear, because it will be a vain wait. Such paragons exist only in the imagination. Life is a compromise and one's happiness in life depends on one's ability to make the best of what is there. Even Joy was beginning to get the point. The men she had fallen in love with, the Shires, Ballys and all the others, had proved to have 'feet of clay'. Peter Bally, George adds, had remarried and had a child, as far as he knew. George saw him from time to time in Nairobi – he was beginning to look very old – and they would have a chat, because he saw no point in always being at loggerheads. Joy, on the contrary, loathed her former husband and had never forgiven him – for what George does not say. But judging by what Dorothy recalls of George's missing letter and knowing how insanely jealous Joy could be, it seems possible that Joy resented Bally's desertion of her. According to Dorothy, 'Joy barricaded herself in Peter Bally's house and behaved quite crazy. She had to be tranquillised to get her out of this house and only when she was told that Peter lived with another woman she gave up to pursue him.' Joy and Peter Bally were still married at this point, since they did not divorce until after Joy met George, but according to Mary Leakey they were already going their separate ways.

On 27 February 1953, George tells Dorothy that he and Joy are not unhappy but that it is not much of a marriage in the sense that they hardly ever make love, despite Joy saying that she wants to have a child. George hopes that the long holiday they are planning in Africa and Europe would improve matters. Then, considerate as ever, he sympathises with his sister-in-law that relations between her and the rest of the family are so difficult and suggests that despite the deep family bond, the intolerance typified by Joy's behaviour is no doubt responsible. He admits to being thought by some to be perhaps ridiculously good-natured himself. On the other hand, he says, if you give people the benefit of the doubt and look for their good side, they often reward you, despite initial let-downs. Although he and Dorothy have never met and whether he thinks she is in the right or wrong, he will never criticise her and will always take her side. Then comes a fascinating passage which shows George at his best: generous, tolerant of others' weaknesses and foibles, and the eternal optimist. We all make a hash of our lives from time to time, he says, and that is when we need the support and advice of friends. Never throw in the towel, Dorle, he says, and never indulge in self-pity. In another fascinating but unexplained aside, he admits he once did so himself, but then he became aware that he was only damaging himself and becoming a pest to his friends.

George asks himself why he has embarked on this long lecture. Dorothy must think him an utter bore. He apologises and changes the subject. Joy is in Nairobi for the hanging of her exhibition in the new museum, opened by the Governor a couple of days before. George's main preoccupation was how he was going to shoot an outsize elephant. He had paid £75 for a licence and he now had to shoot an elephant with tusks of at least 75 pounds a side to make it worthwhile, or else lose the licence and the £75. Even then it was not easy to find an elephant with tusks that big, although there were plenty of smaller elephants, some of which had the habit of invading his garden at night and eating his plants while he slept.

To the outside world and even to people who knew him well, George Adamson was a straightforward, pipe-smoking, whisky-drinking game warden more at home in the bush than in a drawing-room: a man of few words and simple feelings. Yet underneath, and so well disguised as to be virtually undetectable, was a sensitive soul yearning for the love that his wife, for whatever reason, so resolutely refused to give him. In Dorle's mind, however, there is no doubt about the reason for Joy's behaviour. 'She was so selfish,' she says with something of Joy's own vehemence. 'She thought only about herself. Fifi was a very selfish woman and a liar too. I felt very sorry for George.'

Pam Carson, a second cousin of George's and a close friend, recalls going to see him in Isiolo in 1959. 'I remember once we walked round the garden together and he was confiding in me and not exactly complaining, but did say that of course Joy "really hasn't been a wife to me for over fifteen years and I could have divorced her many times over." She was a bit of a hot piece, you know, Joy, she was very keen on the gents, dear, you know – *les pantalons très chauds* ...'

'Did she have lots of affairs?'

'Oh, I think a lot. She was always away. I was six months in Isiolo and she was away the entire time, so I never actually saw her. She was on a lecture tour, I remember.'

Joy's passionate nature not only led her to acquire three husbands and a number of lovers but her interest in the opposite sex persisted and in later years translated itself, inevitably perhaps, into a liking for younger men. Elizabeth de Warenne Waller, whose husband Pat was a young District Officer in Meru in the late forties, recalls her first meeting with Joy, whom she irreverently nicknamed 'the Man-eater of Meru'.

'I came into the *duka* [shop] and here was this woman, dressed as always, which I thought was unforgiveable amongst Africans and Muslims, in a three-cornered scarf over two rather saggy bosoms, yellow and slightly grubby, a topee perched on one side of her head and a pair of shorts. That was her general attire. She was in the *duka* making demands, talking to Pat. I came up and Pat said, "This is my wife who's just come out from England." She barely stopped what she was saying to nod her head and turn back to her demands.' Having assembled her list of groceries and had it carried outside, Joy got into the Land-Rover and drove away. 'I said, "Who's that woman?" – I could have used other words – "that bronzed foreigner?" She was freckly, bungy-faced. Pat said, "She's the artist who's painting all the pictures in the district and we have to look after her." Then he added, rather guiltily, "I'll tell you a funny story about her.

'"'I was out on one of my safaris in the district and camped at one of the camping grounds, in my tent, with the usual following of servants and policemen and elders from the village, when who rolls in, to use the site also, but our friend the artist. Unusual procedure, unless by arrangement, to share a camping ground. However, can't be rude to a lady, not that she turned out to be one, for no sooner had her tent been raised and all the necessary preparations for her stay completed, than she came across to my tent with a 'got a light?' type of demand – somewhat surplus to a woman equipped with three tons of baggage and a full retinue of retainers in tow!

'"'Well, a chap can't be completely ungallant, but what a predicament when a woman is a good bit older than you, and quite plain in her intentions whether you like it or not. So after I'd plied her with a few drinks and she got to the 'I'll go and change into something a bit cooler' bit, I sent hastily for the Tribal Police Sergeant, telling him there'd be a bonus for the fastest tent striking operation he'd ever known, as there had been an urgent message and I was needed twenty miles down the road.

'"Without comment and in great haste, poker face prevailing, my tent came down in record time and my boxes and bundles and furniture hurtled on to the lorry faster than believable, followed by the human element complete with sheep, chickens, pots and poles, joining in the general atmosphere of urgency.

'"The disappointed artist emerged only in time to see us disappearing across the clearing in a puff of dust before the dark enveloped us in its protection.

'"So you see," Pat said, "my penance has been a very long list of complaints and demands from a very frustrated lady who hoped that, a newcomer and a greenhorn to the job, I might have been unable to devise escape at such short notice, and would have fallen victim, like so many before me, to her charms."

'There was absolutely no doubt in Pat's mind as to what she wanted. Not only that but he swears that the next camp he went to, she followed him there. He said he struck camp twice that night, obviously under the same sort of circumstances each time. She had quite a reputation with the District Officers.'

Elizabeth de Warenne Waller says that in 1950, when her husband was posted to Isiolo for three months, she met George Adamson again. 'George of course was the Game Warden in Isiolo and we used to meet him in the *dukas*, and I remember going in one day and there was George sipping a beer, feeling sorry for himself. Mohamed Moti [the shopkeeper] was getting all his stuff ready and two other people came in and we all started chatting. As the beer filtered down, George said, "Oh, I had a rotten night last night, young —" who had come for the night to stay with them [the Adamsons] "breezed in"; and apparently Joy had taken the *kiboko* to George and driven him out into the guest house and kept the other chap in the house! And he was drowning his sorrows in the *duka* the next day with a glass of beer! ... This handsome young man spent the night with her while George was in the guest house, relegated to the bottom of the garden.'

Billy Collins, later Sir William Collins, was undoubtedly one of the great loves of Joy's life. It was common gossip in the publishing world that the distinguished publisher and his best-selling author had a tempestuous affair. Irene Stirling says, 'I think she loved him, among many others. She was a very passionate lady. My only first-hand memory of it is when she came to London. Billy had a love affair with Africa as well as with, we think, Joy. He went on camps with them [the Adamsons], and we think they did have an affair, because Joy when she came back on one occasion was very, very unhappy and thought that Billy had been much more serious than he probably was. Billy actually was very frightened of his wife, a very strong character, [Lady] Pierre Collins, very much a power behind the throne, an *eminence grise* if ever there was one. I was sitting in my own little office and Margery [Villiers] said, "For goodness sake, take Joy for a walk." She was sobbing her heart out and so one walked her up and down, I'll never forget, round and about Belgrave Square, just listening most of the time to this torrent of "How can he behave like this when he loves me?" The usual, really, heartbreak, you know, very very unhappy. He'd really given her the cold mitt and didn't want to know at all, only wanted to see her with other people there to protect himself. I mean,

Joy with Paul Radin (left), one of the two associate producers of Born Free, *and Sir William (Billy) Collins, the publisher*

he wanted a bodyguard and she couldn't get through at all. So one just talked rather lamely about his children and Pierre and sort of said, "There, there, there ..." Nothing one could do. It made absolutely no impression. I did say, "Oh dear, I feel awfully sad for you; it's one of these horrid things," and "men are dreadful, aren't they." She was very unhappy.'

Irene Stirling says Joy was also 'very primitive. She couldn't disguise her feelings. In some ways she was quite uncivilised, which was what made her very interesting ... no inhibitions, absolutely none. But her love for Billy was quite real and I would have thought almost certainly they'd had an affair. This was well after *Born Free*. He used to go back to Africa every year, partly for books and partly because he loved Africa. He always went to see them [the Adamsons]. She really did love him ...

'She was a very exhausting person, you know how very emotional people are exhausting, and if they keep the pitch up the whole time they wear you to a frazzle. I remember after quite a short time in Joy's company one was drained and I suppose rather like Billy she fell in love with Africa too, as well as George, I imagine. Africa had a tremendous pull on her.'

Born Free was such a huge success that Joy Adamson was soon in demand as a speaker all over the world, giving hundreds of lectures and showing the film she and George had made. Her English was heavily accented and she admitted herself that her vocabulary was not perfect, so she took elocution lessons. Her tutor sat in the front row and waved a little red flag to slow her down when she started to gabble incomprehensibly. Before her first lecture in London to 3,000 people she was so nervous that she was physically sick. On another day, also in London, she lectured to businessmen in the morning, to women prisoners in Holloway Prison at lunchtime – by the end they were eating out of her hand – and in the afternoon she went to Kensington Palace to have tea with the Duchess of Kent and show her the film of Elsa. It would have been a perfect end to a busy day had Joy not been aware throughout that the royal Pekingese was busy chewing her long gloves, then *de rigueur* for court occasions, to shreds.

After a world-wide lecture tour in 1964, Joy flew back to Kenya for the filming of *Born Free* by Columbia, although she was specifically forbidden to interfere with the shooting. The location was a 750-acre farm at Naro Moru, at the foot of Mount Kenya, with one of the most spectacular views in the country but also one of the worst climates. Filming was due to begin in the dry season, but the gods were singularly unkind and it turned out to be the wettest dry season on record. The director, producers, actors and film crew slithered about in the rain and mud while a debate raged over whether the story of Elsa should be re-created on celluloid by circus-trained lions or untrained lions. As Carl Foreman, the American executive producer, pointed out, however, the argument soon resolved itself. Juba and Astra, the circus lions from Germany chosen to portray the young Elsa, were too old and fat, so they had to be sacked and young untrained lionesses found instead.

The Adamsons at Naro Moru, where Born Free *was filmed, with Virginia McKenna and Bill Travers*

This pleased Joy and George, as well as the stars who played them in the film, Virginia McKenna and Bill Travers, both early converts to the anti-circus cause. Dozens of lions now had to be acquired as rapidly as possible from a wide variety of sources including the private collection of Emperor Haile Selassie of Ethiopia. Carl Foreman says that in the course of the film, twenty-three lions and lionesses of various ages were permanently housed at the camp, plus another seven 'transients'. Then there was the problem of getting untrained lions and nervous actors and actresses to film scenes together. What ultimately developed, he says, was a 'method' school of acting which required Virginia McKenna and Bill Travers and the lions to go on long daily walks together, to build up confidence between the artistes and the lions and to 'play' at various scenes which would be used in the film.

Luckily, two nine-month-old cubs, a male and a female, the mascots of the Second Battalion, the Scots Guards, became available as the regiment was about to go home at the end of its tour of duty. Fortior and Unita, popularly known as Boy and Girl, arrived with their handler, Sergeant Ron Ryves, and soon settled down to their new life. One morning, out for a walk with the Traverses, Boy playfully jumped on Virginia and knocked her down, breaking her ankle in two places. This could have been a very nasty incident, since a lion is apt to consider anyone or anything on the ground potential prey. Like a true hero, Bill Travers came running to the rescue and carried his wife and co-star to the Land-Rover, at the same time fending off two powerful young lions which thought this was all part of the game. As George says, no one would have blamed Virginia McKenna for abandoning the film there and then, but once she was out of hospital and sufficiently recovered she bravely went straight back to work.

Giles Remnant, a young Briton brought up in Kenya who was an assistant to John Jay, the official photographer for the film, before being recruited by George Adamson, says the Traverses 'struck up a rapport with George then that was wonderful. They depended on George totally. When they were out walking the lions, learning what to do and how does a lion respond, they would ask him, "What can I expect?" It was very much in George's hands. But Joy was never allowed on the scene when there was training of the lions. She could arrive in the evening, read the scripts, but she never ever once went on the film set when the lions were due to do their bit. George would never have the word performing. "Lions don't perform." He banned that word from the film set.

'Without George it would never have been possible. Because he understood the animals. He got the animals to do everything that they did. There was no way the animals would ever have done it otherwise. He understood the age, the stage, what you were going to do with the animals, which lioness, which lion could do it. It was all George. There was never anybody else. He didn't get any personal accolade from that film, but certainly George Adamson is a name which will be synonymous with lions for ever.'

George established his quarters in an enclosure next to Lion Camp, the compound where the lions were housed, even keeping some of the more temperamental ones in his tent at night to win their confidence. 'George really was Mr Lion. We had twenty-one Elsas, several odd males and the hyrax of course which was a big feature, Pati Pati. As I got to know George and went out on all the trips with him taking pictures, he said, "Come and work with me training the lions."' When the unit moved down to the coast, 'George drove down with Girl and she wouldn't do anything, so we had to send for Boy. I was told to drive down to the coast with Boy in the back of a Land-Rover so they would act together. They were pining for each other.'

The senior male was called Ugas. He was a magnificent animal and George's favourite, but he and Giles Remnant did not get on. 'Ugas got me on the ground one day on *Born Free* with my head in his mouth and – we always carried a stick – George literally stuck the stick down his throat and said, "This is not edible." We used to give them an invitation to have a go at us because we used to play hide and seek with them. We would hide behind a clump of grass and the lions would stalk you and jump up. Half of them would leap up and give you a big lick, what fun, do it again ... Ugas took it one step too far. I was quite frightened of Ugas, I don't mind admitting it. He was the man-eater in *Born Free*; he's in the opening scene; he ate the woman doing her laundry in the river. There's a scene towards the end in which there's a big fight which we put together and there's Ugas standing on a rock, calling his lioness. Boy actually didn't portray so much.'

Of the three main lionesses, Henrietta was Giles Remnant's favourite. 'She was delightful, you could get her to do anything. Give her a tin of sardines, she would do anything.'

But it was purely George's skill that made Henrietta such a success. When she arrived from the Entebbe Zoo, she was in a pathetic condition, all skin and bone and extremely nervous. She was said to be the sole survivor of a litter of cubs whose mother had been run over by a tractor in one of the Uganda Parks. She was rejected as useless by the director but after several weeks of good feeding and George's loving care, she 'blossomed out into a beautiful young lioness' and became the star performer.

Girl was the youngest, she still had a cub's spots, and Mara, another lioness who arrived in a bad state but was rehabilitated by George, the most mature. 'We put her into the fight against a lioness which came from Naivasha. It was an exercise you wouldn't want to repeat. You are asking animals to go and fight and it went too far. George knew it had to be done and he resigned himself to it, but he hated the violence. George hated any form of violence in the end.'

George told his old friend Willie Hale in a letter dated 10 November 1965 that during the entire making of the film he was constantly on the look out to prevent cruelty to the animals to get them to do certain things. He was not above using a bit of blackmail by saying he would complain to the Chief Game Warden and the Society for the Prevention of Cruelty to Animals if the film-makers offended. He hated to think what might have been done if he had not been there to keep an eye on things. From talks he had with some of the crew, it was clear that in most animal films a lot of nasty methods were used of which the public had no idea. All they knew was what they saw on the screen, not how it got there.

Chapter Ten

FILMING LIONS

The first director of *Born Free* was an American, Tom MacGowan. According to Giles Remnant, 'He brought on circus lions from Germany and used to say, "Tell the lion to walk from left to right, roll the cameras, action ..." and the lion would sit down. He was absolutely apoplectic with rage that this lion wouldn't do what he was telling it to do. It was a circus lion and should have been taught to obey. He lasted a couple of months and got fired. Then James Hill came. Good British stuff.'

James Hill is a soft-spoken, modest man, as well as an extremely experienced director, with among his credits *The Belstone Fox* and *Black Beauty*. 'I think I was quite lucky,' he says, 'when I came in because as you know sometimes the lions behaved, sometimes they didn't, and they seemed to behave quite well the first month or two. For instance, you just want the lion to sit there betweeen Bill and Virginia for a minute and you could be a week on that. If the lion didn't feel like sitting, nothing could make it sit.'

Surprisingly, James Hill says that in some ways *Born Free* was 'one of the most boring' films he has ever directed. One difficulty was the unpredictability of the filming. 'The human element you can control and shoot it, but you were totally out of control if the lion or lioness decided to jump on the table. Now that was a bonus if the actors continued with the dialogue, but it is very hard for them to continue with a bloody great lion sitting there. Sometimes it did happen and it was good. On the other hand, the next days could go by and there'd be nothing at all, just nothing. So it was the lack of control. Sometimes it was good and sometimes it drove you absolutely to despair.'

The only big argument about the script, written by Gerald Copley, an American, concerned the scene towards the end of the film where, in real life, Elsa returned to the Adamsons' camp on the banks of the Ura River with her newly-born cubs. In a remarkable display of trust and affection, she carried the cubs across the river in her mouth to show them to George and Joy. It was an extremely moving moment, brilliantly captured by George and Joy with their own 16 millimetre camera, and which *Born Free* tried to re-create. As James Hill points out, it was 'extremely difficult to do and quite dangerous because a lioness with her cubs is very protective. We had Ginny and Bill here and they were supposed to come walking towards us, which they'd been practising, so they knew which way. We had a kind of shutter

The Tana River, which makes the northern border of the Kora National Park and south of which, in British colonial days, the Somalis were forbidden to graze their herds

Left: *Kora Rock, with Kampi ya Simba's flock of rapacious and cacophonous vulturine guinea fowl in the foreground. George could not bring himself to eat them*

Above: *Kora Tit, so named by George for obvious reasons. It was here, in 1978, that Suleiman playfully knocked the old man down and then nearly killed him*

Below: *The main gate and guest huts, adorned with the odd elephant skull. The open-air loo and shower are to the right*

Left: *Somali camels and their owners inside Kora illegally. George bitterly resented their destruction of the habitat and poisoning of his lions with a cattle dip called Coppertox*

Inset: *The infinitely pathetic carcase of an elephant, slaughtered in Kora by Somali poachers armed with automatic rifles, its tusks brutally hacked off with a chain saw*

Below: *Prince Bernhard of the Netherlands, then President of the World Wildlife Fund, insisted on having his picture taken with George, ensconced upon the elephant-jaw loos*

Right: *Being great scavengers, the marabou storks were always on the lookout for any tasty morsels left over by the lions*

Left: *Tony Fitzjohn, George's assistant, playing with the leopardess Komunyu, which he brought up and eventually released. She was later killed by a pack of baboons*

Right: *It appealed to George's well-developed sense of humour to draw visitors' attention to the bright blue testicles of the male vervet monkeys*

Right: *This dik-dik, the smallest and shyest of antelopes, loved green beans. George always remembered to have a few for him*

The hornbills were expert peanut catchers – according to George they would have made a good cricket side

Inset: *The ground squirrels had expandable cheeks which could accommodate a huge quantity of peanuts*

Left: *Mohammed Maru, the headman, one of the four in George's Land-Rover when they fell into the Somali ambush. By his own account he ran away, although he was carrying George's old .303*

Below: *Ongesa, who was also with George on that fatal Sunday. Badly wounded, he managed to get out of the Land-Rover and stagger a few steps, but collapsed and died seconds later*

Above: *Bitacha, Hamisi's assistant, was with Inge in the Land-Rover when they were ambushed by the Somali Shifta. He was the key eyewitness to George's murder and later identified one of the killers*

Right: *Hamisi, a Sudanese who was Terence's cook for thirty years and who later worked for George, narrowly escaped being eaten by a crocodile. Speciality: macaroni cheese*

which came down very quickly in case they suddenly sprang for her [Virginia McKenna]. Well, she looks at them and there's a little bit of dialogue about them being carefree and going off with their mother and so on. But Columbia said, "No, she must pick them up and cuddle them." Pretty sick-making, this idea. And I said, "No, this is quite wrong," and Virginia said, "This is quite wrong." I mean, the whole point is about the animals going off and making their own life. This was, as far as I recall, the only real argument. It went on for days and days, cables flying about getting shots of cuddling these lion babies, which was quite against the spirit of the film.' In the end, Columbia dropped the idea.

'The film itself, I had very mixed feelings about it actually. Somebody said to me, "James, that's a very sick film, you know, a very

On the set of Born Free. *Joy and Carl Foreman, the executive producer, deep in discussion. They did not get on*

Freudian film." And looking back at it I'm inclined to agree. It's a film about thwarted mother love, I think, if one analyses it. Whereas George was very calm, very gentle and very patient with the lions, Joy was "Come to me, come to me, come to me," very, very nervous, like children with dogs perhaps; and she was scratched really badly lots and lots of times, by the lions or a cheetah or a leopard, all over the shoulders. She used to wear a half bathing costume and trousers and she was very badly scratched. But George as far as I know never had any serious trouble, because he was very, very gentle, very, very quiet. I admired him very much. He said he preferred the lions, actually, because they didn't snore as much as Joy. Quite often you'd see him fast asleep on a camp bed, there with a big lion. George and the lion.'

Joy and Carl Foreman did not get on at all, James Hill says. 'Carl was a sort of megalomaniac, and probably she was as well.' He remembers a row about the fight scene at the end of the film.

'George said, "It'll be more noise than anything else," but in case it got nasty we had some very powerful water hoses. We could have stopped, I should think, a major row with the stuff we'd got around this compound. But Madam said, "You mustn't do it. You mustn't do it because they'll kill each other." George said, "No, no, no." And all the time she said, "Look, you can have someone come and scream, can't you, and say they had a fight." I said it's like making a film about the Battle of Hastings and somebody comes in and says, "The battle is over, Sir." The audience is totally cheated. And in the event they had a bit of a punch-up. One of them got a small scratch. We built up the sound track tremendously, the rows and noise and things; the sound was no trouble. But that she did get quite hysterical about. She'd come rushing in, saying, "You've got to stop it!" and so on. But George would stay very calm. He was a realist, and I said, "We can't really cheat the audience; there's got to be a confrontation, a sort of 'high noon' between these two great animals. It's over territory and once one's established the territory the other will slope off," which it did. "And if they do fight to the death –" but animals very, very, very seldom do. That went off absolutely fine, no problems at all.'

James Hill confirms that although Joy got on well with Virginia McKenna, she hated Bill Travers. Long after *Born Free*, in the seventies, James Hill and the Traverses were visiting George at Kora. One day, they decided to drive over to see Joy at her camp at Shaba, where she was engaged in the release of a young leopardess, Penny, about whom she wrote *Queen of Shaba*.

'George seemed to think that was all right so we drove a very considerable distance to where she lived, a long ride. When we got there Joy came stalking out of the camp like a weird kind of policeman, saying, "You can't come in." It was nearly twilight. So there I am with Bill and Ginny and George; so I got out, walked up to her and said, "What's the matter?" And she said, "George can come in and talk to me if he wants and you may come in, James, if you wish to, but Bill Travers, never!" I went back and Ginny said, "Well, this is the middle of Africa, middle of nowhere! If Bill can't go in, I'm not going in. I'll go over to talk to her." I felt we were in some sort of Kafka play, and I thought, "This is just ridiculous." It was kind of us and them; there was about a couple of hundred yards between us, and I don't like walking about in the middle of Africa in the twilight, quite frankly, I get very nervous about that. So I stayed with George and Virginia walked all this distance and you could see them from a distance haranguing each other; what they were talking about God knows. Anyway, after a minute Ginny came back and said, "She won't let you in, and I'm not going in." So we got into the jeep and drove all the way back to the camp. Very strange. When she got a hate against somebody nothing, nothing could shift her. Really weird, especially at twilight.' (The rules of hospitality, and safety, in the bush in Kenya make it obligatory to offer travellers a bed. But rules did not apply to Joy.)

Of Virginia McKenna, James Hill says, 'She was very courageous indeed; she was a very good actress. She's got a kind of hundred horse power engine. Splendid lady.' Although she had to play a number of potentially risky scenes, James Hill recalls only one moment when he thought her life was in real danger.

'I think there was only one serious moment where I thought, "Oh dear, dear," and that was when we had the camera on not a very high rostrum and Ginny was on the grass with the lion, stroking her. I can't remember what the scene was but she was with the lion, quite intimate with it, and suddenly the lion just went like that and got its mouth on her neck. And I thought, "Shit!" and very sensibly she stayed absolutely still; she didn't move. Bill was there and George was there and I can't remember which lion it was but they came and said, "Now come on, don't be silly, stop playing," like with a cat and it just took its claws out. She was very shaken, she really was, but she came to no harm at all. That was the only time that I thought something nasty might happen, if suddenly she had struck it, it might have gone for her neck. I don't believe for a moment it was being malicious. I think it was just playing, but four hundred pounds of flesh. That was the only time.'

Born Free, he says, 'made a huge amount of money, and Columbia and Carl [Foreman] said they wanted to do a sequel of *Living Free* which in some respects is a better story. So he said, "Go on a recce," and I said, "I don't want to go on a recce, I've just been there." He said, "Well, one of the Columbia people wants to go there." "But I know all the locations," I said. "I've been there," and he said, "Well, his wife's never been to Africa; she'd like to go." Anyway, they engaged me to

Virginia McKenna bottle-feeding 'Elsa', watched by Born Free*'s first director, Tom McGowan, and Joy (extreme left)*

write the script for *Living Free*. It was a very good script; there were a lot of things in it, with poachers and so on which weren't in the first film. I finished and delivered it and Carl said, "Fine," and then it came to "Who's going to cast it?"

'I assumed Bill and Ginny would, you know. Obviously [*Born Free*] had been successful and you don't want somebody else. Carl, I think, had an interest of something like thirty per cent in the film which is quite high, and we said, "Look, if we're going to go into one of these long things again, it isn't that we want a lot of money but we would like a small percentage" and Bill and Ginny and I asked for seven and a half per cent between us which is really very modest, two and a half per cent each. Carl literally threw me out of his office. "You ungrateful bastards!" he said, and that sort of thing and no way would he and Columbia entertain it. Knowing Ginny, I said, "Well, I don't want to do it with anybody else because it's just stupid, and I think we should stick on this. If Carl's getting thirty per cent we three should get seven and a half per cent between us. We really don't think that is greedy." But they wouldn't entertain it. And then they asked me to do it with other people and I said forget it and they did it with Nigel Davenport and Susan Hampshire. She was quite hot on the *Forsyte Saga* at the time and it was a disaster; it was awful. It's full of clips from *Born Free*.'

James Hill does not accept George Adamson's criticism that the script of *Born Free* was so 'sacred' that many charming little, impromptu incidents with the lions were ignored because they did not fit the script. 'We did change things,' he says. 'You have to adapt yourself to the situation on location, obviously. But basically,' he concedes, 'it stayed the same.'

Giles Remnant says that James Hill's style of direction was, unlike his predecessor's, flexible. The method was to 'take it as it happens; you probably get the best shots that way in any case. So on each shot we were told, "Right, this is what you want to do, see if you can get this to happen." Basically, depending on what the animal would do, we set the cameras that way; so the cameras would be set up depending on what the animal could do, rather than on what the animal was going to be told to do. And that's how they actually filmed it. We'd go out in the morning for a walk with the lions and decide what would be the best way to do things and how this would happen, spring a surprise on the animal and watch the reaction. The famous snake scene

– it was a wonderful scene, plastic hose pipe with a plasticine snake's head on it. This thing was on a string and you pulled it out and the lion was meant to show shock horror at this spitting cobra that was in front of it, which it did. The first time it happened it was wonderful but you could never do the take twice. That was really how the whole thing was done.

'The lion fight was a one-off, so there were cameras behind every rock and every corner and you knew it was going to happen, so for three or four weeks beforehand we would bait the lions, walking each one past the cage, winding each one up. We would feed one and not the other and they began to hate each other and that's really how the film was done. A lot of it was spontaneous. The film crew adjusted very, very well. It was no longer, "God, we've got to be behind cages." They'd all run around and get shots and we knew how to do the shots in the end, where the camera people had to be, the loaders, the focus people, the cameramen, all these people. They all loved the animals; none of them ever came to any harm. There was a trial period for two months when these chaps arrived and they didn't know what to do with the animals but in the end they all loved the animals and the animals would just sit there with them during lunch and we'd all have a super time. There was a great atmosphere, great comradeship.'

Another of the stars of *Born Free* was an elephant called Eleanor. She has since made a name for herself as the foster mother of orphaned baby elephants whose mothers have been killed by poachers in the Tsavo National Park. The elephant orphanage scheme is run by Daphne Sheldrick whose husband David was the game warden in charge of Tsavo.

'Eleanor the elephant – she's a very famous elephant now – she hated being away from any party. We had a party at the Mount Kenya Safari Club. There was a bar there and I can remember her coming straight through the french windows one night because she wanted to be in the bar with us. Didn't want to drink, just wanted to be with us. She was a super elephant.

'We used to drive up there, drive up sober and come back out of our minds, in Land-Rovers. George was the worst. He was the leader of all, an absolute terror. He and William Holden [the American film star] and Ray Ryan who owned it, off we'd all go up there; we all had honorary membership. It was absolutely lethal, terrible. I never actually ever once saw George pissed. I've got to say that. But I saw him have quite a few. He had his regular tots but that wasn't a bender. I think he was realistic, he had to live within a budget, he was quite practical. But Joy loathed him drinking at all. She would say to me, "Tell him to stop drinking!"

'We used to tease him. It started on *Born Free* when the bed-hopping ... the midnight traffic was unbelievable. It went on everywhere. I think George had a soft spot for a rather sweet girl at one time. Her fraternisation with George was purely platonic, but she was also getting the real thing elsewhere. I remember George one day saying, "Yes, great fun, but it doesn't interest me. It never has interested me" – words to that effect. Several times afterwards he did actually say, "You know, Joy and I never slept in the same bedroom from the day we got married." They never actually slept together. I think possibly they did try to have a child; it's in the book that Joy had a miscarriage. It may have been the final demise of the relationship. I remember him saying that when they'd married and they were meant to go off on a honeymoon somewhere, Joy decided to go painting on Mount Kenya. George said, "To hell with it," and went off to chase something up.'

George's own views of the nightly antics on location were more caustic. Writing to Willie Hale he said that he had enjoyed the year he spent working on the film because of the lions. If it had not been for them he could not have stood it. He did not dislike the fifty or so crew and technicians on the set, but he admitted they were not his sort of people. Sensibly, he had decided to remove himself from the main camp at an early stage and installed himself next door to the lion camp. Tongue-in-cheek, he says it was much safer there because of the extraordinary nocturnal carryings-on in the main crew quarters. You never knew what you might find if you went to someone's room, who you might find there or what they might be doing. He then proceeds to recount the story of one young lady who climbed up on the roof in the nude and threatened to jump off if her boyfriend did not stop making passes at another female. Never a dull moment!

Giles Remnant says that by the time he got to know George Adamson in 1963, 'he was approaching sixty so perhaps his sexual appetite was somewhat gone. I remember one day we'd been walking in the bush and we arrived in a Somali camp and there was a most stunning Somali girl there, as they can be, absolutely beautiful, and

George was looking at her with a sort of wanton look and I raised my eyebrows and said, "That's right George, quite pretty," and he said: "Mmm, mmm, fond memories," and we left and said no more. You'd never actually pursue it in case you'd embarrass him. One had such a wonderful respect for him, and everything else he knew. But I don't doubt that maybe one day out in the bush when he was a young man …'

Of the making of *Born Free*, Giles Remnant recalls, 'Everything was done on the cheap. It cost them a fortune, as a result. They were out for the money.' At the end of the film, George Adamson wanted to release all the lions to the wild. There were several reasons. 'One, he did not like the thought of them being caged up and he didn't like what had been happening to them during the film. There's a scene where Elsa comes back looking very, very tired, staggering. Well, she was half anaesthetised to get her to stagger; she didn't even know where she was going. It was only George's voice that was calling her. It was a brilliant shot, this lioness staggering across the bush. George was terribly upset by this sort of thing, frightfully upset. A lot could hurt George. When somebody would shout at him and tell him things weren't going right, he used to say, "Well, stuff it, they can wait until it does go right." He stood no nonsense from the film directors and producers. He'd say, "I'll do it when I'm ready, not before." It was entirely a nightmare, because you had the commercial aspect of it. They'd say, "You know, we gotta run on skedule …" And we weren't helped by weather. It was one of the wettest years in history, it rained continually. Filming a desert scene in a quagmire didn't quite fit. If you look at the film it was all done in very green scenes, it's never done in the wonderful raw desert of the Isiolo environment … So that was an added frustration, when the rains came down. But old George didn't stand any nonsense. He'd say, "You want to do it, do it." Bill and Ginny were being paid to do a job. So they were very commercially orientated as well, but a very loving couple.'

Writing again to Willie Hale, George notes that when the filming ended in April, he very much wanted to take on the two lions and three lionesses he had been most involved with and which he wanted to release to the wild. First there was Mara, a lovely two-year-old from the Nairobi National Park Orphanage, who – when he first got her – was so tricky they thought she might have to be sent back. But George was convinced she would be all right and devoted many hours to gaining her confidence, even going to the length of erecting his tent inside her compound. For several weeks, Mara slept on the floor beside George's bed and in this way he completely won her over. Another, slightly younger lioness called Henrietta, who came from Entebbe Zoo, also shared George's tent from time to time. So did Girl, who was also about the same age, and her brother, Boy. The nights, George says with his customary understatement, were not notable for their tranquillity but – and this is the extraordinary thing – none of these lions, which he had known only for a short time, ever gave him a moment of fear or even anxiety.

Henrietta had to appear in a bedroom scene. To get her accustomed to the bright lights and the rest of the paraphernalia in the room, George suggested that they should stay there together. No sooner was she established than Henrietta caught sight of a blue chamber pot under a bed. At once she got a paw to it and sent it flying across the floor, like a kitten playing with a ball of string. Then she got her paw inside the pot and skated round the room with the gerry attached. George had to take evasive action. But when the scene was filmed, the gerry was replaced by a waste-paper basket, which George thought a mistake. Henrietta's big scene involved her sitting on top of a Land-Rover as it drove sedately through an African village, past a bus full of tourists. Everyone thought this would cause no problems because Henrietta adored lying on top of the Land-Rover. When all was ready the Land-Rover set off with Henrietta queening it in her preferred position. The cameras started to roll – and then Henrietta caught sight of a chicken in the street. She was off the top of the Land-Rover like lightning and after the chicken, to the consternation of villagers and tourists alike, until she ran it to earth. She then proceeded to carry the chicken back to the top of the Land-Rover where she solemnly ate it. Since this was not in the script, which was sacrosanct, the whole scene had to be reshot. As luck would have it, no sooner was the retake underway than another foolish *kuku* stepped out from behind a hut and Henrietta, practice making perfect, caught it in a trice.

Not being quite so hungry, Henrietta took her time eating the second *kuku*, which drove the director and producers wild – the bill on location was £2,500 a day. Finally, the scene was completed but only by dint of fastening the remains of the *kuku* to the top of the Land-Rover.

Henrietta was the funniest of all the lions on the set and a very attractive character. All George's attempts to get permission to release her and Mara came to nothing through stupidity, blindness and small-mindedness, he says. Mara went to Whipsnade and Henrietta was returned to the rotten life she had had in the Entebbe Zoo. The Chief Game Warden of Uganda, Tennent, tried to be helpful and, George thought, would have let him have Henrietta, but the idea was vetoed by his black minister. It was left for two Scots Guardsmen to prefer freedom to a life behind bars for their regimental mascots, and they let George have Boy and Girl. The remaining lions were all sent to zoos in Britain and America and George felt particularly bitter that the film company did not put a penny towards their rehabilitation. He had to cover the initial outlay himself, from his own meagre funds. They even refused to lend him one of their special Land-Rovers fitted with a cage.

George's fiercest barbs were reserved for the producers of the film, who, he said, had no concern for the well-being of the lions who had done them so proud. All they were interested in was money and, once the shooting was over, they were anxious to have the lions disappear at as little cost to themselves as possible.

Chapter Eleven

A GENTLEMAN IN THE BUSH

George ended up with only three of the twenty-four lions which took part in *Born Free*: Boy, Girl and Ugas. At his own expense, he transported them to the Meru Reserve, a remote and beautiful piece of country north of the Tana River.

Giles Remnant, who accompanied the Adamsons to Meru, recalls, 'When we left Naro Moru to go back to the wild in Meru Game Reserve, George was the happiest man you could find around. He was a different person. He had a love affair with the bush. He could read the bush, the same as a sailor can read the sea. He would walk twenty miles a day, every single day of the week. It was a busy routine. We were up at five every morning, a thermos of tea, off we'd go with the lions for walks. Or if the lions decided to stop somewhere he'd leave them and we would walk on. I saw scenes which I'll never forget. George loved it; he could read what was going on; he could smell what was happening in the bush. He could tell exactly what was going on without a word being said – if there were elephants up front, from the tracks on the path, the stillness, whether the birds were singing – George could interpret immediately what had happened. That was his life. He could smell the rain coming, from the grass or the plants that predict the rain is around the corner, or if the rain had finished. If certain animals were back in an area, he knew it all, wonderful! He was an absolute authority on the bush.

'I recall a scene which I will probably remember to the day I die. We heard the Cape hunting dogs [wild dogs] chasing something. We were standing on the edge of a big dried-up river bed and this beautiful greater kudu arrived on the other side of the bank, panting, being chased, and these dogs came up and were baying it. George shot the dogs. He shot four of them, spontaneously. The kudu just stood still. The rest of the pack then disappeared. This animal just looked across the river at us, panting, and then quietly walked down to the river to take a drink; it was absolutely out of breath. George just said, "That's my good turn for the day." I always remember it, because it was the most magnificent sight. He said, "That's what you should do. Those animals don't have the right to chase the most beautiful animal, the most magnificent animal in Africa." To George the kudu was the finest animal, there was nothing to surpass it. I agree with him. It was a wonderful sight. I learned a lot from George; he was a gentleman in the bush.'

Those early days in Meru, from 1965 onwards, were happy ones. George set up his camp for the release of Boy, Girl and later Ugas at the foot of a small rocky hill called Mugwongo, in the centre of the reserve. Joy had her own camp where she was busy rehabilitating her cheetah, Pippa, a few miles away. To begin with Joy tried to persuade George to give up his lions and join her in her work with cheetah and leopard, but he refused and their virtual separation dates from this time. Apart from a brief spell in 1969, when George had to leave Meru and had not yet moved to Kora, they never lived together again. Although they had frequent rows at Meru, George's sense of humour seems to have risen triumphantly above all but the stormiest of scenes.

'When Joy used to turn up at the camp, George used to wind her up,' Giles Remnant says. 'He would sit there stirring his tea very noisily, rattling the spoon against the cup. You could see her going quietly red with rage, and she would say, "George, George stop that! Your noise drives me vild!" He'd beat his spoon on the cup and then, with a loud clatter, throw it in the saucer. And she'd say, "George, you

Pippa, Joy's cheetah, at Meru

know it makes me so vild," in her Austrian accent. But he used to do it every time just to wind her up. It was a love-hate relationship.

'We had a houseboy called Korokoro, who was a Turkana. Joy used to come round to the camp to do the mail and lecture George. A row would take place, frightful heated arguments, and we all kept our distance while George went, "Alright, alright, I'll do that, I'll do it, alright." She would be screaming and shouting and bits of paper would be shovelled across the table into different piles – there used to be a lot of correspondence, fan mail, Elsa Trust, Collins, or whatever – and then Joy would get up and disappear and as she went over the horizon, Korokoro would always arrive with a glass of Scotch on a tray for George, whatever time of day. Dear old Korokoro, he would arrive at that moment, with the Scotch. There was nothing ever said, no thank yous or anything, George just used to take it and drink it, any time of day, even if it was breakfast. Because Korokoro didn't understand you shouldn't drink alcohol before sundown. It was medicinal, purely. That's why I've got that shot of the lions with the whisky bottle. We sent it to Joy, saying, "Even the lions have taken to whisky." It made her go right through the roof!

'Joy had an appalling temper. But for George it was in one ear, out the other. As long as he had his tobacco, fill up the pipe, glass of Scotch, forget the woman, he was happy. I can remember George one day hiding in the bush. We had come back to camp to see Joy's Land-Rover. George said, "Oh God, she's here. What does she want? Did you lock the food boxes up? She's raiding the place." One imagined the worst. So I was told, "You go back and find out what she wants." George sat in this gully and the lions followed me into camp, and Joy said, "Vair's George? Giles, vair's George?" I said, "Joy, he got left behind, he's walking slowly ..."

'"He's sick?"

'"No, he's not sick. He's walking at his own pace; he saw a nesting bird or something."

'Joy said, "Ve must go and vind him." I was so young and gullible, I didn't want her to know that George was actually within twenty feet. So we then had to set off on this stupid hunt for George, with Joy marching off ... She used to wear these khaki semi-boiler suits; the top half was a boiler suit and then these shorts. We went marching off into the bush calling George. "I hear his voice." Then he was playing hide and seek with us. It went on for half the morning, this bloody stupid game, she getting more and more irate, George getting into quiet hysterics, thinking it the funniest thing he'd ever done. When she found out she gave him absolute hell. She'd only come over to show him a letter or something, probably from Collins, that was the only reason, but the morning was taken up with this stupid hide and seek.'

Surprisingly, Joy would retaliate. 'It was a real wind-up. But he always wanted to know she was alright. If he didn't make contact with her, he would worry about her. He'd always make sure a share of the provisions [from the local *duka*] went to her as well as him. If you'd come back with the post, she had to get her post. It was no use going back to the camp and hanging on to it for two days, it had to go to her at the right time. Is Joy okay? When she was sick he always used to go over every day. There was a bond. If there hadn't been Joy, I don't know what the alternative would have been. He had a wonderful sense of humour. You could sit there crying your eyes out all evening, if George got on to what we called a "When we" session.'

George Adamson's bushcraft undoubtedly saved Giles Remnant's life one day. 'We were out walking,' Giles recalled, 'and the lions were mucking around in the bush. One wondered what was going on. We walked up and this spitting cobra came out and bit me on the shin. George said, "We better do something about that. Sit down." I was in a state of shock; I was nineteen or twenty. George got out his penknife, an old Swiss Army knife – he always carried it – and stuck the blade in his pipe, then literally went "shhhht" down my shin and pushed out the poison. He said, "You'll be alright, no trouble with that," and put the ash of his pipe on the wound. I've still got the scar on my shin now. He said, "Now you sit down and wait. I'll leave the lions with you." Meanwhile this bloody serpent is still pissed off, hanging around, and I always remember George's care, although it was very matter of fact, his care about what was happening to me. He did exactly what should have been done. He wasn't going to shoot the snake. He said we'd imposed on the snake's territory, not vice versa. He said, "If it's in my tent, I'm going to shoot it, but if we're out in the bush, that serpent has as much right as we do."'

In his belief that man had no God-given right to lord it over the rest of creation, George Adamson was well ahead of his time. Having lived virtually his whole life close to nature, he understood the need to respect the natural scheme of things. Man, in his view, had no right to upset the balance. Every creature on earth, however lowly, had its place and its right to exist.

To begin with at Meru, George had only Boy and Girl; it took him several months to obtain permission from the National Park authorities to rehabilitate Ugas, who had been transferred to Nairobi animal orphanage after the end of filming at Naro Moru. When George arrived to pick up Ugas, he was told that in the four months he had been there he had become dangerous. George found him, on the contrary, extremely friendly, and when he got him back to Meru, Ugas, now a huge lion, showed his delight by rubbing his great head against George and moaning softly in a paroxysm of pleasure. Inevitably, since Meru is ideal lion country, they soon ran into trouble with the local wild lions. One, the biggest and fiercest, was christened Black Mane by George.

One-eyed Ugas: 'the gentle leader of the pride'

'I can remember Black Mane very vividly,' Giles Remnant told me. 'We had a camp laid out with six-foot chain link wire fencing round it. This was very early days and animals are very territorial. I remember waking up one night and feeling this hot breath next to me, and I said, "Oh Boy, go and lie down." I was in a sleeping bag. I turned on the torch and it was Black Mane beside my head. I shot to the bottom of my camp bed. I wasn't the bravest of people. The lion got a shock and literally leapt straight over me! But he worried us for months, and I remember George saying, "I've had enough, I'm going to go out and shoot him. He'll either kill a human or there's going to be a tearing nasty fight, but that animal is fearless now." It wasn't just because of his own lions. "That animal is a dangerous animal," George said. He was an old and magnificent beast but he would charge you just like that.' Black Mane attacked both Boy and Ugas and he killed Girl's cub. 'You can't blame the poor chap, he was defending his patch, his territory,' Giles Remnant explained.

'We got lots of hangers-on at Meru, animals that decided, "This camp is good news, I've got a sanctuary, a haven of security." There was an old rhino that used to come and live beside the camp, and an elephant – it was a bloody nuisance – it used to follow us. We had our own wadis [dry riverbeds]; George had his wadi where he'd go off to do his morning ablutions and I had mine, and this elephant used to follow us. Morning ablutions are sacred; you don't want any interruptions. I used to hear these terrible shouts from George Adamson. "Oh, bugger off! Get out of here, you bloody thing!" All the animal was doing, it wanted to know that there was a human nearby. He used to come for a walk with us, always kept a distance of fifty yards, we could never touch him, but fifty yards and he'd be there. I took a picture of the lions lying on the road and the elephant standing next door to them, quite happy. We'd go for a twenty-mile walk and the elephant would walk with us, trundle along. Or we'd leave him in a spot; he'd find a really juicy green bush and we'd leave him and we'd always come back and pick him up.'

When Ugas arrived, Giles Remnant left. He had been attacked by Ugas during the *Born Free* filming and he knew it could happen again. They were simply not compatible. George then turned for assistance to his godson, Jonny Baxendale. Shortly after his arrival, Baxendale went to visit Joy in her camp. 'I could see her as I drove in,' he says. 'She was screaming out, waving her hands and screaming at one of her African staff. I said: "Well Joy, what's the matter?"

'"These people, they're all so stupid."

'"So let's sit down and have a cup of tea and talk about it." I could see there was a serious problem. Anyway, tea arrived and she screamed something else at the man in Swahili and I looked at her and said, "Joy, I know what the problem is. They don't even understand what you're saying, because I don't know what the hell you said myself then. What are you trying to tell him? I tell you what, why don't we solve this problem. You tell me in your best English what you want them to do and then I'll tell them in my best Swahili. That should do it and I think everything will be fine." Then she started screaming and shouting at me, which was okay. Anyway, we did solve it. I remembered that when I came into the camp the cook had had a bloody great carving knife in his hand. I said to her – it was ironic as that was the way she was killed – "Joy, you can't *turkana*" – which is a lovely word – "you can't insult these people like this. They're from a northern tribe and they're not going to take it, from you or from anyone else. So I suggest you really slow down a bit and try a different technique because they're not going to take this from you. I hope you realize that the cook was about to have you with the carving knife," I said. So that did actually shake her a bit. "Just be very careful," I went on, "because I wouldn't put it past them. So I suggest you're really careful about the whole situation. You're on your own." She was totally on her own. "I don't think you should *turkana* them like that." And of course this is exactly what happened in Shaba [Joy's camp from 1970 until she was killed in 1980]. She owed the guy 125 shillings, refused to pay him, told him to get out of camp, never wanted to see him again, wouldn't give him a lift, so he had to walk out. A young Turkana guy and he was very proud. He wasn't going to take that sort of nonsense. He did leave camp, came back two weeks later to collect his money. He knew that she went for walks in the evening and of course she did "a Joy". She screamed and shouted, "Get out, I never want to see you again," so he pulled out his knife and that was the end of Joy. A hundred and twenty-five shillings was nothing to her but it meant everything to him.'

When he arrived in Meru at the end of 1967 from England, where he had been flying and mapmaking, Jonny Baxendale was a sanguine young giant of twenty-five. It was just as well. He was thrown in at the deep end. George, who had recently been charged by a buffalo which he had shot and wounded, announced that he was going to Nairobi to have a hernia operation. He was lucky to be alive. Buffalo are notoriously dangerous when wounded and George had been knocked to the ground and narrowly escaped being gored. Before it expired, the young bull trod on his foot and broke a toe, as well as rupturing him. In a typically casual way, George asked his young assistant to take over.

"'Can you monitor the lions, look after them and record everything they do?' 'Well,' I said, 'yes, certainly, no problem at all.' The first evening I couldn't find them anywhere. So within a day of George leaving I'd completely lost them. Then I heard them roaring at night, so I went out, followed them and found them and spent most of the night with them. The next morning I walked with them to their

George crossing a flooded stream near camp in Meru

nearest lying-up place. All I had was a pair of shorts on, that's all I used to wear. We walked through the forest to the swamp and decided to sleep under this tree. I was exhausted. I'd been up all night. They chose a tree to sleep under so I decided I would take a nap as well and then walk back to camp. So I took a nap under this tree with the lions, which was very comfortable, using Girl as a pillow. I was woken by the lions all moving, so I sat up and there were four people in a minibus who were really excited because they'd found some lions. But when I sat up, they simply couldn't believe their eyes. I'll never forget the expression on their faces. So I leapt to my feet, dusted my pants down and trotted off towards them and they took off, absolutely took off. I was quite worried about the whole situation so I ran back to camp, jumped in the Land-Rover and went to Leopard Rock [Reserve headquarters]. But I never found them again. I don't know what went through their minds, finding in the wilderness this lovely pride of lions and then some half-naked human stands up, who'd been sleeping with them; that didn't make sense. And I never ever found out who they were, because I was determined to explain the situation. The expression on their faces! They started the car and took off! I was petrified because George had left me in charge of the lions for quite a while, ten days or so, so I went everywhere with them, everywhere.'

Chapter Twelve

AT MERU

George had two ways of dealing with Joy's intemperate outbursts. In public, being a perfect gentleman, he would say nothing and blandly turn the other cheek. In private, occasionally at any rate, he might remonstrate more forcefully. But he had a third defence, which in the earlier days of his marriage he used to good effect. He loved practical jokes and who better to play them on than the irascible and in some ways gullible Joy. According to Jonny Baxendale, Joy was frightened of only two things: punctures and elephants.

'She just couldn't change a tyre, so she was petrified of having punctures. She always had to have someone in the car with her everywhere she went just in case she had a puncture. And the other thing she was frightened of, amazingly, was elephants. So George and I had this little technique; Joy wants to come round at the weekend and we really can't be bothered to put up with all the hassle, all the screaming and shouting. I used to leave camp when Joy arrived generally, because I knew she would scream and shout at George. George could take it but I couldn't, so I would just go for a walk with the lions or something, we'd go up on to the hill. So we'd convince Joy, George chuckling away on his pipe: "Just tell Joy that there's a lot of elephants on the road, and of course if there're elephants on the road they're always pulling thorns across the road and she'll end up getting lots of punctures." The combination of the two guaranteed that Joy would never turn up. She had to go round the long way and she'd always say, "Are there still lots of elephant there?" and I'd say, "Well Joy, they're thinning out a bit; it's not too bad but we'll let you know."

'The only thing Joy said that I reckon was very correct about George was that he drove like a rhino. George would light his pipe and he would go along in top gear, with the thing juddering, hit every hole, boom, boom, boom! Joy would say, "George! Stop the car, stop the car! You're driving like a rhino!" She had a neck problem; she wore a collar. "I can't take it! Jonny! George, get out, get in the back. Jonny's going to drive." And George would. "Yes, alright."

'George liked to keep a record of what the lions were doing and this was the major part of his diary. So I used to stand in the back of the pick-up and I'd be looking around for the lions, and very often they would hear the car come up, and George would be in there with his pipe, driving. On many occasions – I can remember three occasions – we'd be going along and I'd suddenly hear "pff, pff, pff, pffoo" behind

Rhino starting a charge on George's Land Rover

Head down before impact

After impact: honour satisfied

me and I'd turn around. The first time I thought it was a puncture, the tyre going. I turned round and there was a damn rhino behind us. So I'd lean over and say: "George! Go! Rhino! We're being chased by a rhino, go like hell." "Oh!" he says, and he stops! He puts his brakes on, Bang! Crash! and then the rhino would run off. And that was one of the rhinos. And George said, "God, that was a rhino. Why did you tell me to stop?" "George, I said go like hell; we've a rhino after us." So we go off again. And you know it happened three times and every time George stopped. On two occasions we got hit, really hit; on one occasion it was two rhinos so we got a double-barrelled session, and then on the third occasion we didn't get hit at all. Finally, I said, "George, I promise you if we get a rhino after us next time I'm not going to say anything because it's better if you just keep going than stop." Because you know he was a bit deaf, especially when he was driving. I used to lean over and say, "George, stop! stop! Lions or birds" or something. So when I leant over and said, "George, go like hell, rhino after us," he probably thought, "He's seen something," and would automatically stop. And I couldn't persuade him. I would say to him, "This evening, George, we were chased by a rhino and I said nothing and we didn't get hit." And he chuckled; I don't think he believed it.

'If you keep going with the old rhino, he gets quite close, but as long as you're getting out of the way he's quite happy. But if you stop! There were a hell of a lot of rhino in Meru in those days! Nothing left now. I took a series of pictures of a rhino coming, hitting the car and going away. I thought, I've got to persuade George that I did see it coming.'

Jonny Baxendale, who was older, larger and stronger than Giles Remnant, did not have any trouble with Ugas, who by this time had only one eye: the other, thought by George to have been damaged by a spitting cobra, had to be removed by surgery. 'Ugas was an incredible lion, huge, very nice-natured, much less excitable than the others. Between them, he and Boy, who was a lot younger, they managed to establish their own territory. With the lionesses they made a nice little pride and then they had cubs.

'But,' Baxendale says, 'in order to survive with creatures like that you have to understand them. There are two times when a lion is particularly dangerous: one's when he's got a small portion of meat; you

Girl and her new-born cub, Sam

Out for a first walk

Quite hard work, really, having a baby. (Sam, alas, was later killed by Black Mane, a wild lion whose territory they had invaded.)

see it in the wild when they get a wart hog or something, they won't share it with anybody, and anybody who comes anywhere near them gets into trouble. The other time is when a lioness is in season; the lioness purrs and it's the only time a lioness purrs. It's the most amazing sound. And of course she loves everybody and this aggravates him more than anything. She's always trying to greet me, and everybody. We had this with Girl; Girl would come up purring and flopping on the ground and rolling upside down and of course when Boy came round the corner you just check out extremely fast or get back in your car. If you came within forty paces of Boy and his girlfriend or Ugas and his girlfriend you could expect a charge. They would probably go for you. Of course you wouldn't survive something like that.

'The reason George survived all these years is that he literally thought like a lion. If you live with them that long, you really get to understand them. There were very few times that George ever or even nearly got into trouble. The thing was always to remain standing. And George had a little stick that he could smack them on the nose with.

George and Boy: the best of friends

With lions you've just got to show disapproval. If you don't want to play, you show disapproval and then they'll lay off. Otherwise the game continues and they grow into really big, heavy animals, and they sit on you.' Physically, George Adamson was quite short, but immensely wiry and extremely fit from a lifetime of walking across the vast, arid expanses of the Northern Frontier District. His calm, unflappable temperament and lack of any sort of fear made a perfect combination for dealing with any sort of wild animal, above all lions.

'George had a lovely deliberate movement, because of course amongst cats you must always be very deliberate, you mustn't move fast or jump. You couldn't make George jump under any circumstances. He was totally unruffled, always. That's why I find Joy so amazing and I wonder whether she really did have a particularly good rapport with the cats. She was fanatical of course, she loved them, and of course the good thing about cats and wild animals was they didn't answer back. Joy liked that.'

Jonny Baxendale had a soft spot for Girl and compares her with Elsa. 'Elsa was a really lovely creature, she was a unique animal. And I know

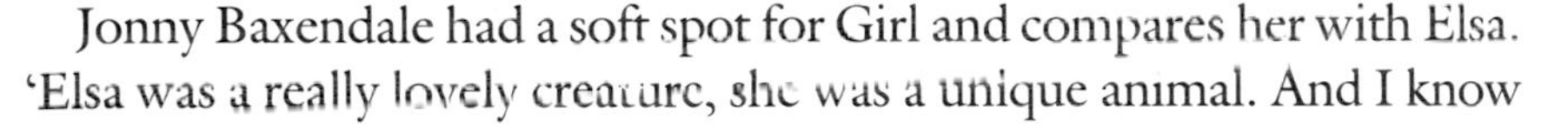

Jonny Baxendale and George with Boy, Girl and Ugas (left). Jonny's comment: 'Joining in on the kill for some fresh buffalo steaks.'

from our lions that some of them are far more affectionate than others. Girl was another one, Girl was incredible. I went back many years later. I didn't tell [Peter] Jenkins [the game warden at Meru] this, because I'd made a promise to Peter that if I ever went back to Meru I wouldn't pet the lions – both George and I promised – we wouldn't feed them, pet them or have contact with them. I went back nearly two years later on a safari and I was with these people just looking at our old camp site at Mugwongo. There was nothing there, just Sam's grave [Sam was Girl's cub, killed by Black Mane]. We were walking through the grass there and suddenly I heard a yellow-neck [spur fowl] fly up and I turned round and walking through the grass straight for me was this big lioness. I said to everybody, just quietly, "Into the car." Then I

Astonishingly, the lioness Shuki allowed George to come right up to her lair to see her new-born cubs. Jonny Baxendale, who took the pictures, says he never saw anyone get as close

One of Shuki's cubs, eyes barely open

looked at her through binoculars and I recognised her straightaway; it was Girl. I looked around, couldn't see any of the other ones. I thought, this is really going to be an interesting episode. I nearly got in the car, and then I thought, "No, I know Girl." So I braced myself against a tree and then I called her as she came closer, just to make sure I was right. She stopped and her little ears came up, and then she came bounding through the grass. I didn't know whether I was going to be greeted or eaten. It was quite an interesting experience. And I tell you what, she jumped up and put her paws on my shoulders, went round and flopped over, it was amazing, and she started purring. I thought, bloody hell, where's that male? But there wasn't one around. She was just so happy. It was so amazing that I actually said to the other people,

Jonny Baxendale recalls feeling extremely nervous, but Shuki did not seem to mind

Lionesses are, notoriously, at their most dangerous when they have tiny cubs, but Shuki clearly welcomed George's attention: indeed, she looks positively ecstatic

"If you feel that you'd like to get out and say hello to Girl, do so," because she hadn't changed a bit in two years. That was really food for thought because even George had had no contact with Girl. We sat there for about twenty minutes, then she got up and walked off in the evening light and that's the last I ever saw of her. I went back there a few times on my own hoping the same thing would happen but it never did.'

'She recognised your voice?'

'Yes, I think she just hadn't heard that call for such a long time. I just said "Girl! Look!" George always said "Look!" We always had something for them or we would call them, "Look!" I couldn't wait to tell George.'

Jonny Baxendale witnessed another example of the extraordinary trust George Adamson could establish with particular lions, even going beyond the trust Elsa displayed when she had her first litter of cubs.

'Lionesses, even tame lionesses, are very protective of their cubs and I think George was the only person ever allowed to see cubs only hours after being born. The lioness won't even allow the male, or any other lioness, anywhere near her cubs for quite a long time. They don't bring the cubs back to the pride until they're quite mobile, and initially she's quite careful about who approaches the cubs. Then after about half an hour they all get a sniff of the cubs and then it's all over, they're all friends and playing.'

Jonny Baxendale took a remarkable series of photographs of one of George's lionesses called Shuki showing him her new-born cubs. 'That was the very first sight we had of the cubs, it's a classic of George getting close. I sneaked up and managed to get a picture of these tiny things. When they've apparently got no ears, no ears at all, they're very new.' At first George simply sat with the lioness, who was very friendly, and then she allowed him to see her cubs. Jonny crept up behind and took a sequence of photographs.

'She had two little cubs, tiny little things; they couldn't really walk, their eyes had just opened. You know, he had never dared do that before. That was the first time he really tried to sneak in. First they sat on the rock, you see. It was one of the greatest moments of his life, being able to get to the cubs at such an early stage, when none of the other lions had been permitted to go anywhere near them. It was a remarkable feat.'

About the same time as Jonny Baxendale arrived in Meru, a new game warden, Peter Jenkins, the brother of Daphne Sheldrick, took over the Reserve. He had a wife, Sarah, and two small children, a son called Mark, who was almost four, and a baby daughter, Siana. Each time they visited George's camp, Jonny Baxendale recalls, the lions became particularly uneasy. Everyone knew, George better than anyone, that all big cats are fascinated by small children and lions are no exception. 'One never knew whether they wanted to play with them or eat them. I should think they probably wanted to eat them. So we knew how critical the situation was.' At the time Boy had been gone from the camp for several days, trying to establish his own territory.

'Boy had disappeared and I was driving back from the park headquarters. I went to see the Jenkinses, dropped off their mail because I'd just come from Nanyuki, and was on my way to Joy's camp when I met Boy just walking down the road. So I stopped and he greeted me. He was a huge lion, enormous, and I said, "What are you doing here?" I thought, Now, how can I get him back? Anyway, sure enough, he got on to the roof of the car, on to the cab. I thought, This is a problem, I need to go to Joy's to drop off some supplies. [Joy had Pippa, the cheetah, at her camp.]

'So I stopped there and got out a rather warm beer, I remember, and thought, well, if I sit here long enough he'll get bored and get off the car. I sat on the front of the car, on the bonnet, and he was sitting right above me and it was a beautiful evening. Then I heard a car coming up and it was Peter and Sarah coming back from Joy's. Peter pulled up right beside me. He was in a new car that he'd just got and it had low-cut doors and there was Peter and the two kids and Sarah. It was late in the evening and the two kids were beginning to squeal a bit like they always do. Peter pulled up right beside me to give me a letter that had come in from the council, some document or other. I said, "Well, I'm just sitting here because of Boy. I need to go to Joy's camp, but if I go to Joy's camp with Boy on the roof she'll really be ticking for weeks [because of Pippa]. So," I said, "I'll just sit here until he gets off." We were just discussing how far he was from his territory.

'Up to this point the relationship between the Jenkinses and George had been fine, although Peter was always guarded about this Adamson project. He didn't like it from the start, but he had inherited it, plus the rest of the park and the chaos in which it was at the time. The road

Boy: utter contentment

system was non-existent; it was quite a handful as a park, a very wild and wonderful place but very underdeveloped.

'I remember noticing Boy looking in through the windshield and of course the kids were just here. Then he got up and started moving so I got off too. It wasn't done quickly, it was just done very deliberately; he just stepped off on to the ground and immediately up on the side of Pete's car and reached right past Peter and tried to pull Mark out. I tried to block him because I wasn't in any danger.'

Peter Jenkins' recollection is rather different: 'I stopped about a hundred and fifty, a hundred and twenty yards from the Land-Rover because I had George's mail and some fresh provisions for George and Jonny. I had a new Toyota Landcruiser and I knew these lions had a habit of climbing on to vehicles and I wasn't very keen for this five-hundred pound lion to climb on to the top of my new Landcruiser and smash the canvas to pieces. So I stopped and Jonny walked down the road and came up to my car. We had special doors without windows, we'd had them modified, and I got out of my vehicle and handed this cardboard carton to Jonny and a bag with some mail in and then got back into the driving seat while we talked.

'It was getting dusk then and I saw the lion get off George's car on to the bumper and on to the road and then start walking, not towards us but cutting away diagonally down to the river which was behind us. So he actually wasn't coming down the road; he left the road and he was sort of angling away; we were here and he was angling out like that. When he was slightly ahead of us, forty or fifty yards from the road, I said to Jonny, "Stand on the running board and I'll move forward."

'Sarah was on the left hand side with our daughter Siana, who was probably not a year old and was asleep, and Mark was leaning on the middle seat but looking out the back. Neither of the children were making any noise at all. Whether the lion saw a small being in the front of our vehicle or not, I don't know, he was almost broadside to us then. But he suddenly turned and he never growled, never made the usual sign of a lion charging, he just came.

'He got into the car. He was inside that vehicle before I had time to react and shut the door. The door was open and I had one leg up. It happened so quickly. I suppose it took me a split second to realise exactly what he was doing because I'd never seen that behaviour from him before. I knew the lion quite well. I don't know what happened to

Jonny at this stage but the next thing was the lion was through the door, over the top of me. I can remember the terrible lion smell. He pushed me right in the back of the seat so I was completely smothered by his mane and all I could hear at that stage was Mark screaming. I can distinctly remember getting my left hand underneath him and I can remember feeling his gullet, I'd got him here and I was trying to push him out. Well, of course that's like trying to move Kilimanjaro. Fortunately it was that particular model of Landcruiser that had the starter on the right hand side and I was able to get my other hand underneath him and turn the key – I always leave my vehicles in gear when I stop, out of habit. It started immediately being a new car and I let the clutch out and he sort of scrambled out and fell on to the road. I looked down and there was blood everywhere. So I never stopped.'

Jonny Baxendale has an equally stark recollection of those few, agonising moments. 'Peter managed to start the car and I just said to him, "Go! Peter, go!" realising the horrific danger that was now imminent. Peter took off and Boy's back feet which were on the ground went flying and Boy came out of the car – I expected Mark to come out with him, fortunately he didn't. And I realised the damage was done, it was done just like that. Peter and I, both of us were experienced and we were just careless about it. He had really low doors so it was easy for Boy to reach across [to Mark]. Peter fortunately was able to start it, because it was a new Toyota, start it and take off. I had a rifle with me and, as Boy recovered – Peter and Sarah didn't stop, they just took off to headquarters – Boy was standing in the middle of the road looking back at me, kind of, What the hell was that all about? I'll never forget looking at him down the 'scope sights, that's how I saw him. I very nearly shot him right there and then, because I knew it had to be. I knew this was not good news.

'But I didn't. I decided I'm not going to shoot him. We can find him any time we like and if anybody was to shoot him, George should shoot him, it wasn't my duty to do so. So I just jumped in the car, spun round, went back to headquarters to find out what happened.'

Peter Jenkins must have driven off in a white heat of horror and rage, although today his recollection of perhaps the worst moment in his life is a model of lucidity. He and his wife Sarah are remarkably unbitter.

'Sarah got her scarf off and tried to stem the blood which was coming out of Mark's arm in vast quantities. The roads were very bad then and it was about a fifteen-minute bone-shaking drive going flat out to Leopard Rock where we arrived just after dark. We carried out immediate first aid and then got him up to the hospital at Mau. They carried out an emergency operation and the good mission doctor there said, "No problem; you're very lucky. The bone's not broken, and the artery's not cut." It was the left arm, the left elbow, just above the joint. Canine went right through. And he was clawed in the head and bled badly from the head but those weren't very serious wounds. Exactly what this lion was trying to do I don't know because he could have easily just flipped him right out. Anyhow, the whole thing happened in a fraction of the time it's taken me to tell you. They operated and the doctor said, "No problem; you're very lucky; the nerves are okay; with penicillin and a lot of antibiotics he'll be fine." I said to the doctor: "Are you absolutely sure about this?" and he said: "Absolutely sure," and then I said to him, "Well, I have taken the liberty of alerting the flying doctor to come up in the morning." And he got very po-faced then and said, "Well, if you feel like that then do it." And it's just as well that we did because by the next morning he had gangrene.

'He was then flown to Nairobi and re-operated on by one of the top surgeons in the country, he's now a very well-known plastic surgeon, who opened up the wounds. Well, actually the flying doctor opened the wounds up here and all this black stuff came out. So he was operated on again in Nairobi that afternoon and about two weeks later they did another operation, sewed him up and he developed gangrene again. And the second time he nearly died. That incident retarded him [at school] for about fifteen years, which a well-known paediatrician subsequently told Sarah would happen.'

Sarah Jenkins says, 'I think the worst thing was the nightmares that he had. Even now.'

Peter Jenkins adds: 'Even now he gets them if he's tired. He doesn't know what it is, it's always something big on top of him. He can't of course remember anything. He was nearly four, just under four. I'm told by quite a number of professional hunters who've been chewed up by lions that it's a thing you never get over, psychologically. People who've been chewed up by leopards, it doesn't seem to worry them. But I've talked to quite a few hunters who've been badly bitten by lions and most of them have never really recovered. It's always there.

'That incident had disappeared into the background of my memory until I had to help move a girl, in her early twenties, who was badly chewed up by a lion in the Aberdares a few years back. I had to help get her out of a Land-Rover so that the nurse could get her ready to be taken to Nairobi by the flying doctor. She had that terrible smell about her from the lion – it's a carrion sort of smell, a disgusting sort of smell that you never forget. Just handling her, she was still alive, helping lift her out of the vehicle and on to the ground, so the nurse could treat her, the smell actually sticks to your clothes, you feel like burning your clothes. Mark's incident came right back as if it happened last night, just handling that girl, the lion smell. I've smelt lions before and I've shot lions, but until you're actually associated with somebody who's been eaten by a lion – in this case it was Mark and of course I was covered in lion smell. It had never really worried me until I actually had to move this injured person. So I guess there is something psychological about a lion attack. It is such a damned big powerful thing.'

Mark, fortunately, seems to have made a complete recovery. He followed his father into the game department and today leads one of the crack anti-poaching units in the Meru area.

As a result of this incident, Wilfred Thesiger, the distinguished explorer and author, denounced in a letter to the *East African Standard* George Adamson's attempts to return to the wild lions that had been born or raised in captivity. Thesiger wrote, 'These animals have no fear of man and they are incompetent killers. When they cannot kill, these animals will turn on the easiest prey available – man ... To return a tame lion to the wilds is to turn loose a potential man-eater.' George Adamson's response was typically matter-of-fact, although Jonny Baxendale says, 'It's the first time I actually remember George being really genuinely upset and irritated. He knew Thesiger very well. I remember George just quietly saying to me one evening, "I find it amazing that somebody can write about this project and me and the lions, because all he knows about lions is down the sights of a rifle."' Thesiger was a great hunter in his day and admits to shooting more than seventy lions in five years in the Sudan before the Second World War. Later, when George had moved to Kora, his cook, Stanley, went outside the wire one night, was mauled by Boy and later died of his wounds. Thesiger again launched into print, firing off another letter to the *East African Standard*. It was, Adamson says, 'largely a compound of prejudice and ignorance'.

The end of George's stay in Meru was as clouded as the beginning had been sunny. Ken Smith, who had taken over from George at Isiolo, often drove over to see the Adamsons.

'I was there when they had the most fearful rows. George was just such a quiet chap. Sometimes it was small things. "Why did you bring only one goat when I ask you to bring two?" And before George could say, "But that was all I could get," she'd cuss and swear: "You, the mighty great hunter, kill these innocent creatures and then you leave me to look after them [their offspring] and you won't help to feed them or bring anything for them." Then she'd go into paroxysms totally out of control and go up and pound him. What does one do, one stands aside, and this happened many times. There was another incident at Mugwongo, again a small insignificant thing that he'd done or hadn't done and she got hold of a kitchen knife and threw it at him. At close range! George had to duck!'

Ken Smith was so frightened by Joy's behaviour that night that he fled from George's camp and took refuge with the Jenkinses in their house at Leopard's Rock.

To add to George's troubles, Boy was badly injured, probably by a buffalo, and fractured his shoulder. This needed a series of operations to pin the bone together and George spent a great deal of time and money arranging for vets to be flown up to Meru.

The operations must have been difficult enough – manhandling such a huge lion, especially when anaesthetised, cannot have been easy – without having Joy playing up as well. Carol Byrne, a young friend of the family, remembers being at Meru when Boy had a big operation performed by three vets: Mike Richmond and Sue and Tony Hartshoorn. 'Just as the operation was about to start, Joy came rushing in with two lion cubs, tiny little things that the mother had abandoned or whatever. She was terribly agitated that they were not going to survive, and that a great deal of attention was being given to Boy but what about these poor little things! She started feeding them mouth to mouth, with milk, spitting the milk into their mouths: I don't think they were that ill. Anyway, there was this huge sort of drama going on, or two dramas! Boy's was relatively calm, it was rather like a construction site; people had something to do, like surgeons anywhere: "Take this, take this, you hold that ..." We were just standing right on the outside looking on with Joy trying to get her bit of attention, hands in the air, shrieking, screaming, and everybody trying to be icy cool and calm in the other place with this lion flat out for its operation.'

The repercussions of the Jenkins incident and Boy's accident finally forced George to leave Meru. Boy was flown to Naivasha to convalesce while George planned his next moves. It was an unhappy time, made more so by Joy's increasingly difficult behaviour. Even George's famous sense of humour began to desert him.

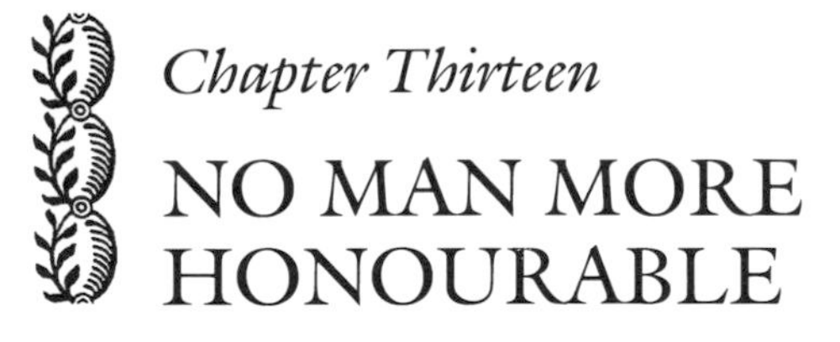

Chapter Thirteen

NO MAN MORE HONOURABLE

After a nightmare journey in a small plane from Meru, Boy was put in a pen to convalesce in the grounds of Elsamere, the house Joy had bought on the shores of Lake Naivasha with funds from the Elsa Trust. George occupied a small wooden cottage nearby. The long, low, white clapboard house with big picture windows, set in fifty acres of rough garden and forest, looks out over the lake with its flocks of white pelicans and herds of hippos, some of which would wander up on to the lawn at night. Black and white colobus monkeys and eagle owls lived in the trees round the house and brilliant blue Malachite kingfishers darted among the papyrus. It was a beautiful spot but relations between George and Joy, now living in unaccustomed proximity, deteriorated sharply.

Early in March 1970, George was telling friends that the atmosphere at home was particularly unpleasant and that on one particular day he got no lunch. That evening he went out to have a drink with neighbours.

Elsamere, the house Joy bought on Lake Naivasha with some of the proceeds of Born Free. *It is now a museum and memorial to Joy*

When he returned in time for dinner, he found the front door locked on Joy's orders and he had to get the servants to let him in. While he was having some cold supper in the kitchen, Joy suddenly appeared and told him to leave. When George demurred, Joy began to shove him about, so he got up and slapped her face. Then he told her that Elsamere was not her personal property but belonged to the Elsa Trust.

The next day, after lunching with the Hales at the Lake Hotel, George returned to discover that Joy had summoned her lawyer from Nairobi and told him she wanted a divorce. George was advised to make contact with his own solicitor without delay. For good measure, Joy had trotted out a long rigmarole of George's alleged sins, including the characteristically hysterical accusation that she was frightened he might do away with her.

Two days later George accompanied Joy to Nairobi and was left sitting in the car for two hours while she went in to see Peter Johnson, her accountant and one of her trustees. To George's surprise Joy came out having been persuaded by Peter Johnson to buy a second-hand Peugeot because it was cheaper to run than a Land-Rover. George found this a pointless economy, since Joy was by then a rich woman and the Trust was worth millions.

At this juncture he was planning a safari with Ken Smith and Ray Mayers to the north in his quest for a suitable home for Boy. But Joy was dead against the plan, complaining that she did not want to be held responsible for Boy in George's absence, and she became very worked up at the thought that she would be left on her own without a driver, cook or houseboy. So, reluctantly, George abandoned the idea.

Later that month, he was in Nairobi seeing his solicitors, Daly and Figgs, about the divorce. He told them he would not fight it, as long as Joy was not going to demand alimony or leave him with a big bill for lawyers' fees. He also stipulated that he should be allowed to keep his own personal things including his silver, furniture and books. Their advice was to wait for the divorce petition, accept it, make sure they got a copy and leave them to do the rest. Curiously, the petition never arrived. Possibly Joy got cold feet or allowed herself to be persuaded by her trustees that it would be bad for her image and that of the Trust.

Relations continued stormy. The next day, when some Germans arrived to see Boy, Joy was downright rude and virtually told them to leave. Later, more visitors arrived to talk about the Northern Frontier

District, on which he was an authority. Again Joy interrupted the discussion to announce that George had lots of work to do and they must not detain him any longer.

Joy's bad temper persisted. She pestered George about hippo coming into the garden and made him build a gate to try and stop the nightly incursions. George found this laughable as nothing will stop a hippo – certainly not a rickety fence and a wooden gate – and the garden was a joke in any case. That afternoon, as George was having tea with the vets, who were looking after Boy, and two other visitors, Joy came storming into the room and ordered him to get on with the hippo gate. Rather than provoke a row, he did as he was told and with the help of one of the servants finished the job. Next day, Joy's mood underwent a complete transformation, changing abruptly from aggression to self-pity and making George abandon a plan to visit one of the islands in Lake Naivasha.

He still continued to scour the country for a home for Boy. Every time he found what he thought was an ideal spot, he would run into the problem of domestic stock – herds of African cattle, sheep and goats which Boy would have enjoyed slaughtering but which a benevolent government could not allow. So the search went on, with just a hint of desperation beginning to creep in.

George returned to Naivasha on the evening of 27 April to find Boy in good health and pleased to see him. Not so Joy. She was in a bad temper and straightaway brought up the question of the divorce, demanding that George make a sworn statement promising that he would not behave in a violent manner towards her and to be a loyal husband. She was so nasty that George cut short the conversation and departed, wondering if she had been at the bottle.

In June, he was in the north, near Marsabit, continuing his quest for a home for Boy. At one point, driving along the Shaffa Dika road, he went as far as the swamp and recognised the spot where on an earlier occasion, after some other argument, Joy had thrown a rock at him. In August, she was in hospital in Nairobi and George went to visit her. He found her in a particularly bad mood, having heard that the Elsa Trust had agreed to pay him £2,500. Joy was absolutely against this and was also furious that a friend called Lilian Ashley had given his brother Terence and himself 200 shillings each (about £10) – just one more confirmation of Joy's extraordinary meanness to George.

***

By the middle of the year, George's search for a new home had narrowed to the Garissa region, of which his old friend Ken Smith was now the game warden. They finally settled on a place called Kora, on the Tana River, its banks well wooded and the bush behind well stocked with game. The main geographical feature was a group of lion-coloured rocks two or three miles from the river, the largest, Kora Rock, towering four hundred feet above the surrounding landscape. It was ideal for George's purpose. Permission was obtained from the Chief Game Warden and the Ministry of Wildlife and Tourism, and George's brother, Terence, who had been working on a big cattle ranch near Tsavo for several years, started cutting roads through the thorn bush.

On 6 August, George flew over Kora, saw the Rock for the first time and decided to make his camp at the foot of it. He was excited by the prospect of living there. The move finally took place at the end of August, Joy seeing to it that the event was as fraught as she could make it. She was 'nagging and difficult about Boy being taken away' and on the day of departure, 'created quite a scene and urged Paul Sayer [one of the vets] not to give Boy clearance. But he was firm and said Boy was perfectly fit enough to travel.' With Boy and a cub called Katania in a cage in the back of the Land-Rover, George and a friend drove through the night to Kora, arriving about eleven the next morning, 1 September. Both lions were 'very exhausted and chafed, particularly Boy who had a large piece of skin off his forehead.' Shortly afterwards

Joy on a rare visit to Kora. An equally rare picture: on the banks of the Tana with Boy

the lion Christian arrived. He had been found by Bill Travers in a shop in Chelsea, having been bought as a cub at Harrods by two young Australians, Ace Bourke and John Rendall. Bill Travers planned to make a film of George releasing Christian to the wild, along with Boy and Katania.

Joy arrived in Kora to spend Christmas and at first all went well. On Christmas Day, George went for a walk with Boy and Christian round Kora Hill while Joy put up the decorations. But the happy atmosphere did not last long, Joy becoming bitter and moody and railing against Sue Harthoorn, one of the vets, and of all people, her publisher Billy Collins, with whom she had had a passionate affair. Finally Joy rounded on George and, apparently returning to the theme of divorce, told him she wanted him to 'pack up'.

Despite the tantrums at home, George did not forget his lions, making sure they had enough to eat. He noted down the fact that a young lioness, Susie, was one year and eleven months and that Katania would have been eight months old on Christmas Day. George kept a meticulous record of the age of his lions, even after, as with the cub Katania, he had completely lost touch with them. She had disappeared one night when crossing the river with Boy and Christian, and was most likely taken by a crocodile.

The rest of Christmas went off better. They went out for walks with the lions and fished in the Tana. There was one unfortunate incident when Boy snapped at Joy and grazed her slightly on the arm. Boy thought he was going to be fed and Joy was slow getting inside the gate.

There is no record of Joy's reaction: it was the sort of mishap which she would take in her stride. George was aware that his self-appointed task of rehabilitating lions and returning them to the wild entailed a certain amount of danger, not because he was afraid his own lions would attack him but because they might innocently land him in trouble. If something were to go wrong and he were to die, George was at pains to impress on his friends, he wished to be buried at Kora beside Boy, and nowhere else. If necessary, a doctor could be flown up to sign the death certificate. (In June 1971 Boy killed Stanley, George's cook, and George was forced to shoot his favourite lion.)

Boy and his twin sister Girl were born on 26 August 1963. Christian was born on 12 August 1969. George chronicled the lives of his lions with more care than most fathers bestow on their children. They were, indeed, his children.

On 2 January, the Adamsons drove to Elsamere and the next day,

Carl Foreman, the executive producer of *Born Free*, called with his wife Eve. Foreman and Joy had a lengthy and acrimonious discussion about the script of *Living Free* (the sequel to *Born Free*). But they could not reach an agreement; indeed each threatened the other with legal action. George, sensibly, stayed well clear. A few days later, Carl Foreman and another producer, Paul Radin, had another script conference with Joy. Again, feelings ran high and they could not agree on how the film should end.

Back in Kora, George was joined by Simon Trevor and his wife Leila. Simon was about to start shooting *Christian the Lion*. He is now a famous wildlife cameraman who, after making *African Elephant* in 1969, has worked on almost every major feature film shot in Africa since then, including *Out of Africa*, *Gorillas in the Mist* and *White Hunter Black Heart*. He also made for television *Bloody Ivory* and a series of documentaries for *Survival* including *Elephants of Tsavo*. Early one morning, as they were having breakfast, Hamisi, Terence's cook, came up breathlessly to say Boy had attacked one of the African staff outside the camp. George raced out, was unable to see anything in the dark, but heard a human cry about fifty yards away. Eventually, he spotted Boy dragging the unfortunate man along the ground by his shoulder and, without hesitation, shouted at Boy and went for him with the only weapon he had, an electric goad. At that point Simon appeared in his pick-up; Boy let go of his prey and slunk off.

A Christmas card from Kora. Boy, George's favourite lion, shows off his impressive jaws

George omits one detail which Simon Trevor remembers vividly. 'I legged it for the gate, met George coming at an angle with his electric prodder. At that precise moment, George, and you can work out how old he was then, but he was no young 'un [64], went arse over tip on a guy rope, full run, full length down and I went to help him and he was up, up again like a shot. If I'd done that I'd have been groaning on the ground, from loss of wind, but he was up and off, threw open the gate. I went for the vehicle, it all happened very quickly. I saw George's torch. I started the car and raced through the bush. When I arrived there was George facing Boy who was about to go for George. Boy had his tail up and he was about to go. I didn't know that at the time but after it was all over George said to me very quietly, "You know, I'm glad you came in the car because Boy was about to have a go at me." George had his prodder, that was all. No rifle, he didn't have time to get his rifle.

'When I arrived there was the bloke (a Turkana called Muga) lying on the ground, and Boy standing not over him at this stage, he was a few feet back from him. George was closer to the man than Boy and I raced up past George in the car and went at Boy and he backed off a bit. Now the guy was lying near the car and George came forward and said, "Get him in the car," very quiet but I knew his tone of voice, so I got hold of this bloke, and said, "Get up. What the hell's the matter with you?" Now I did that because I know in urgent situations there's no good showing sympathy and this bloke looked a bit surprised, so I said, "Come on, get up," opened the door and "get in here." So he got up and got in and he had these bloody great holes in his head and blood everywhere. I slammed the door on him and I got in and George said, "Take him away." I didn't question him because of the rapport I had with George, although I knew I was leaving him with Boy. I knew he wasn't going to be a hero for no reason. He told me afterwards, again, that he could see that Boy was calming down. Once he lost sight of the victim, or the meal, or whatever you like to call it, it defused his adrenalin; it was like reality coming back to a man who's lost his temper.

'Anyway, I'm driving back, trying to get the car backwards through the bush, this bloke's starting to moan. "Oh, shut up," I said. "What's the matter with you? Nothing wrong with you at all." And he looked at me and said, "What's this then?" and he put his finger in through his mouth and out through his cheek. I said, "It's just a little hole, what's the matter with you. Just a tiny hole." So he pulled his finger out and then he suddenly grabbed hold of me and said, "If I die, you tell them I fought the lion. You'll tell them?" I said, "Yes, of course I will but you're not going to die. Do shut up, will you."

'I got the car round and went back to the camp where my wife Leila was. Leila was a nurse. We opened the door of the car and this bloke stepped out and just fainted. We patched him up as best we could. He had two bloody great holes in his face, one in the top of the head and one lower down, so I think [Boy's] mouth had gone right across here. An hour later we drove to Garissa hospital and I went in to the doctor and said, "Look, I've got a man who's been badly bitten by a lion." So he said, "Well okay, sit him down on that bench over there," and there were four or five on the bench – at the end of the queue, in other words. I said, "But this bloke's been bitten by a lion," and this African doctor turned to me and said, "So what? So have all those!"

'So it didn't only happen in George's camp. There were four or five guys who'd been bitten by lions who'd been brought in in various states of mauling. Ten days later that man [Muga] walked eighty miles back to George's camp, and the only thing that worried him was, was he going to get his wages for the days he'd been away!'

Why did Boy attack Muga? Simon Trevor says it was almost inevitable; he had broken all the rules: 'This man had gone out in the dark, which is the lion's time. A lion's character changes after dark. It becomes sneaky and very dangerous. A man had gone walking upright, then squatted down, turning his whole image into prey, probably with his back to Boy which is an absolute trigger.'

George's view was that, left to his own devices, Boy would have killed and probably eaten Muga. It was incredibly foolish of Muga to have left the safety of the camp when he knew there were lions all around. In fact, he had been told by the other members of George's staff to stay inside the wire. But he refused to listen, saying the lions did not frighten him.

Simon Trevor, who had been a game warden in Kenya before he became a cameraman, had the highest respect for George's expertise. 'George very rarely spoke quickly or urgently, with any urgency in his voice, but one day he and I and somebody else were out filming the pride. One of the lions was up in a tree which had a branch pointing out and it walked along the branch – I was filming it. The branch broke and the lion fell ten feet to the ground and George said very quickly,

"Don't laugh at her." I always remember that, and this lioness got up, wasn't hurt because a lion doesn't hurt itself falling, and it looked, it *was*, annoyed. I'm not saying it was waiting for somebody to laugh. I don't believe that for a moment. But what I believe is that it was ready to take it out on anybody who might annoy it. If you spoke any words at that moment, especially a hysterical laugh – some people might start rolling around laughing – it could have attacked purely on instinct. George knew lions so well. He also believed the theory that lions work on the most immediate reaction that comes to mind. You might have a lioness that's very hungry and has two tiny cubs. Now at the moment, her mother instincts are the strongest; therefore she will stay and protect them. But gradually hunger comes in and eventually takes over and becomes number one reaction. Then she'll go away and hunt and expose the cubs to danger. Once she's fed, suddenly that mother instinct returns and she comes rushing back.

'Falling out of the tree and the sudden anger – lions like a lot of animals have sudden anger or surges of adrenalin or aggression which are triggered by various things – it could have been triggered by falling out of the tree and hitting her head. After all, we get angry, don't we, if we knock our head on the door or something: we get really angry. It could have done that and she could have taken it out on me. Now I think all that went through George's head, in an absolute flash, and that's why he had to make sure. It only lasted five or ten seconds and then the lion looked around and the moment was past. But George was so quick.

'To the uninitiated person he was perhaps foolhardy in the way he dealt with the lions. He was the first to admit when he made a mistake. But a lot of his actions were definitely calculated. Definitely calculated. He's been condemned a lot, particularly by hunters for taking risks. I've had the same thing with elephants. Hunters have said to me, "You're stupid, what you do." But then hunters only ever see an animal over the end of the barrel of a gun. And that's the one time an animal, in defence of itself, will attack. So they're obviously biased and most, I should think ninety-eight per cent of hunters, don't understand animals anyhow. They really do not understand the behaviour of animals, and I can prove that in a hundred different ways.'

Simon Trevor recalls another occasion when he and George were walking through a sand *lugga* (dried-up river bed) in Kora and came to a place where some wild lions had killed a warthog. 'We walked along the drag mark. I had a wonderful rapport with George. I'd been in the bush – I have to say nowadays, a long time, I'm getting a bit long in the tooth myself – I went into the bush when I was sixteen. Both George and I had our eyes on the spoor and we both read the same thing and our eyes came up and centred on a bush ahead. We both knew that the lions were in there, at which moment the whole bush seemed to be shaking and there was a lot of incredible growling coming out of it. What I didn't know, but George did, was that the distance from the bush was not within the danger attack distance. So when I looked at George – I had a rifle, because we were actually looking for meat for the lions at that stage – I was ready for the lions to come out. George had his rifle over his shoulder and he was lighting his pipe. And he's saying something like, "Shut up, you silly old buggers," mumbling to himself.

'But he knew all along it was very, very unlikely that they would come out at us from a hidden place. If we'd gone forward, yes, we'd have been pushing them to the limit. Then they would have probably attacked because we were in this *lugga* and there was no retreat. Or possibly they would have attacked us: you can never say for sure. But George knew all this, again, you see, he knew. Now interestingly, the moment I saw him doing this I knew he'd summed it all up, so I relaxed. When he'd finished lighting his pipe, he didn't turn his back – this is the difference, again, you see – and walk away. We backed up. Because if you turn your back this again triggers an instinct in the lion, as he knew so well – that one I knew – this is the degree of George's experience with animals and lions particularly. All the time it was calculated. It was not foolhardiness.'

In the six months Simon Trevor spent filming at Kora, he and George would set out from the camp with all the lions after breakfast and 'walk all day, miles'. During his stay, Boy was attacked and nearly killed by two wild lions. 'You always have two males that defend a territory. That's what George always wanted for Boy. He wanted Christian to grow up to be the brother. And of course the two wild lions that came for Boy were the two holders of the territory. One faces the intruder, and the other jumps and bites at the base of the spine; behind the front legs. That's what cripples these lions. Vicious. God, frightening. When I filmed it [on another occasion], unbelievable.

That's exactly what happened to Boy. He [Boy] could just, just walk. But he came back to George and George fed him for the day and [gave him] water and we managed to get him back into the *boma* and then he was safe inside the *boma* and we flew the vets up …

'By taking them out repeatedly, they did learn enough to exist; they learned to kill for themselves. This was remarkable in many ways. If the lions were around the camp it would be a question of waiting for them to go. They wouldn't follow us because lions, basically, are extremely lazy. If they were at camp at dawn, then they'd more than likely go off somewhere so then you'd just go with them – you became one of the group.

'Other times, if they weren't around the camp, George might have heard them roaring at night, so he'd know the direction. You'd go out and you'd find the spoor, track them down, and that was always quite something. For one thing, you never quite knew when you were going to see the wild lions. I was always hoping for film of them but I only saw them once with George ever and I never got a shot of that. Two, when you did meet lions, you had to ascertain that they were George's lions – sometimes you met them really close – so there was a lot of tension in the first few minutes. I remember one particular case, George and I were walking along a sandy river bed and there was a highish bank and George suddenly stopped and we looked up and there was the head of this lion with its ears down, just over the bank. George went very tense because it was very close and suddenly this head came up and these great big eyes and it turned out to be Boy, but for a moment, quite a long moment, he didn't know it was Boy. Then another head came up; of course it was Christian; he wasn't doing his bit properly, he should have been much more alert. I remember feeling quite a tingle on that occasion. They could have been wild lions.

'It was interesting to watch them going about things, how they reacted to things, how incredibly attuned a lion's senses are to picking up what's happening in the bush ahead of you. Most of it by hearing, hearing in thick bush, but sight in plains country. They have both, but phenomenal sight. They can see vultures way, way, way up. They look for vultures as a means of finding food. They're great scavengers.'

On Sunday, 6 June 1971, George woke early to hear Boy roaring near Elephant Lugga and later took the rest of the lions for a walk, watching them disappear into the rocks as the day grew hot. At about

10.30 A.M. he was having breakfast in camp when he heard the sound of Boy drinking nearby. A few minutes later someone gave a cry and George rushed out to find Boy had attacked Stanley, the cook, about 250 yards away. Though Boy dropped his victim as George ran up, George was left with no alternative but to shoot the lion. Together with Kimani, another member of the staff, George managed to lift Stanley to his feet, but after a few yards the cook collapsed, unconscious and bleeding heavily. They took him to George's hut and laid him on the floor. A deep wound at the base of his neck indicated that his jugular had been severed, and he died as they were examining his wounds. George put Boy's body in the back of his pick-up and buried him on the edge of Elephant Lugga under Christian's Rock. That evening, when he collected the lions, they were very quiet – as if they knew something untoward had happened.

George was closer to Boy than to any other lion, including Elsa. Elsa and Joy were virtually inseparable, particularly when she was young, whereas Boy was very much George's lion and with his sister, Girl, the founder of George's first pride. When Boy got into trouble, first over the Mark Jenkins incident, then when he mauled Muga and finally when he killed Stanley, George stood by him, arguing that if people behaved stupidly they could not blame a lion for acting naturally. When Boy broke his shoulder and later was nearly killed by two wild lions, George nursed him back to health, often sitting up all night with him. He missed him sorely, confiding to his diary five days after his death: 'So difficult to get used to not seeing Boy sitting on Camp Rock and not hearing his roars echoing in the hills.'

Joy visited Kora two or three times when Simon Trevor was there. 'She was quite polite in telling me to push off so she could be alone with George. I think there was no doubt at all they loved each other – a real love-hate relationship. I would describe her as an extremely talented person who was totally frustrated by not having children of her own. Being Austrian and a very, very nervous, highly-strung person, if she'd had a child of her own she might have turned it into some monster, but she needed that [to have a child] desperately, for whatever reason. I think that that affected her tremendously and I think that it went on to make her feel inferior, to give her a complex about not being able to have children. She took it out on people and bestowed on animals the love that I suppose she wanted to bestow on a child. It's rather like the case of Dian Fossey, who studied gorillas.

'If it hadn't been for Joy Adamson, Meru Park wouldn't be there today. Just as, for better or for worse, the gorillas wouldn't be there today if it hadn't been for Dian Fossey. Joy could have driven around in a Rolls-Royce and had a flat in London, New York or Tokyo and anywhere else, and could have lived in luxury, but no, she gave a hell of a lot of money to wildlife. For whatever reason – I don't think we have to diagnose the reason – I think we should look at the positive side of what she did, exactly the same as George. I think we should look at George's work, or his lifestyle as being his own business. He didn't mess anybody else up. Some of these hunters who went there with their clients who ended up with Elsa in their tents, they didn't have to go. So what are they moaning about? He was an old man in the end who wanted to live with lions; he didn't take money from anybody in any way that wasn't honourable. You couldn't have found a more honourable man than George.'

Chapter Fourteen

A LONELY PHILOSOPHY

One day in 1972, a tall, swashbuckling Englishman arrived at George's camp at Kora and asked for a job. He had originally answered an advertisement from Joy, who was planning to rehabilitate leopards at her new camp at Shaba, north of the Tana River, and wanted an assistant. But she had to change her plans and sent the young man, whose name was Tony Fitzjohn, to George instead. Educated at Mill Hill, a Roman Catholic school in north London, Tony had worked variously as a photographer, night club bouncer and Outward Bound course instructor and had knocked about South Africa before landing in Kenya. At the age of twenty-six he was willing to turn his hand to anything.

George Adamson needed someone who combined the qualities of a Man Friday with those of mechanic and game warden and who, most important of all, was prepared to do all this for no pay. Apart from the

Tony Fitzjohn and Bugsy. His bark was worse than his bite

all-consuming needs of the lions, there were several vehicles to be maintained; a radio, fridge and various other pieces of equipment to be kept running; and stores and mail to be collected every couple of weeks from Mwingi, ninety miles away. There was not exactly a rush of applicants and Tony got the job. He turned out to be an ace, although George was sometimes tempted to call him a knave. But whatever Tony's faults George would have found it difficult, if not impossible, to run Kora without him. George himself was a brilliant improviser, never happier than when tinkering in his workshop, an expert at repairing and patching, especially Land-Rovers and their component parts.

Even Simon Trevor, who was well used to the shortcomings of life in the bush, was amazed at the lengths to which George had to go to keep Kora running. 'I'd say to George, "That tube looks a bit grotty,

Tony and Bugsy – an old softie at heart

George," when he's sitting out with a foot pump. But the spring has broken so he's attached a piece of string to his knee, so when his foot comes up the pump comes up. "There's nothing wrong with it," he says. "How many patches has it got?" "I don't know." When you count, it has seventy-two patches on it! And he's still using it; he didn't have any money. There was that side of it, you know. Joy was bloody mean, [she] really was. I think right deep down she did it for the fear that when he was independent he would no longer need her, not physically but emotionally. She was trying to keep him, because she was terribly fond of him.'

Tony Fitzjohn had to acquire the same survival skills and luckily was an immediate success with the lions. In George's view, he shared many of the characteristics of young males of the species: he was handsome, strong and playful. George likened him in particular to Christian, although Tony never gave George as big a fright as Christian did. Christian loved to ambush George, playfully of course. One morning he went too far, knocking George down, sitting on him and grabbing his head and neck in his jaws. When he let go, George was 'so bloody angry' that he seized a stick and went for the culprit, who promptly ran away. Soon afterwards, he did the same thing to Tony, smacking him with his paws and dragging him along the ground by his head. When he was finally able to get up, Tony was so enraged that he punched Christian on the nose as hard as he could. As with George, Christian did not retaliate but went off and sat down some distance away looking hurt – but not as hurt as Tony. The two victims came to the conclusion that Christian's bad behaviour was caused by loneliness and frustration. Tony sometimes suffered from the same complaints and every so often would go on a bender to which George would turn a blind eye. One of these benders led to a particularly nasty incident with a lion called Shyman, one of the dozen or so which now made up the Kora pride.

On 12 June 1975, Tony returned to Kora after a visit to the relatively bright lights of Garissa. George records that he got back about 4.30 P.M., slightly drunk.

His first action was to go and see the cubs in their compound. He came back with his shirt torn by Arusha, a young lioness bred in captivity in the Rotterdam Zoo, who had playfully knocked George down and broken his pelvis a few months before. Tony said she had just killed a guinea fowl. A little later Tony went back to have another look at the cubs. George could hear quite a bit of growling going on, as if the cubs were disputing possession of the guinea fowl, when Haragumsa (George's cook) appeared in a state of great excitement to announce that Tony was being attacked. George, thinking that the cubs had managed to get Tony on the ground and were giving him a bad time, grabbed a stick and ran to the scene where, to his shocked surprise, he found Tony being attacked by a grown lion. George charged, chasing the attacker into the bush and noticing that one of his paws was covered in blood. Tony managed to stagger to his feet only to have Arusha, who thought it was all a game, try to jump on him. When George had chased her off he managed to get Tony, who was badly mauled round the head and neck and bleeding a lot, back to his hut. Terence appeared and began to clean up Tony's wounds while George radioed the flying doctor, who said that it was too late to get to Kora before dark and he would come next day.

Tony had a restless night and George sat up with him for most of it, dosing him with antibiotics and valium. Tony had lost a lot of blood and was very weak. Next morning the journey to the old airstrip, about ten miles from camp over very bumpy roads, was agony for him. He finally took off around ten. Two days later, just before eight in the morning, a lion called Shyman, about whom George had always had reservations, came into camp, behaving in an odd manner and growling aggressively at the other lions. George noticed he had congealed blood on his muzzle. After much heart-searching, George concluded Shyman was the culprit and he would have to shoot him. He could not be trusted any more. He shot him through the brain and buried him next to Boy.

While all this was going on, three rifle shots were heard not far from the camp – obviously poachers – and over the next few days George found the carcases of two rhinos, one a large cow, both minus their horns. The news from Nairobi was better. Tony was making a good recovery. He had been extremely lucky. If the wound in his neck had been a millimetre deeper, it would have severed the artery and the jugular vein.

A couple of months before Tony's near-fatal mauling, George himself had a nasty experience, although in a letter to Willie Hale he dismissed it as a stroke of bad luck. One morning, Tony and George had set off to take their four cubs for a walk. Tony went on ahead, and some ten minutes later George saw them on top of a rocky ridge about a mile from camp. Then, rather unwisely, instead of going up to meet the cubs in the normal manner, George decided to play a game of hide-and-seek. Arusha, aged 16 months and weighing about 160 pounds, responded at once, ambushing George and throwing him off balance. He tripped and fell painfully; all four cubs, thinking this was part of the game, piled on top of him. At this point Tony managed to distract the cubs' attention by rolling rocks down the slope. George got to his feet with some difficulty, but was unable to move. Tony, however, was able to carry him to level ground, while the cubs continued to try and play. When they eventually tired and rested in the shade, Tony ran back to the camp and fetched the Land-Rover, leaving George propped against a tree with a big stick in his hand to discourage the cubs. Next morning, George was taken to hospital by the flying doctor, where he learnt that his pelvis was broken.

Over the years, George came to look on Tony as an adopted son and hoped he would carry on his work with the lions at Kora after him. But in the end this proved to be impossible. Tony, like Joy, was too volatile and temperamental to maintain smooth relations with anyone for very long and he repeatedly fell foul of local officialdom. George put it down to 'continual harassment' but there were undoubtedly faults on both sides and in 1988 Tony was declared *persona non grata* and told he would have to leave. With Kora closed to him, Tony and his American girlfriend, Kim, decided to move to Mkomazi, in north-east Tanzania, to embark on a study of wild dogs and cheetah. Whatever the final verdict on Tony's contribution to Kora, he did stick with George, through thick and thin, for more than sixteen years.

Whereas George, being a generous spirit, was always ready to forgive Tony, his brother, Terence, a lifelong bachelor and a much more prickly character, could not stand him. The feeling was mutual. Terence often fell out with brother George, too. One of their fundamental differences concerned lions. For George they were the noblest animals on earth. For Terence they were unreliable and downright dangerous. One day Terence's conviction that they could not be trusted was confirmed in a horrifying manner. He and his workmen had been rethatching a roof at Kora, and early the next morning he stopped his lorry just outside the main gate and got out to set fire to the debris. He then committed a cardinal sin: he failed to make sure there were no lions about before bending down and trying to light the damp pile. Without warning, a lion materialised from the bush and sprang on top of him, pinning him to the ground and seizing his head in its jaws. Terence's African labourers jumped out of the lorry and rushed to the rescue, shouting and throwing stones at the lion which let go of Terence and backed off. Alan Root, the photographer, who was staying at Kora, and George heard the commotion and came running out in time to see a lion called Shade beating a retreat into the bush, leaving Terence lying on the ground with blood pouring from his face.

He was a terrible mess, with holes in his neck and face where the lion had bitten him, and through one gash in his cheek his teeth were visible. They wrapped him up and did what they could to disinfect his wounds. Alan and his wife, Joan, bandaged Terence's head in cotton wool, loaded him into their plane and flew him to Nairobi. Joan had her arms round him for the entire flight. Despite his injuries he was conscious enough to be able to tell her that he had never before believed Livingstone's story that he felt no pain at all when he was mauled by a lion. But he now knew it was true because Terence himself was in no pain either, although he did feel desperately cold and kept shivering uncontrollably.

The doctor told Terence on arrival at the hospital that he had already performed the same sewing-up operation on both Alan and George, but Terence was not impressed. The only thing that interested him was that he was going to have his first hot bath in more than twenty-five years. Although terribly mauled, Terence had been lucky. Shade's teeth had just missed the carotid artery and jugular vein and narrowly missed destroying one eye, although Terence was left unable to blink the eyelid. It took another operation to put that right. But he never really recovered and at the end of his life – he died in 1986 – he looked frailer and older than George, although he was a year younger. Terence was undoubtedly an eccentric but he was also a first class botanist, extremely knowledgeable about elephants and a handyman *par excellence*. His achievement in building Kampi ya Simba and hacking

Kora's roads and airstrip out of the inhospitable thorn bush was truly remarkable.

Ken Smith, who once went to stay with him in his 'hut' near Marsabit, said: 'As George had that kinship with lions, so did Terence with elephants. He took me all round, we saw all Marsabit and particularly an elephant that later came to be called Mohamed [a huge old bull with enormous tusks, one over eleven feet long, now preserved in the National Museum in Nairobi]. Terence was probably the first European to see it. He was a fascinating chap, a teetotaller, he could only talk work, work, birds or whatever, no gossip. I stayed there two or three days and on the third day he produced one of these four-gallon petrol "debbies" [tins] that they had during the war. I saw him working at it, tapping it, and I said: "What's this for, Terence?" He said: "I'm going on leave. I haven't been out of the country for thirty years and I want to go to Canada. I don't know why, but I just want to have a bit of a break." So he proceeded to open this four-gallon debbie and inside was his demob suit, the one and only suit he had!' It had been in the tin, buried in the ground, for twenty-odd years.

By 1978, George Adamson had fourteen lions, lionesses and their cubs at Kora and was finding it increasingly difficult to feed them. The price of camel meat kept going up and it was impossible to buy a reasonably sized camel, which kept the pride in rations for less than a week, for less than £40. He wondered how much longer he could carry on, but he never doubted that it was worth it. He had his reward, he used to say, from being able to watch his lions going about their daily business and living happily as a family, without constraint. In the evenings mothers and offspring cubs would troop down to the camp where George would contentedly sit and watch the cubs playing with endless energy, racing about, fighting, ambushing one another and being cheeky to their elders and betters. It was a delightful sight, especially if the alternative was life-long captivity in some zoo. George felt that alone justified all the hard work and occasional criticism that he had to put up with. As the fame of Kora spread, he received several offers from America and Denmark of unwanted lion cubs, air freight paid. But what about the subsequent expense, he used to ask. People simply did not understand how much it cost to rehabilitate lions and return them to the wild. So, regretfully, he had to say no.

That same year, at the age of seventy-two, George had another stroke of 'bad luck' which could well have proved fatal to anyone less tough and lucky than him. He had at Kora two big cubs, Suleiman and Sheba, a brother and sister, eighteen months old, whose mother had been killed. They were not accepted by the other lions and had to be kept in a special enclosure. Early one morning, George let them out as usual and went up Kora Tit to look for the lair of a lioness called Arusha who had just had cubs. Ten years later, this is how George described to me perhaps the second most frightening experience of his life:

'I left the Land-Rover at the bottom, climbed up the hill and looked around but couldn't find them. I was about to go down again when suddenly Suleiman and Sheba appeared in a very playful mood. It's on a very steep slope there, and while I was fending off Sheba this young lion [Suleiman] jumped on my back. I couldn't keep my footing and I sort of fell sitting down, with him on top of me and he grabbed hold of me by the neck. I had a stick and I tried to beat him off, over my head, but that made him angry and he started to sink his teeth into the back of my neck. He became even more angry and was sinking his teeth in farther and farther. So I thought, Well, if I don't do something you're going to kill me. Luckily I'd taken a revolver with me and while he was on top of me I drew my revolver, thinking that if I fired two shots over my head that might put him off. I pulled the trigger twice and there were just two dull clicks. I thought, Good God, I've forgotten to load this blasted thing. I broke it open while he was still on top of me and it was fully loaded. I put it up again and fired off a shot but it had no effect whatsoever. He merely sank his teeth in deeper. I thought, I've got to do something otherwise he *is* going to kill me. So I put the revolver over my head and shot him.

'He immediately let me go and went off and collapsed about twenty feet away, looking a bit startled. I thought I'd better get down to the Land-Rover, which was at the bottom of the hill, as soon as possible because I was bleeding profusely and before I started feeling too groggy to drive it. I made my way down to the Land-Rover and drove to camp. Luckily my brother Terence, who'd been on safari, arrived just a few minutes after I got in. So he attended to the wounds in my neck and the flying doctor came (next day) and picked me up and took me off.

'You know, that evening Sheba arrived alone and I felt very worried about Suleiman not turning up, because I thought maybe he's badly injured. But in the morning he arrived and he seemed to be perfectly alright. Remarkably the bullet had gone across the top of his shoulder – I could see it lodged under the skin on the other side – and he was almost alright and also he was perfectly friendly.'

Four months later, after leading a happy life on the banks of the Tana River, poor Suleiman came to a violent end, killed by a big bull hippo which he and his sister Sheba rashly decided to take on. George saw both of them one morning and gave them a good feed of meat, so it was not hunger which made them attack the hippo. He went to visit them a couple of days later and found Sheba alone. She was calling in a strange way and George, with all his experience, knew immediately there was trouble. Sheba took him down to the river where he found Suleiman lying dead, with appalling wounds to his back and stomach. From the evidence in front of him – trampled bushes and deep marks in the soft earth – there had obviously been a terrific fight and George concluded that the hippo had caught Suleiman up against the trunk of a huge acacia tree and almost bitten him in half.

As George well knew, a lion's life is never without risk, especially when it is young and inexperienced. But at least Suleiman had not disgraced himself: he had put up a tremendous fight and had died like a lion. It was also clear to George that Sheba had watched over Suleiman's body for two nights. He could see the footprints of crocodiles leading up from the river, trying to get at Suleiman's body, and how she had driven them off. George buried Suleiman close by, just above the flood mark, while Sheba sat and watched him.

Astonishingly, Sheba would not leave her brother's grave, and after several days George was forced to trap her to get her back to camp. A few weeks later, Tony Fitzjohn reported that he had seen a badly injured hippo in the river not far from where Suleiman had been killed. Next day George drove down to inspect and found a hippo on the bank under a small shady tree. He looked decidedly groggy so George drove closer, got out of the car and examined him through his binoculars. Without warning the mighty beast let out a terrific snort and charged. George leaped back into the car but before he could start it the hippo smashed into him broadside and heaved the vehicle up so high in the air that George thought he would overturn it. The enraged hippo then bit the left front wing and finally, honour satisfied, retired to his tree. A few days later George came on him in the open: his back was a mass of deep claw marks and his right foreleg was badly damaged. George was convinced this was indeed the hippo that had killed Suleiman.

Life at Kora was certainly never dull and sometimes dangerous. The threat of attack by Somali Shifta or poaching gangs, which became increasingly bold and ruthless, was never far away. In January 1979, a gang of armed Somalis attacked a safari camp run by a young neighbour, Chris Matchett, on the north bank of the Tana, about twenty miles from Kora. Luckily for them, Matchett, his French wife and little daughter, who were on their way back from Nairobi, had a breakdown which delayed them and almost certainly saved their lives. But his young German assistant and an African employee were killed and three others wounded. Matchett was ordered by the government to close his camp. George, who expected to receive the same instructions, was reprieved but only on condition that he improved security and installed a guard of fourteen rangers. George grumbled at what he considered a piece of blatant bureaucracy, describing the ruling as a bloody bore which would merely interfere with his life to no advantage. He would much rather, he told friends, rely on his lions to provide a bodyguard.

There were rumours that an attack was also planned on George's camp. One day, George sent his driver, Moti, to Asako, the nearest village, to buy a camel for the lions. Moti was stopped on the road by some friendly person who warned him that a gang of thirteen Shifta were waiting to ambush him, hijack the Land-Rover and attack George's camp. The reason they did not, George says, was that when the Somali elders heard about the plan, 'They told the young men that on no account were they allowed to attack the camp because they were making so much money out of selling me camels at exorbitant prices.'

Apart from marauding Somalis, the only creatures which George considered *persona non grata* at Kampi ya Simba were scorpions and poisonous snakes. They tended to invade the camp in the rainy season and were most unwelcome in the living quarters and the outdoor lavatory, especially at night. The 'loo' at Kora was simple but practical, a clever adaptation of the old, upcountry 'longdrop'. The seats consisted of two upturned elephants' jaws – an old hunter's trick, according to George – which were comfortable to sit on and suspended above a trench dug in the sand. Sitting quietly on the elephant's jaw one day, reflecting on the vagaries of the world, George felt something on his bare leg and, glancing down, saw to his horror that a scorpion had climbed up it. Moving with great care – a scorpion is extremely poisonous – but also with great speed, George knocked it off and killed it without being stung. 'A very unpleasant creature is a scorpion,' he observed laconically.

One distinguished visitor, Prince Bernhard of the Netherlands, was so taken by the loo that he insisted on having his picture taken alongside George, each of them perched decorously on their respective elephant jaws.

On another occasion a huge Egyptian cobra, seven feet four inches in length, invaded the African staff's latrine. The alarm was raised and George despatched it with his shotgun, although, he says, 'In some ways I was sorry because I don't think it had any sinister intentions. But it's dangerous having these creatures in, so I can't welcome them.'

Least welcome of all was the spitting cobra, so called because it blinds its prey by spitting venom at its eyes from a considerable distance and with remarkable accuracy. It is also highly poisonous. During one rainy season two British girls, Julie and Carly, arrived at Kora after cycling from Glasgow, all the way across Europe, through the Egyptian desert to Kenya, and stayed for a week. One day, one of the girls was sitting in the mess hut admiring the view, when suddenly, a snake fell from the thatched roof right on top of her. In the resulting pandemonium, it bit her on the finger. 'Luckily,' George told me with a chuckle, 'it was not a spitting cobra but a striped sand snake, which is harmless. Of course, she didn't know it was harmless and she let out a scream. I came rushing in and then we happened to look up and there was a spitting cobra up in the roof.

'I think what had happened was that the spitting cobra had come after the sand snake, and the sand snake, in fright, had dropped off the ceiling onto the girl. You couldn't have a spitting cobra as near as that so I got a shotgun and, eventually, with some difficulty, managed to shoot it: whereupon a stream of blood came down and landed on the dining table, followed by the corpse of the snake!'

Throughout the seventies George and Joy saw less and less of one another, exchanging increasingly infrequent visits, whether to Kora or Shaba. Although George always remained loyal to Joy in public, it was clearly a great relief not to have to cope with her incessant lectures and tantrums. Simon Trevor, who spent a lot of time at Kora during this period, says, 'I could see he always looked forward to her coming but the moment she arrived he regretted it. As soon as she was gone it was like a burden lifted off him; he was like a young boy for a few minutes. Then after the weeks and months went by he was quite pleased to see her again.' Ray Mayers was more cynical. 'When he [George] was at Kora, somebody said to him, "Isn't it your wedding anniversary?" George said, "Maybe," and they said, "Well, aren't you going to see Joy?" and he said, "No, she's fifty miles away. Thank God."' This may be apocryphal and Ray Mayers was almost as old as George when he told me the story, so his memory may have been faulty, but it has the ring of truth.

Except for the odd anniversary and Christmas, which she set great store by, Joy was remarkably self-sufficient. She had the ability to become totally absorbed in her latest project, and so it was with the leopard programme which she started at Elsamere. In May 1977, she wrote to her sister Dorle in England that she and her 'very nice USA assistant' were busy taking Penny, the young leopardess she wanted to rehabilitate and study, for walks in the hills, 'mornings and afternoons on the leash'. But there was not enough space round Naivasha. 'I am getting desperate to find the right place where we can then camp for 2–3 years to study several litters. George is doing lion rehabilitation some 400 km from here and has also a full programme, so we see each other less often.'

In September 1977, Joy moved to Shaba and was writing enthusiastically to Dorothy about her new home. She was camping out, she said, in a beautiful reserve near Isiolo where she and George had lived for twenty-five years when he was the game warden in charge of the Northern Frontier District. Penny was now nearly two years old and ready for a mate, but as there was a shortage of male leopards in the area they had had to import one. Unfortunately, they had been unable to keep track of him after he had been released, although all the signs were that he and Penny had mated. As to Penny, she was to all intents and purposes a wild leopard ranging over an area one hundred miles square and with her own base about six miles from Joy's camp. Every morning, Joy would track her down by means of the radio collar she wore – a system George used with his lions for several years. Then Joy and Penny would spend two hours together, with Penny just as affectionate as she had been when she was a cub.

By the end of the year, Joy felt the experiment was going well. By

Joy's 1977 Christmas card from Shaba: out walking with the leopardess Penny. Joy wrote, 'She is two years old, lives utterly wild but is still very affectionate when we locate her within 160 square kilometres of rocky mountain.'

now it was the rainy season and, driving around, she often got stuck in the mud. Keeping track of Penny was a full-time business, given the size of her territory. Joy, however, felt it was extremely worthwhile since she had learnt a lot about the behaviour of leopards, which had such a bad reputation among the general public. She was anxious, clearly with another book in mind, to present a true picture of these extremely intelligent and interesting animals, quite unfairly labelled as the most dangerous of all the big cats.

The year 1979 started disastrously for Joy. In January she wrote to her sister that she had broken her left knee a few days before and would have to wear a heavy plaster from crotch to ankle for a month. This was a serious drawback as she could only just drag herself about with the weight of it, and it was extremely uncomfortable, biting into her flesh and making sleep difficult. But Joy was lucky in that there was a mission hospital about fifty five miles away which looked after her and saved her having to go to Nairobi. She hated the thought of that, almost as much as George would have done, since the hospital would have kept her in bed and, being used to the limitless space of Shaba, she would have been driven mad: being confined to a small room gave her claustrophobia. The rains were heavy but that was fun since it made everything muddy and wet. On top of everything else Penny had had a miscarriage. Her first litter was due on Joy's birthday on 20 January, but it was premature and Penny was missing for seventeen days.

Joy's camp was thirty-seven miles from Isiolo, which she usually visited once a week to collect her post and supplies, but in the rainy season the roads were often impassable. On two occasions she was stranded overnight when her Land-Rover became bogged down in the mud, and once she had to walk for miles to camp to get help. But she did not seem to mind, feeling that she would be amply rewarded if, for the benefit of mankind, she could unlock the secret of how Penny controlled her breeding.

Despite Joy's mishaps, one can only admire her amazing energy, boundless curiosity and, surprisingly, sense of humour. Few people would regard floundering around in the mud in the Kenyan bush during the rainy season 'fun'.

While nothing was too much trouble when it came to Penny, Joy was far less inclined to put herself out for a member of the family.

When one of her nieces, Ulli, wanted to visit Kenya, her reaction was anything but welcoming.

Joy made every sort of excuse for not having her niece to stay. First of all, it was so hot in Shaba that to cool down, Joy said, she had to go into the shower fully dressed several times a day and let her clothes dry on her to get enough energy to work. Then her camp was not designed to accommodate guests, and in any case she could not look after Ulli as she would be busy with Penny during the day and in the evening she would be working to all hours on her typewriter. On top of that – and this sounds like a specious argument – Joy says she was under contract to the government not to run a bush hotel and to have as few visitors as possible, so as to interfere as little as possible with her 'research'. Elsamere, her house at Naivasha, was let to prevent it being burgled and she had only been back there once, for a few hours, in the past two years. She hardly ever went to Nairobi, a seven-hour drive over bad roads, since she was far too busy. If, however, Ulli wanted to see Kenya without her aunt's help, then she had to warn her that it was 'VERY expensive' compared to Britain and cost SH600 (about £30) a day to stay in a lodge in a National Park. Ulli would have been a brave girl indeed to have ventured out to Kenya on safari after that sort of encouragement.

The climax of the year, as far as Joy was concerned, was the birth of Penny's cubs, and she was ecstatic that only three days after their birth Penny led her and her new assistant, Pieter Mawson, a young South African, to her lair to see them. She wrote to Elspeth Huxley telling her how happy she was. The birth was also the climax of her book on Penny, entitled *Queen of Shaba*. Shortly after the event, she posted off the final pages of the manuscript and the best of the four thousand photographs she had taken of Penny to Margery Villiers in London. A few days later her camp was destroyed by fire and Joy lost virtually everything – her furniture, crockery, cutlery, food and, much more seriously, all her books, papers and remaining photographs. Joy was alone in the camp – it was a Sunday – when there was an explosion in the mess, probably caused by a faulty fridge. The whole area was exceedingly dry and in a few seconds the fire had swept through the mess tent, spreading to the rest of the camp at terrifying speed. Joy rushed about helplessly, trying to save what she could. She was most upset by the thought of all the small animals that had died, including

Georgina (Doddie) Edmonds, George's devoted secretary and helper for seven years. He loved her dearly and left her all his diaries

Above: *One of the cubs shows scant respect for George's beard. Behind them is the high wire fence that surrounded Kampi ya Simba and the bush beyond*

Above left: *Inge Ledertheil and George Adamson, with two of the three cubs whose mother had been shot by a farmer. George was killed by Somali Shifta a few months later, going to Inge's rescue*

Left: *Carla Loeffelholz, from Minnesota, one of the many pretty young women who flocked to Kora, attracted by the guru-like appeal of George's personality*

Right and opposite: *George on the Tana at Asako, the village where he bought camels and goats for his lions. One of his Somali killers is said to have come from the village on the opposite bank, Mbalabala*

Right: *Armed with .303 and thermos flask, George is ready to set off on safari*

Below: *At dusk, George would open the wicket gate in the wire and go out to feed the lions, calling them by name, always in the same way: 'Come on, Growe. Look . . !'*

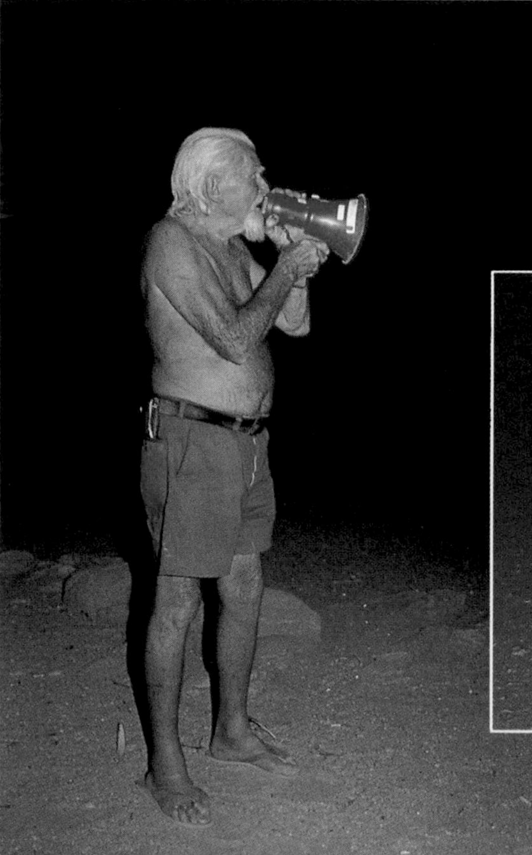

Below: *Growe, the twelve-year-old matriarch of George's last pride at Kora, getting a juicy leg of goat*

Above: *Lighting the Tilley lamps, an evening ritual as fixed as the rotation of the stars in the sky above Kora*

Right: *The 'Lord of the Lions' and the author observing the hallowed ritual of the eleven o'clock gin while out looking for the pride*

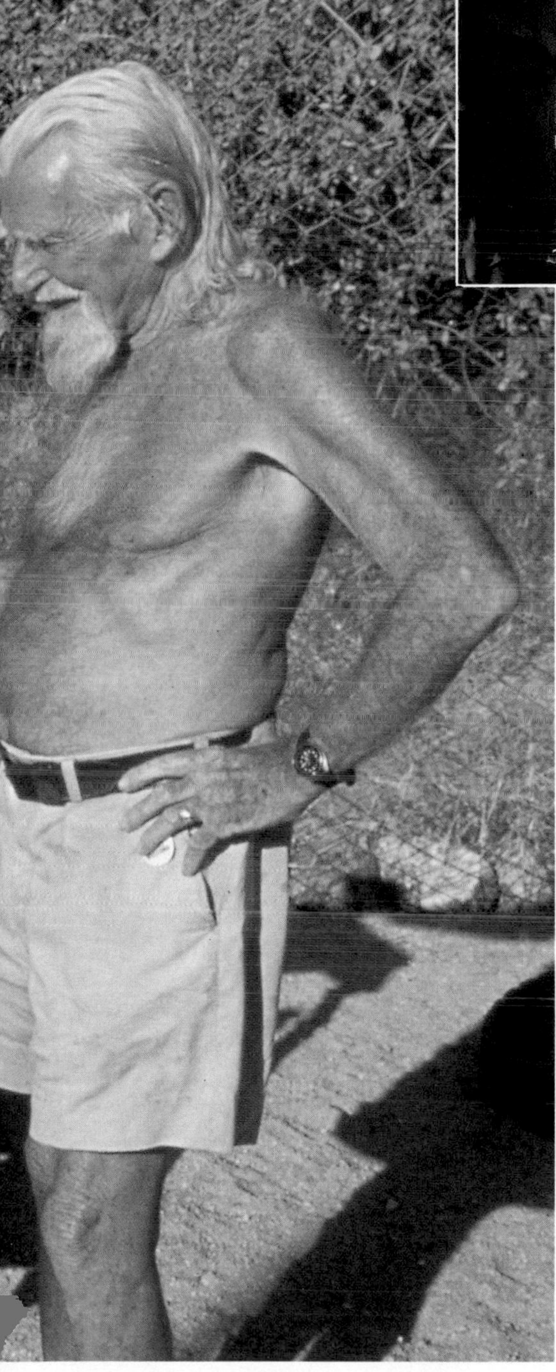

Left: *Celebrating his eighty-third birthday at Kora with friends and a glass of champagne. Afterwards George liked to go and have a dip in the Tana, despite the crocodiles*

Above: *George's funeral at Kora; Richard Leakey, the Director of Kenya's Wildlife Services, and an honour guard of game rangers*

Below: *Jonny Baxendale's wreath which according to Major Dougie Collins, had been blown some distance away and which one of the lions must have picked up and put back on George's grave*

One of the cubs keeps watch over George's grave, the day after the funeral

her pet rabbits for whose incineration she bitterly blamed herself. Always a highly-strung, excitable person, the disaster of the fire made her almost uncontrollable and she had frequent and very public rows with Pieter, her assistant. Because of this, when Joy was murdered shortly afterwards, suspicion fell initially on Pieter Mawson.

Brian Jackman of the *Sunday Times Magazine* happened to be on safari in the Shaba area and, knowing that Joy lived there, decided to visit her.

'This was two months before she was murdered. These big, tough macho African safari operators, Jock Anderson and another chap who ran the camp at Shaba at the time, were really rather nervous about going up to meet her. Finally we all plucked up courage and we shot off to her bush camp. There she was with her rather frizzled hair, approaching her seventieth birthday, her leg from ankle to crotch encased in plaster where she'd broken a knee. Her bush camp had just burnt down, her gas fridge had just exploded, she'd lost a manuscript and half the pictures of her leopard, Penny – she was writing this book about her at the time. She welcomed us warmly – in spite of all the fear and trepidation; everyone had said, "God, she's a terrifying woman!" In fact she was charming. We sat down under the shade of a tree and we drank a couple of beers and we talked, or rather, she talked at us, at me, for four hours I suppose. It was rather heady, high-flown stuff that she had this intuition; she knew, she and the leopard knew what they were thinking, it was getting into those rather strange realms. She had rapport and a sort of sixth sense; she could second guess the leopard and the leopard knew exactly what she was thinking. Nevertheless she wore these leather guards around her arms which were very heavily scarred: "For God's sake don't mention my scars." Obviously from going in with these leopards, you know what they're like, those horrendous claws. But she was a pretty tough, indomitable old character.'

Undeterred, Joy pressed ahead with plans to fly to Paris to take part in a television programme with Brigitte Bardot. In a letter to her sister, dated 30 December 1979, Joy wrote that she had just returned from a hectic three days there. After a showing of *Born Free* there was a ninety-minute studio discussion between the two 'stars', Brigitte Bardot and Joy, plus two other people representing the conservationists on one side and spokesmen for a mixed bag of interests including zoos, circuses, trappers and National Parks on the other. According to Joy the programme was to be shown internationally on 1 January 1980. There followed a typical Joy diatribe. 'As France – like all Latin countries – are VERY Catholic & the Bible does not refer to being kind to animals these countries are very cruel to them & do little to preserve them.' That was why, Joy adds, she had undertaken this exhausting and rushed trip in the hope that it would do some good. Paris was freezing cold and wet and she spent most of the time at the television station, so the trip proved to be no holiday. On her way back she spent a few hours at London airport with her publisher (Collins) and her lawyer discussing her new book on Penny, which was due to appear in September, as well as two small gift-books on the eagle owls and Colobus monkeys of Elsamere. The BBC would also soon be showing a film about her in what Joy called 'The World Around Us' series, which she was anxious for her sister to watch.

She then reports that she had two serious burglaries at her camp before leaving for Paris, in which one of her Leicas and a number of other valuables were stolen. The police were still hunting for the culprit who Joy was convinced must be one of her staff. On a happier note, she writes in praise of Penny, a wonderful mother to her two cubs, now seven months old. They were completely wild and Joy counted herself lucky if she caught a glimpse of them now and again far up among the rocks where they lived. Penny did her best to persuade the cubs to make friends, sitting in the midst of them and flirting with Joy and her assistant to show the cubs that they were to be trusted. But the cubs refused to be won over and determinedly kept their distance.

Finally, Joy explains that George was unable to visit her for Christmas. It was a long, expensive flight – in fact it only took an hour and would have cost George nothing – and in any case, there was no one to look after his twenty or so lions. (The Adamsons always spent Christmas together, and Christmas 1979, the thirty-seventh anniversary of their first meeting on Willie and Morna Hale's roof in Garissa, was intended to be no exception. Unfortunately the pilot friend who offered to take George to Shaba was called out on an emergency at the last moment and the trip had to be cancelled.)

Joy's last words – the last words she was to write to her sister – express the hope that the coming year would be a good one for all of them. Four days later, on 3 January 1980, Joy was dead. The news did not reach George until the next day. He had gone downriver to Boy's Lugga to look for one of the lions when a plane buzzed the camp. By the time George got there the plane had gone but, as he told me later, he knew at once from his brother Terence's face that something terrible had happened. 'He told me that a friend of ours, Peter Johnson [Joy's accountant and one of her trustees], had stopped to tell me that Joy had been killed by a lion. I didn't believe that. I couldn't think how that could have happened.' Peter Johnson flew on to Shaba to collect Joy's body and take it to Nairobi.

George says he was 'convinced that it could not have been a lion' and he was proved right. A post-mortem carried out in Nairobi on 5 January came to the conclusion that Joy had been killed, not by a lion, but by a sharp weapon such as a *simi* [short sword]. In other words, Joy had been murdered.

A week before, her old friend and literary editor, Margery Villiers, received a letter from Joy saying she was frightened that she was going to be killed. Mrs Villiers told her close colleague and friend, Irene Stirling, about the letter but did not show it to her. Irene Stirling remembers, however, that it was taken very seriously. Margery Villiers immediately alerted Billy Collins and he, Irene Stirling thinks, passed it on to the police for them to take action – presumably by alerting the Kenya authorities. Joy's letter has since disappeared.

According to Pieter Mawson, who told Jack Barrah, George's old assistant, Joy's behaviour on the day of her death was quite unusual. In Jack's words to me: 'He [Pieter Mawson] said that that day her behaviour was most extraordinary, because she encouraged this leopard to come to her and broke down all the previous stuff [training]. She was releasing this leopard, encouraging it to go wild again. On this day, the day she was killed, she encouraged it to come to her again and started playing with it. She had abandoned all that! Then she came back and instead of getting her films together and typing she went and sat under a tree, gazing into space. Pieter came up to her and started talking and she just turned on him and said, "If anything happens to me, will you promise to look after Penny?" And he thought this was the most extraordinary thing and said, "Of course I will." She just gazed into space again, didn't even unload her camera, didn't write up her diary, didn't do anything.

'It was a habit of hers always to go for a walk in the evening and get back in time to listen to the BBC news at seven o'clock. Pieter always used to go with her. So as she set off on this walk, she turned round to Pieter and said, "I want to walk alone today, Pieter; don't come with me." Only time she had done such a thing. So come about quarter past seven, no sign of Joy, which was strange because she was always back by seven to listen to the BBC. So he then went to look for her and found her dead on the path only about a hundred yards from the camp. His immediate supposition was that she'd been killed by a lion because she had this wound here [under her left armpit] and he was only a young fellow. He whipped her in the car, took her to Isiolo, then went to Meru. They did a post-mortem in Meru Hospital and they found this stab wound. Then Pieter became suspect for having murdered Joy. He really broke down about this. He was in a hell of a state. Peter Johnson and I flew down and flew him out the next day. The police had said to him, "You don't leave camp," and all the rest of it. We just flew down, picked him up and brought him back. Then he went for a job in Botswana, rolled his Land-Rover and killed himself. Extraordinary behaviour on Joy's part that day.'

It is almost irresistible to conclude from this story, especially when taken in conjunction with Irene Stirling's account of the missing letter to Margery Villiers in which Joy said she feared for her life, that Joy experienced a premonition of her own death.

The police interviewed all Joy's staff, including Pieter Mawson, who because of his very public rows with Joy was the prime suspect, initially at least. But fairly soon their inquiries began to concentrate on a young Turkana called Paul Ekai, whom she had sacked in early December and whom she suspected of being responsible for the two robberies at her camp. Paul Ekai had disappeared and it was not until about a month later that he was spotted nearly two hundred miles north of Shaba and, thanks to some smart police work, arrested. Two days later he made a full confession, admitting that on the night of her murder he had gone back to Joy's camp to demand his back pay, which he claimed he was still owed. When she started to argue, he lost his temper and stabbed her. At his trial, Paul Ekai withdrew the confession, claiming it had been extracted under torture. But the court upheld it and, nearly two years after the event, convicted him of the murder. The penalty was death, but since he was deemed to be under age, he was sentenced to be detained during the President's pleasure.

When she was told of Joy's death, her sister's impromptu reaction, reported in the local newspaper, was: 'I'm saddened but not surprised.' Writing to the author much later, Dorle referred to Joy's 'miserable' treatment of her African servants. 'Isn't it surprising that Fifi was really the only non-Nazi in our family – very much pro-Jewish – and she treated the natives in Africa so abominably!' In a separate letter, she gave the following verdict on Joy's marriage to George Adamson. 'It was a pity that his wife had so little time and consideration for him and he was left lonely, without a real marriage partner for most of his life.'

Joy summed up her own philosophy in a letter she wrote to her sister on 30 October 1975. It might well stand as her epitaph:

'If I am in trouble I rather bite my tongue off than to ask for help. I have tried all my life to make myself independent of other people after I had trusted – and been let down more often than I could bear. It's a lonely philosophy, but it saves hurts.'

Joy adds that she had no other wish than to do something to repair the mistakes 'we humen' (sic) have made in our exploitation of nature and wildlife and therefore, she says, she is giving all the money Elsa made back to the animals.

Chapter Fifteen

RESTING IN ARCADIA

The funeral was held in Nairobi on 8 January 1980, with swarms of photographers, journalists and cameramen in attendance and with George, who must have loathed the whole occasion, looking unhappy and out of place in a suit and a tie. Among the journalists there that day was Brian Jackman of the *Sunday Times Magazine*, who had visited Joy at Shaba a few months before she was killed. George seems to have taken an immediate shine to him and invited him back to Kora: it was the start of a friendship which was to produce some memorable articles.

'I couldn't believe my luck, to fly back with the old boy to see his lions. That was my introduction to Kora. We flew into this dusty little strip, [Tony] Fitzjohn charges up in a beat-up old Land-Rover and I'm suddenly in the midst of all this thorn bush and the cackling hornbills and the burning heat and these big red rocks floating up above the bush, and I thought "My God, this is something, this is the place." Very much that dry, thorny, Hemingway's Africa and not at all like the green, grassy Mara, Serengeti kind of Kenya which I'd been used to.

'George said, "Right, let's go." He really wanted to get out and see what had been happening to his lions. So Fitzjohn drove us all out

Kampi ya Simba, from the top of Kora Rock. George's hut is at the back, on the extreme left, with the cubs' compound directly in front of it

through the bush towards the Tana river and said, "They're down here somewhere. They killed a waterbuck today and they should be still around." So we drove up and George gets out of the Land-Rover and starts calling, like someone in the park calling their dog. "Arusha! Arusha!" This is the big old matriarch and all of a sudden this huge lioness comes drifting out of the bushes, blood all over her muzzle from this waterbuck kill, sees George, shambles towards him, stands up on her hind legs, puts her huge paws over his shoulder like that and he puts his arm round her. "Oh, Arusha, old girl." She's sort of going, "Waoah, waoah," you know, making those lovely leonine grunts, and they're just like old pals. George shouts back to me, "Don't get out. I should stay in the Land-Rover if I were you." I thought, "My God, I'd absolutely no intention of getting out." I was sitting in the front passenger seat and eventually Arusha jumped down from George and she came nosing around the Land-Rover and came right up and stuck her head into the window and I realised for the first time how huge the head of a full grown lioness is. Absolutely enormous. And the cliché, you could actually feel her hot breath, rather smelly. Then she just drifted off. That was Day One in Kora.'

On 1 June 1986, Major Dougie Collins, sometime soldier, author and professional hunter then living in retirement in Lamu, received an SOS from Ken Smith on behalf of George Adamson. Would he fly to Kora and help George, now virtually on his own, to run the place? As Dougie explained in an unpublished account of his stay with George, entitled *The Old Man and his Lions*:

'Evidently George had suffered further losses since his wife had been murdered at her own camp several years ago. His only brother Terence had died two months previously. It was the self-effacing, hard-working, indefatigable Terence who had cut all the tracks and roads in the Reserve, had built Kampi ya Simba as well as keeping the tractor and ramshackle Land-Rovers going. To add to his misfortunes, his energetic and mercurial assistant, Tony Fitzjohn, together with his attractive and hard-working girlfriend Kim, were on the move to Tanzania. Ken asked me if I would team up with the old man and help out. Such a request needed no consideration from me.' A week later, Dougie flew in a small plane from Manda Island, the airstrip for Lamu, to Kora.

'I had not seen George for some thirty years. Now in his early eighties, he looked fit and tanned although I had heard that his eyesight was failing. With his long mane of silvered white hair, moustache and neatly-trimmed beard, the familiar figure still looked the same and all in all I thought the years had dealt with him in kindly fashion. We entered the camp – a compound of a couple of acres, nestling at the foot of an enormous volcanic rock, one of the many of these frowning Inselbergs that are a feature in this particular sea of bush. The *makuti*-roofed primitive living quarters, mess, kitchen, stores and workshop were enclosed by a twelve-foot-high wire fence and inside one had the impression of occupying a large zoo, with the freed lion and leopard, all released in the wild as part of their unique programme, roaming at will outside. I was to find out that these great cats would pay friendly visits for camel and goat meat when they found the animals they normally preyed upon had disappeared due to the depredations of the poachers.

'Over a frugal lunch on my first day with the slight wind rattling the palm-frond thatch above the mess, tame ground squirrels, dik dik, hornbills, doves, go-away birds and vulturine guinea fowl shared our food, for all animals, both great and small were welcome, watered and fed at this St Francis-like sanctuary. Afterwards the Old Man lit his pipe and put me in the picture. I learned that poaching was worse than I had believed possible. In the years 1960 to 1970 gangs of them, well-armed with automatic weapons, had descended on Kora to wipe out the entire population of some one hundred and fifty rhinoceros. As also the leopard. The once magnificent elephant herds had been reduced to pitifully small groups, mostly cows and calves, scattered and scared. Gone too were most of the buffalo, waterbuck, oryx, gerenuk, Grant's gazelle and reticulated giraffe in spite of the Game Department and anti-poaching unit's efforts to protect them. They were, and are, fighting a losing battle against the odds, for the poachers are better armed and more mobile than themselves. The threat from these poachers and marauding Shifta from over the Somalia border still remains, and whether in camp or sleeping out in the bush, a loaded rifle or revolver is always kept close at hand. The only connection with the outside world is the radio, and all supplies, petrol, diesel, foodstuffs and other necessities are obtained from Mwingi, ninety miles away on the main Garissa/Nairobi road. Every other day, a Land-

Rover loaded with empty drums is driven to the nearby Tana River to be filled with its chocolate-coloured water for drinking and cooking purposes.

'The lion-stocking programme has now come to an end and the Old Man would like nothing better than to introduce rhinoceros to this area where they were once so plentiful – but only if they could be adequately protected . . . As to the Old Man's achievements over the years, many of the originally released lions have died of old age, been poisoned or poached, or wandered off outside the Reserve, but many offspring are still to be found at Kora and they in turn have produced cubs. As an old White Hunter I was, understandably so I think, sceptical of my old friend's efforts to rehabilitate both lion and leopard and of his belief that lions can communicate with man. I am no longer so.

'In the early days of my lengthy stay there I was invited to accompany him in finding one of his prides: Coretta (C is favourite), Boldy and Cindy (named, apparently, after Cinderella, for she was so beautiful and shy) – three fully-grown lionesses, and also three half-grown cubs – the offspring of Coretta. The Old Man told me he had a feeling that they may be hungry due to the scarcity of game. We set off on our short safari one late afternoon. I was to drive a battered-looking Land-Rover containing the carcase of a camel he had purchased at an exorbitant price. I eyed the front tyres with some trepidation as they were worn down to the canvas. I say "with trepidation" for when approaching lion in my hunting days to photograph them the last thing I wanted was a flat tyre to prevent me making a hasty retreat if necessary. I followed the Old Man driving his own Land-Rover over the winding, bumpy, rock-strewn track. It was growing dusk when we finally stopped on a plain some fifteen miles from camp. We had a welcome sundowner by the side of the vehicles. It was now almost dark.

'The Old Man turned to me with a confident smile and said, "They won't be far from here." Producing a loud-hailer he then called Coretta three times. I checked my watch. Within three minutes I noticed a large, lithe yellow shape approaching out of the darkness. The shape approached closer.

'"Coretta!" He smiled as he walked over to the lioness. "Come and greet her, Dougie." Other ghostly shapes now emerged to sit around the Old Man in a circle. The whole pride of six of them. I declined his invitation, hastily poured myself another whisky and made ready to jump in the Land-Rover, for I had not his sublime faith. I thought the whole episode uncanny, for how could he know that the pride, especially at hunting time, would be exactly where he thought they would be in such an enormous area of wilderness? Lighting his pipe and puffing away happily, the Old Man now sauntered back to the cars.

'"We'll turn round to motor back to a belt of trees on the edge of the plain," he said. "There is a chain round the carcase of the camel. I'll point out the tree. Back up to it and we'll tether the loose end round the trunk, then you start up, drive forward a little to pull it out of the car and they can feed there." I did as he asked but the chain was fouled up and after some time, vainly working in the dark, we gave up. The pride had now caught up with us and were growing restive. They looked hungry. The Old Man was quite unperturbed. Calmly puffing at his pipe, he said:

'"It really doesn't matter. We will camp here for the night and they can feed in the back of your Land-Rover!" I felt quite relieved when he made the suggestion that we both sleep on the top of his own Land-Rover where he had two mattresses and an ingeniously constructed superstructure with shelving for drinks, thermos of coffee, soup and sandwiches.

'That night under the stars proved to be exciting and exhilarating. Having fed continuously during the night just under our noses, the whole pride moved off at first light. A battered kettle was produced, tea, milk and sugar. I made a fire and brewed up. Some meat still remained on the camel's rib cage and I had little difficulty in kicking this out of the back of the Land-Rover. The Old Man eyed this unsavoury-looking mess speculatively to remark that they would be ready for another meal when they had slaked their thirst from the river.

'"On the way back to camp we'll give it a tow. I think I know where to find them again," he said. Even now I was not wholly convinced of his quite remarkable powers of contacting the pride. During the fifteen miles from camp the previous day, I had noticed dozens of tracks leading to the river. As we towed the rib-cage back he unhesitatingly chose one of them and there – as we neared the river, lying in the middle of the sandy track – the whole pride sat waiting for him. After that I was totally won over.

'A couple of months before my arrival at Kampi ya Simba, a Japanese television team had been filming a documentary on the Old Man's lions. They called their film *Saint Lion*. Fulsome praise indeed for George Adamson, but a title I would not disagree with.'

There was indeed something saintly about George Adamson, his flowing white locks making him look like an Old Testament prophet, although his philosophy was much closer to the New. What struck me most about him when I first met him was how wonderfully tolerant he was of other people's foibles and failings; he was perhaps the nicest man I have ever known. His personality and way of life exerted a rare fascination, especially on the young. They flocked to him for a variety of reasons, but all of them, in their different ways, found in Kora a peace and understanding they failed to find elsewhere. George Adamson's Kora was a kind of Shangri-La, a Never-Never Land; but also, in its harsh way, an earthly paradise where the lion, it seemed, might lie down with the lamb, or if not with the lamb at least with man.

One of Tony Fitzjohn's former girlfriends, Carol Byrne, who visited George at Kora as a young woman in the seventies, is still very conscious of the healing power of his personality. 'One evening I was with George on that rock he used to like to go and have his drink on; it had a lovely view. We were sitting up there one evening, we hadn't seen any lions for an awful long time and suddenly this huge lion gave me a great shove and it was Lisa. The sun was just setting, it had been absolutely perfect until that moment. Then for me it wasn't quite so perfect. I had total trust in George. I was never frightened when I was with George at all, because I assumed he was in control. He didn't have a gun though that day because we hadn't seen the lions for so long. He just told me to stand up. '"Whatever you do, don't get pushed over," and he called for [Tony] Fitzjohn and we were trying to battle this lion off. They rub against you and can knock you over.' Tony Fitzjohn came up the rock to join them and said, '"We'll go back with Lisa between us. You walk ahead but just walk very slowly." And every time she looked as if she was trying to walk after me the two of them closed in on her. That's how we got back.

'Over all the years, in the later part of his life he'd acquired a great deal of wisdom. He was somebody who was at one with nature, with his own life, and that's very attractive to people who are searching, who don't know who they are, or where they are. I certainly found myself talking to George about life, the problems in life. He had a good philosophy and he'd sit there puffing away. There would be a silence and then out would come this total wisdom and you'd think, "Well, I wonder why I didn't think of that."'

The African bush, for those who do not know how to survive in it, can of course be a dangerous place. George knew how to survive in it, better than almost anyone. His godson, Jonny Baxendale, said of him: 'I know of no one in my lifetime who was in such total and complete harmony with his environment. George had such a rapport, not just with the lions but with the squirrels, with those guinea fowl. Monitor lizards came marching into his camp, things that you wouldn't think would have any contact with human habitation. And anything that happened, like the rivers flooding and you couldn't get out, everything was totally accepted. George was never surprised by anything that happened in nature, even the disasters, like one of the lions [Suleiman] being killed by a hippo. All this power was part of it. I don't know anybody who was so totally at ease and so totally self-contained as George.'

I first met George Adamson at the beginning of February 1988. Nick Gray of Yorkshire Television and I flew out from London to Nairobi overnight and then, transferring to a small plane, headed north for Kora, 150 miles north-east of Nairobi. After about three quarters of an hour we caught our first sight of Kora Rock forty or fifty miles away, a white blur against the grey-green of the bush, and watched as it rapidly became a great sand-pink pyramid, surrounded by lesser pyramids, framed against the wide sweep of the Tana River. We buzzed the camp, a little group of low, thatched huts nestling at the foot of the Rock, insignificant in the immensity of the thorn bush. As we circled the second time a tiny brown figure in shorts came out and waved: it was, unmistakably, George. We landed, bumping and skidding along the rough airstrip, and taxied over to the edge of the strip, parking beside a big acacia tree. Nailed to it was a roughly hand-painted sign, which said, 'Lions on Road. Buzz Camp. Wait at Plane [roughly drawn] until picked up.' Underneath it said 'Kampi ya Simba'.

A few minutes later a Land-Rover came bumping along the road and drew up beside the acacia. Out stepped a short, wiry, deeply-tanned old man who greeted us with a broad smile, his eyes still blue and mischievous despite his eighty-two years, and helped to load our bags. I was flattered that George himself had come to meet us. Over lunch, a simple affair of cold meat and salad, we sat and talked about the film we proposed to make about his life. He was amenable to all our suggestions, said he was looking forward to doing it, made no demands and exuded serenity and a sense of humour. That evening he drove us to the river, down one of the roads hacked out of the bush by his brother Terence. Leaving the Land-Rover at the end of the sandy track, we walked to a rock overlooking the Tana, about a hundred yards wide at this point, its dark brown flood rolling smoothly past us in the evening light. George had come suitably prepared to offer us a sundowner: beer for Nick and whisky for himself and me. When the thermos ran out, George sent me down to the river to fill up a glass with the brown water of the Tana. He chuckled at my slight hesitation – it looked very cloudy – but the last whisky of the evening did taste very good, like a peaty malt. We drove back to camp in euphoric mood.

Just before our departure, I said casually to George: 'I don't suppose you'd ever want to raise a lion cub again?' His reply surprised me.

'Oh, yes, I certainly would. In fact, I'd like nothing better.' He became unusually animated. 'I've been thinking about it for some time. It would be a marvellous idea.' Nick and I looked at one another, the unspoken question hanging in the air. Was George too old? Would he really be up to looking after one or more lively little lion cubs? Would he be able to take them out for walks as they grew up, until they were two years old or more and able to hunt and kill for themselves? George puffed on his pipe, looking serenely determined. I knew the answer was yes.

So next day in Nairobi, we called on Dr Perez Olindo, then Kenya's Director of Wildlife. After discussing the general outline of the film, to which he gave his blessing, I said, 'You know, what would really make this film a great success is one thing.' He looked at me deadpan from behind his desk piled high with files.

'Yes?'

'A lion cub. For George. You know, it would somehow re-create, rekindle the magic of *Born Free* ...' I struggled with words, anxious to make the best possible case. He smiled. 'There is no problem. Lion cubs we have plenty of. And for George, we will do anything ...' He waved his hand and stood up. The interview was over. Would he be as good as his word? I was hopeful, but sceptical. Many people in official positions promise favours lightly, but seldom deliver. In a long journalistic career, I had taught myself not to expect too much. It came, therefore, as a surprise and an exciting one when I was told that George had acquired not one cub, but three! The fact that the cubs were triplets was, of course, purely fortuitous – their mother, as we have seen, had been shot for raiding cattle by a farmer who lived at the foot of Mount Kenya and whose first thought was, 'Let's get George to look after them!' Perez Olindo was contacted and gave his permission. George was excited and intrigued. It made the film, and I like to think the cubs made the last year of George Adamson's life infinitely more rewarding. It was, after all, the last return to the wild.

George's ritual in the evening at Kora was as regular and fixed as the slow rotation of the stars in the sky above him. On one of the last nights we spent together, in September 1988, when we were completing the film about his life, he appeared at dusk from his hut still clad only in shorts and sandals and installed himself in a comfortable camp chair by the wire. From there he could look across the bush to Kora Rock and Kora Tit, from where the lions would suddenly appear, padding majestically through the dusk, their stride and carriage in the wild truly one of the magnificent sights of this world. George sat and waited for them with his pipe in his mouth and a glass of whisky at his elbow. A couple of his men carried up the cold box with the camel meat and George opened the wicket gate in the wire and went out to feed the lions. In 1988, as at the time of his death a year later, Growe was the matriarch of the pride which included her daughter One Eye, One Eye's daughter and son, Maggie and Denis, and their various offspring. George flashed his torch, and immediately the beam was reflected by seven and a half pairs of eyes, One Eye – nobody knew how she lost the other eye – being easily identifiable.

George walked out quietly into the half-darkness and called. 'Growe! Come on then, Growe. Look!' She came forward, the great muscles rippling under the smooth skin, into the light of the torch, regally sure of herself and George. When she was about six or seven feet away George tossed her a piece of meat which she snatched up with a growl of pleasure, shaking it hard to remove the grit, and stalked off with a superb swing of her haunches. He used to feed her by hand, until, as he ruefully explained, she nearly took his little finger off with one of her claws, not intentionally, merely out of impatience. 'But it would be all right to do it if I had a leg of goat,' he said stoutly. He then called the rest of the pride, one by one, his Africans standing watchfully behind him, a young assistant with a rifle a few yards away, just in case. It would have been easy for the old man to trip in the half dark. As they came up, some with a rush, some like the cubs, cheekily confident, George would dole out the chunks of meat, talking to them in a quiet voice all the time, knowing each one by name. You could see that he loved them in a practical, no-nonsense manner and treated them as equals.

When the lions had been fed, George walked back to his seat to enjoy his whisky, gazing out into the darkness, his pipe between his teeth, making desultory conversation, radiating contentment. Before it got too dark, he wandered off to light the Tilley lamps, a task which he clearly enjoyed and which he always did himself, priming them, pumping up the pressure and then hanging them up, one in the mess hut, one in the tree outside. They glowed peacefully in the great bowl of the African night, two tiny beacons of hope and civilisation. Sitting at the table at the edge of the darkness one night, we talked about the world, about Africa, its people and its animals.

'There are far too many people in the world,' he said. 'A short time ago they reckoned that there were five thousand million or something. The world's overcrowded. That's what leads to all the wars and uprisings and all the symptoms of over-population. It doesn't matter how clever the human race may become, eventually nature will sort it out and achieve a balance.' He paused to relight his pipe and then continued, his voice, as nearly always, gentle and reflective.

'Mankind is probably the most destructive creature that's ever lived on the face of the earth. Look what we're doing to the world now. But I think people are waking up to the fact that if we go on like we are now, life's not going to be worth living. The quality of life is rapidly disappearing. I know probably a lot of people think I'm a crank, but I rejoice in being a crank.' He gave his self-deprecating little chuckle.

He was pessimistic about the future of wildlife, especially in Kenya. 'One of the factors against wildlife is the incredible birthrate in Kenya, one of the highest in the world. Eventually, if measures are not taken to control the birthrate, the country won't be able to withstand this human pressure. When it comes to humans and wildlife, wildlife has to give way. That's really one of the alarming things about the situation. I believe that people are being educated now in family planning ... but to me it is a bit late for the wildlife ... [although] Africa without its wildlife would be a very different and dull place.'

He poured us another whisky and got up to fiddle with one of the lamps. The soft light burnished his white hair and turned his face into a golden icon. He took a sip of whisky and gazed into the darkness.

'If they want to have wildlife in this country, they have got to be absolutely ruthless with poachers.' The old man's voice took on a sudden vehemence now. 'As far as I'm concerned, I think that the life of one elephant is worth probably the lives of at least a hundred humans. It should be a capital offence for anyone to shoot an elephant.' It was uncharacteristically extreme, but only a few days before, and only four or five miles from his camp, we had inspected the pitiful remains of a cow elephant and her tiny calf, lying obscenely spreadeagled in the bush not far from where George himself would find his death less than a year later. Both mother and calf had been shot with automatic weapons, and their tusks – in the case of the baby they must have been pathetically small – hacked off with a chain saw.

As someone who had lived a life of exceptional freedom, I wanted to know if personal freedom was his greatest ideal. 'Yes, but freedom for animals of the wild. I don't think so much about the freedom of human beings; it's the freedom of animals. I think that animals, whatever they are, have just as much right to live and enjoy their lives as we have. Something that appals me is animals in captivity. I think that in this day and age it's a disgrace to the human race to have animals in captivity.'

The lights were getting low, hissing quietly now in the warm darkness; the lions were silent except for the odd snarl over a piece of meat; the moon was rising, a silver huntress, over Kora. The stars and the odd satellite wheeled above us, a reminder that the world is indivisible and that much of it is torn by war and strife. But here, for a moment, was a glimpse of an earthly paradise, where one man, at the end of his long and adventurous voyage, had, like a latter-day Ulysses, finally come to rest in his own Arcadia.

Chapter Sixteen

AMBUSH

When Inge set off for the airstrip in the Land-Rover at 12.30 on that fateful Sunday, 20 August 1989, the future looked as bright as the day itself. The night before had been one of the most magical she had ever experienced at Kora, or indeed in her whole life. Not only had the whole pride turned up at Kampi ya Simba and enraptured George and his German guest with their majestic roars, but the knowledge that Kora was going to be gazetted as a National Park had made George, and Inge for him, doubly happy. Suddenly, in the space of a few minutes, Inge's happiness was to be shattered for ever.

Making their way through the bush only a mile or two from camp were three armed Somali Shifta-cum-poachers. Whether they were simply travelling through the Reserve on their way from one place to

George's Land-Rover, with the legend 'All Aboard the Nightingale', in which he was killed

another, whether they were intent on robbery or on poaching elephant, or whether, just possibly, they were out to murder George Adamson, we shall probably never know. Whatever the explanation, the events of that day are etched in Inge's mind, burned into her memory as if by acid.

'About halfway to the airstrip – it's about seven kilometres from camp – I suddenly heard a bang behind me on the right. At first I thought a tyre had burst because just about every day we had punctures and had to change the wheel. But the Land-Rover was driving normally. Then I heard a second bang, and I thought, it's the exhaust, because the exhaust was broken and every so often it used to backfire. Then ahead of us, on my right, about eighty metres in front, I saw a man in uniform carrying a gun coming out of the bush and flagging me down with his hands. I thought, there's a ranger in front of me and shots behind me, I'm in the middle, so I should duck down because there's shooting going on. It was clear to me that the man in front was a ranger, because he was wearing a uniform and the rangers were in camp the night before. So I thought he was a ranger.

'I was crouching down behind the wheel. I'd stopped but left the engine running because I thought if I switch off it won't start again. Then I straightened up again. The people were in front of the Land-Rover, one in uniform, the other two in ordinary clothes, and Bitacha was standing in the road with his hands up. I thought, if I get out, I'll faint. Then they started shooting at the Land-Rover, at the tyres and in front, at the engine, very loud, several shots and the tyres went pssshhh!'

When the sound of those shots reached his camp, George Adamson left in a hurry. He would have guessed immediately that the shooting was the work of Somali Shifta or poachers. He would also have known that, almost certainly, they would be carrying automatic weapons, that they might well be deserters from the Somali army and that they would be tough and completely ruthless. Only a year before, they had ambushed and shot dead three Kora game rangers just outside the Reserve. He knew better than anyone that the Shifta, who had terrorised the northern frontier area of Kenya since the days of the British, killed easily. Whenever a gang raided a village or robbed a bus, they usually massacred all their victims; partly to eliminate potential witnesses; and partly, in the words of George's doctor, Andrew Meyerhold, an Austrian who has lived in Kenya for many years, because they *like* killing.

On that Sunday morning, several thoughts would have raced through George Adamson's mind: clearly the Land-Rover Inge was driving had been ambushed, so either she and Bitacha, the African with her, had been killed or wounded; or, at best, they had been taken prisoner and were now at the mercy of an armed gang. In the opinion of George's old boss, Willie Hale, now living in retirement in Hampshire, George's response was predictably 'quixotic'. Fired, he says, by a chivalrous impulse to rescue a damsel in distress, George, like Don Quixote, would have 'charged the windmill'. 'And don't forget,' Willie added, 'George was Irish.' Although normally extremely calm and self-controlled, he could occasionally 'go pop'.

Delaying only to take his revolver, which he always carried, and to tell his head man Mohammed to bring his old .303 with only four rounds in the magazine, he climbed behind the wheel of his second Land-Rover, bearing the legend 'All aboard the Nightingale', and set off with Mohammed and three other members of his staff, Hassan, Ongesa and Kiya. He must have thought speed was vital, or that his mere presence would be enough to save the situation; otherwise he could have opened the strongbox in which he kept three guns, a heavy .458 elephant rifle; a .264 high velocity rifle, which could stop anything up to and including a buffalo and was well-supplied with soft-nosed ammunition; and a double-barrelled shotgun. Mohammed, who had alerted George to the shooting, bears out the sense of urgency.

'I told George that those Shifta were enemies and asked him to drive slowly. But he was furious because he thought that Inge had been killed by the Shifta bandits. He was in a fit of violent rage.'

Inge, meanwhile, was only beginning to realise that the three men who had stopped her were not rangers. 'I switched off the engine, and then the one in uniform came to my side – the window was open – reached in and grabbed my watch. It had a bracelet which you have to undo, and he got it off. I must say for someone from the bush, who doesn't have that kind of thing, he was very clever with the watch. Bitacha was standing on the other side, about four or five metres away, and one of the others, the tallest of the three, came to that side and reached in to where there's a kind of box, in which George kept his binoculars and everything for a picnic. Everything was kept there. Straightaway he took George's torch, then the case with the binoculars; he ripped out the wire that charged the torch; there was some tobacco; he took everything. Then the one in uniform, on my side, opened the door and made me get out.'

From this point on, Bitacha's account differs sharply from Inge's in several significant respects. Firstly, Inge says the three Shifta had only two automatic rifles between them: Bitacha says equally adamantly they had one each. Secondly, Inge makes no mention of the Shifta breaking Bitacha's leg and says she did not know it was broken until much later. Thirdly, she makes no mention of George Adamson drawing his pistol and firing at the Shifta and indeed says that if he did so, she never saw it. Fourthly and most importantly, she denies she was raped, whereas Bitacha says quite categorically that Inge was raped by 'the short man wearing ranger's uniform'. Of the other two, one was tall and had on what Bitacha describes as 'a chief's uniform', a thick, dark-green or dark-blue pullover as worn by the army or the police, and the third man was dressed in a khaki shirt and black trousers. This third man, Bitacha adds, was known to both himself and George, which is not surprising as he came from Asako, Bitacha's own village near Kora.

After the short man in ranger's uniform pulled Inge out of the Land-Rover, she managed to shake him off and ran towards Bitacha. As she clung to him for protection, the short man came after her and hit her with an iron bar. 'It was at that point,' Bitacha says, 'that the [short] man [in uniform] took the woman away. As he was going he saw me and hit me with the iron bar on the leg, three times [badly fracturing his thigh]. Then he took the woman to the bush. I heard him tell the woman to take off her underpants and clothes. He raped her. He did not take her far. I could see them clearly. One of the other two men [the tall man], whom I knew as the man from Mbalambala [a village on the north bank of the Tana River, opposite Asako], said that I should be killed. That I should be shot. The other man said, "Let the man who took the woman finish his business and then we will kill them together. After all his leg is broken and he'll stay here, lying down. He can't move."'

Although Inge denies she was raped, she described to me in great detail the ordeal she had to face when she was forced to get out of the

Land-Rover. The man in uniform began to demand money. 'I said "nix money, no money" and turned out my pockets, I only had the keys from the store – I was wearing a pair of Bermuda shorts and a T-shirt – but I didn't turn out this pocket because I had a flick knife in it so I didn't show that. "Nothing, no money," just the keys, no money. I must have told him eight or ten times we had no money, "nix money," and then suddenly – we were standing beside the Land-Rover – he pointed to a kind of leather case to the right of the sun shield which was used for holding a knife. He pointed to it – apart from "money" he didn't speak a word of English – he pointed to it. I said I don't know who has the knife, perhaps he has, and I pointed at the other bandit. So then he shouted to the other one and he shook his head – he probably asked him if he had the knife – and he said "no." Then he shoved his rifle hard into my stomach and kept pointing at the leather case, and I said, "No, no money, no this." He kept going on about the knife. The other two were talking to Bitacha and then the one in uniform, standing next to me, kept shoving me back with the rifle, along the road, quite a way, maybe forty or fifty metres, and all the time:

'"Money ..."

'"I haven't got any."

'So after about fifty or sixty metres he tried to push me with the rifle off to the left into the bush but I refused to go. I just stood there. Then the tall bandit came up and they swapped the rifle and the tall bandit shoved me again, but hard, into the bush on the right. He started to hit me in the face with his hand and with the rifle and I kept going backwards and then I fell down and got up again, and then the other one, the one in uniform, came back. I kept looking over at Bitacha. He was all the time beside the Land-Rover with the third man, squatting down on his haunches, one bandit in front of him. I could see him because it was dry bush. The other two bandits spoke to one another but not in English.'

Finally, Inge says, the Shifta dressed in ranger's uniform took over from the tall man, after again swapping the rifle. 'The small one started again and I kept showing him my empty pockets, that I had nothing apart from my T-shirt and the key, and then I discovered that perhaps when I fell or was shaken, I had lost my knife. I didn't have it any more. It was a flick knife, black, and when you pressed it a long blade shot out. It was very sharp. It's the sort of thing I wouldn't normally have, but it was very practical; it fitted into my pocket and I used it to cut the meat for the animals, because there wasn't a single sharp knife in the whole of Kora. So I always had it on me. Then suddenly it was gone, it must have fallen out of my pocket.'

By now George was on his way and, according to Mohammed, was driving as fast as he could over the bumpy bush road. Mohammed gave his account of George's confrontation with the Shifta three or four months after the event, in Swahili, to Sue Gardner, a British Airways stewardess who was a frequent visitor to Kora. Not unnaturally, it presents the narrator's actions in the best possible light and should be taken with a pinch of salt, to say the least. For example, Mohammed says he was sitting in the front of the Land-Rover; Bitacha says he saw him jump out of the back.

'He drove the car at high speed,' Mohammed says. 'I think he was doing sixty kilometres an hour or more, and he kept pressing his foot on the accelerator. I asked him not to go so fast, as the Shifta bandits might be on the road waiting to shoot us. He wouldn't slow down; he kept going fast. I held on to his hand and said, "George, don't drive so fast." But he refused to slow down and changed up into third gear.

'I looked ahead and saw a Shifta bandit far away, aiming at us. I said to George, "Stop. I see a Shifta over there." But he refused to stop. The windscreen was hit by a bullet and fragments of glass fell on me as I was sitting in the front seat. I realised then that it was better to save my life, as George was not going to stop the car.

'I jumped out of the car while it was still going very fast. I fell on the ground and rolled over three times and then passed out. When I regained consciousness five minutes [sic] later, I saw the car was speeding into the middle of the Shifta bandits. I took the gun [George's rifle] and checked it to find that it had only four bullets in it. I thought at least I should save George's gun because if I tried to fight with the Shifta and used all the four bullets, they would have been able to kill me and take the gun. So I tried to escape.

'While I was running away, I heard someone calling me from behind. I stopped, lay down on the ground and tried to see who was calling me. I looked round and saw Hassan approaching. He had also jumped out of the car. I asked him if he had been hit by any bullets. He said, "No." I told him that George had been killed [this would appear to be hindsight] and that we should run to the camp and see who was available there and then run to Asako [about 20 miles away].'

Hassan's account is so similar to Mohammed's that one has to conclude they compared notes.

'After travelling for a short time, we saw a man on the road. He was wearing a kind of uniform, like a game warden's uniform. We told George that there was a man on the road but George did not want to listen. He just drove on. At that moment the man began to shoot at us, but we drove on and he continued shooting at us as we drove towards him. I then saw Mohammed grabbing the gun [rifle] and jumping out of the car. But we continued driving towards the man, and he kept shooting at us. Then I also jumped out of the car and fell over and the shooting was still going on.'

Inge, who insists she saw neither Mohammed nor Hassan jump out of George's Land-Rover, says the small man kept hitting her with his rifle. 'I fell over again. There were lots of bits of wood on the ground and I was going backwards, so I fell over again, and he bent down and hit me in the face and then I got up and saw George.

'I can't remember exactly; either he had stopped or was driving very slowly. I didn't hear him [coming] because the wind was still blowing very strongly. I was standing about four or five metres from the road and George was perhaps ten metres away in his Land-Rover [to Inge's right]. The bandit had his back to the road and he apparently noticed that I was staring at George and he turned round and ran to the road, over the road to the other side, making a kind of triangle, the bandit in uniform, George and me; the other bandit was somewhere on the road and Bitacha was still up there. I looked at George and he looked at me square in the eye and then he either moved forward or he was already driving along slowly. My Land-Rover was somewhere in front of him and, as George drove away, Bitacha came running to my side of the road, and then the one in uniform shouted something that I didn't understand to the tall one and then came the word "Adamson!" and George kept going and Bitacha, who was heading in my direction, ran behind George, sort of round the Land-Rover and straight into the bush. You know they wear these loincloths, he had pulled his up to the thigh and ran. He was gone, here, into the bush.

'When George drew abreast of me, we looked at one another and then, just as George drove past me, the bandit [in uniform] was sort of behind him, behind the Land-Rover; then the shooting started. The shots were one after the other and the glass splinters from George's Land-Rover flew in all directions, from the side and behind George. I only heard the shots. The tall one was some distance away; I didn't look at him at all, but I think he ran forward. He also started shooting. Both of them. Just as George drove past me, the window shattered and the shots flew past me, and one of them ran beside him and George kept driving and I watched George drive off the road to get past my Land-Rover, and then I thought, now he's going to break through, and I started running and got behind a tree. Suddenly I heard a cracking noise, exactly the sound a vehicle makes when it runs into the bush, and I thought George had lost control of his Land-Rover, run off the road and skidded into the bush. The engine stopped. There was one shot, and then another shot, and then I ran again, behind an anthill. I heard a few voices but faintly because the wind was so strong and then nothing more. And I lay there.'

If Inge *was* raped, as Bitacha insists, it would explain her otherwise curious lack of precision about those crucial, final moments of George's life which one would expect to be indelibly printed on her memory. For example, she says she cannot remember, when she first saw George, whether his Land-Rover had actually stopped or was driving along slowly. Then there is her rather bizarre claim that Bitacha, whose leg was badly fractured in three places, was able to run at speed some distance into the bush. Bitacha says he was in such pain that when he tried to run his legs gave way and he collapsed. Then, describing the shooting, she says, 'I only heard the shots. The tall one was some distance away; I didn't look at him at all.' Her vagueness is hard to explain if, as she claims, she was standing up, facing the road, watching the scene unfold in front of her. But it makes a great deal of sense if she *had* been raped, as Bitacha says, and was still lying on the ground, with only a partial view of what was happening on the road. Dr Richard Leakey, the Director of Kenya's Wildlife Services, who went to the scene next day, told me that judging by the scuffle marks on the ground beside the anthill, and a scrap of Inge's torn clothing caught on a bush nearby, he believed she was raped.

In comparison, Bitacha's account is remarkably clear and consistent. After describing how the Shifta in ranger's uniform had taken Inge into the bush and raped her, he says, 'Shortly afterwards, we heard the sound of an approaching vehicle [George's Land-Rover]. They were standing over me with their guns. As the vehicle came nearer, the two men with me shouted to the man in the bush and told him to come quickly. They told him to come quickly in Somali. He left the woman behind and came running. When he joined the others, the [tall] man in chief's uniform told the other two, "When the vehicle comes into sight, don't shoot the tyres, shoot the driver!"

'At that point, the vehicle appeared. It was as far as that tree. [Bitacha, who was interviewed near Kora eight months later, pointed to a tree forty to fifty yards away.] George did not see Inge. She was lying in the bush, behind some tall grass. He couldn't possibly see her. When the vehicle appeared, all three bandits attacked at the same time. The one who had a chief's uniform had a Kalashnikov [AK 47]. I saw all the shooting. The bullets hit the top part of the vehicle; others hit the windscreen. They showered the vehicle with bullets. When they reached this open space, the vehicle came to a brief halt. I then saw Mohammed and Hassan jump out. They ran away. They were in the back of the vehicle; George was in the front. When they ran off, George put it into gear – I could see both George and Ongesa. He started off fast and then slowed down. At that point he took out his pistol and fired about five times. He did not hit anyone; they were too far away, and when he started shooting, they ran off and took cover. He shot with one hand while he drove. I don't know exactly which man killed George, but I think it was the tall man who took cover in the bush to one side, behind the vehicle. He went to the side and shot from there where he had taken cover. The two in front only shot at the windscreen, but they ran away when George started shooting at them. It was the man who was shooting from behind who killed George. At that point the vehicle careered off the road and went into the bush. I got up and tried to run, but I had no strength in my legs and fell. Inge stayed where she was, where she had been raped. She did not move. I stayed there, silent, having seen George killed.'

Bitacha says the three Shifta went over to George's Land-Rover and took his pistol, but did not drag his body out of the vehicle. They also took his watch and knife and a car light. While they were searching the Land-Rover, the light aircraft, which had buzzed George's camp and landed at the airstrip, took off again and appeared overhead.

'It was the plane we had gone to meet. It first flew over us and then over the camp. It then came over us a second time. The Shifta were frightened and ran. I then saw Ongesa jump out of the vehicle and fall. He did not get up again. When he jumped out of the vehicle he was dying. After the plane had flown off and the Shifta had gone as well, Inge came over to see the old man [George]. She cried and went back into the bush. I saw all this while I was lying hidden, in pain. I vomited. I had no strength. I stayed where I was and Inge stayed where she was until six o'clock. I fell asleep in the sun. It was six thirty when a vehicle arrived from the Game Department. They stopped the vehicle and came on foot. They went first to Inge. She was frightened. They assured her they were game officers ...'

Bitacha is convinced it was the arrival of the plane which saved the lives of Inge and himself. 'They did not kill us because they were frightened by the aeroplane. Otherwise, having finished off George, they would have killed us.'

Chapter Seventeen

THE LIONS' LAST FAREWELL

With the departure of the Shifta, frightened off by the appearance of the small red aeroplane which Inge Ledertheil and Bitacha had originally set out to meet, silence settled on the bush again, broken only by the sharp buzz of flies and an occasional bird call. The sun burned down pitilessly from a cloudless sky on the two, shot-up Land-Rovers and on the body of George's old retainer, Ongesa, face down on the ground. In the dry, tropical heat, thick pools of blood congealed rapidly on the seats and floor of George's Land-Rover and began to turn black. His body, still behind the wheel, began to stiffen with *rigor mortis*. Kiya lay dead in the back. The two survivors, Bitacha, in great pain, and Inge, deeply distraught, lay motionless, praying that the Shifta would not come back to finish them off. Inge hid behind an anthill from where she could see only the top of her Land-Rover.

'Nothing happened,' Inge's account continues, 'and then I started to cry for the first time. Before that I hadn't wept and I hadn't screamed. I was absolutely calm and then I started to cry, and I thought that at any moment George must come and shout "Inge". [This conflicts with Bitacha's statement that after the Shifta had gone, Inge went over to George's Land-Rover and then went back to the bush in tears.] I thought, perhaps he isn't calling my name because he doesn't know where the bandits are. Perhaps he's hiding like me or he doesn't know what the bandits are going to do. Absolutely nothing happened at all. Then I thought, perhaps he's dead, but that can't be true because why should they kill George? Why? Because it was money they were after. Then I thought, they've gone to the airstrip for the tourists; they want money and jewellery. They knew there were people there because Bitacha had told them, and I thought, my God they've gone there, or to the camp, and since everything was quiet I thought of everything possible, except that George was dead. The thought only crossed my mind once and I immediately put it away because I simply couldn't imagine such a thing. Then, there was nothing for a long time, only the wind, or was that a car? Someone's chasing you! It was crazy, the whistling, I've never known such a wind in Kora.'

Inge saw the plane go over and says she waved at it but without getting up; the pilot did not see her. Aboard were a German Lufthansa engineer from Frankfurt, Werner Schillinger, a local pilot called Naveed Rasul and several members of a Lufthansa crew on a stopover in Nairobi. Rasul, who knew Kora well, says that normally George

Adamson or one of his staff would pick up the new arrivals five minutes after they landed. 'This time we were on the ground for forty-five minutes and then I decided, there's got to be something wrong. So we left the passengers on the ground and I and Schillinger took off to go and check at the camp whether the car had left to pick us up.' Schillinger says they took off at 1.30 and made a circle over the camp. They saw no one and that worried Rasul. 'Where had they all disappeared to?' They started to follow the road back to the airstrip and saw one Land-Rover on the road. It was the One Ten Land-Rover that Inge had been driving.

'We couldn't see anyone in the One Ten. I mean, not a soul. Then the other Land-Rover we saw in the bush, and there was a body, what, fifteen or twenty feet away in front of the car, lying on his stomach with his hands forward. It was a black man wearing a yellow T-shirt [Ongesa]. And that was obviously, you could see, a shooting.' Their immediate priority, Schillinger says, was to pick up the passengers.

'After landing we had a discussion with the passengers, and they said, "Well, that must be a trap, so let's go out right away."' They took off at two to fly to Meru Game Park, a short hop across the Tana River, but on the way they again circled over the two Land-Rovers. They saw no living person, only the body in the yellow T-shirt.

On arrival in Meru they 'alerted everybody, the police, the army, the anti-poaching unit, but unfortunately all the bosses were not there so they couldn't make a decision.' Schillinger says they landed in Meru 'at two fifteen, two twenty, and right away we were running to the police station there, reporting everything, and finally we gave the offer to take some police or army to Kora. But they said, "No, you are forbidden to land in Kora again."'

After the sound of the aeroplane's engines had died away, Inge continued to lie prone behind her anthill, in a state of shock.

'I kept wondering if I should stay where I was or if I should go and look for George: I didn't know if the bandits were still there but I kept thinking, If they've gone, George will come and find me. I was sure George would come looking for me; and then I thought it was better to stay hidden, or that he was having trouble walking, that he'd had a fall, broken a leg or something. All the time I tried to decide if I should stand up or not. To be honest, I must admit I was too cowardly to stand up. I kept thinking he must call, and if he calls I'll hear him. And I thought, if the plane flies to Nairobi, it will take at least an hour, another hour to find someone in Nairobi, police or whatever, and another hour to come back; that makes three hours. In three and a half hours a helicopter or some other plane must come. I wasn't surprised that no one came from camp because we had the two Land-Rovers. The only one who can drive is Moti [the tractor driver], and if they came in the tractor, they'd be like targets in a shooting gallery. I [also] presumed that Bitacha had run to the camp. I started to count, but by the time I got to four hundred, I didn't know if I was up to seven or three hundred because I kept trying to decide if I should stand up. What should I do?

'I had cried a lot and it was awful because I was covered in insects and ants and they went up my nose and everywhere else, and the tears, it was ghastly. I didn't notice that it was hot, but the insects were all over my body and I was itching all over, the ants and mosquitoes on my face where I had cried, in my mouth and nose, everywhere, and I was lying face down, with my arms out. I only moved once, when the plane came over, otherwise I just lifted my head to look. I didn't move, didn't turn. I thought three and a half, maybe four hours until help comes from Nairobi; nothing will happen in camp. I kept counting but since I was always thinking of something else, what had happened to George, I couldn't concentrate. Then with my left hand which was in the sun, I started to lay out little bits of stick and counted: one minute, sixty sticks. And I don't know how many thousand I had got up to, counting with my right hand: 'One minute, two minutes, three minutes.' I thought it must be three quarters of an hour, or an hour, but the sun hadn't changed at all, because the shadow of the sticks was just the same. I either hadn't counted right, or had got in a muddle. Obviously I was in a complete muddle and I kept wondering if I should move, and I thought, No, they haven't killed George, and if he's had a fall, that's not so bad.

'If he was sure about things, he would call me. I won't do anything. Help will come either with the plane, or Bitacha's back in camp, so I decided not to move. Time passed very slowly. I noticed the sun was going down, but I had no idea whether it was half past four or half past five. Then suddenly, after a long, long time, I saw, on the other side of the road, a good bit to the right, a man coming out of the bush in ranger uniform, carrying a weapon. Naturally, I thought, now they've found me. I lay absolutely still. He was looking in my direction and he started to walk in my direction, and I was sure he'd seen me.

'But several others followed him, and then he called out, "Help you" or something like that. And I thought, There couldn't be four or five bandits in ranger uniforms; and he called again "Help you" or whatever, and I called back, "Ranger?" which was stupid, because whoever it was would have said, "Yes." Anyway, he shouted "Yes," and the four or five came quickly over to me and lifted me up, or I stood up, I can't remember. I only said, "Quick, go to George," and pointed to where he was. They all ran to where George was and then Moti came along the road and he took my arm, and we went over to George. I sat down on the edge of the road, right where we were. I couldn't stand any longer. I watched three of them, bending down, kneeling, with a water bottle. They were some distance away, on the same side as I had been on. And I thought, George must be there; the sun is hot and they're giving him some water. Then a ranger came up, and I asked him: "How is George?" And he said, "He's dead."

'I started to cry. Moti asked me: "Where's Bitacha?" And I said, "Isn't Bitacha in camp?" "No." I showed him where Bitacha had run into the bush and Moti drove into the bush, not very far, and I saw him lifting somebody up off the ground. I ran over and saw Bitacha lying there with his foot twisted. I thought he must have fallen when he was running and broken his foot. So we lifted him into the Suzuki [George's white pick-up which Moti had driven to Asako to alert the rangers] and I sat in the back. We drove on to the road, and all the rangers came up to me.

'They began to question me: how many bandits, weapons, whether they had pistols, what they looked like, that kind of thing. Then Moti came up and said, "Ongesa is dead." "Did the bandits go to the camp, then?" "No." I didn't understand. Ongesa dead and the bandits weren't in camp. Then a ranger came up with some spent cartridge cases. The head ranger looked at them and said, "That's a German weapon [G 3] and that's Yugoslav [AK 47]. The German weapon is very good and shoots a long way." Then he asked me if I could drive my Land-Rover back, but I didn't want to. So I asked if nobody else could drive and they said, "Yes, yes." So I didn't have to drive. First they changed the tyres, but as usual it wouldn't start. There were four or five rangers with me in the Suzuki and they all went over to the Land-Rover and pushed it. Then I asked the time. It was a quarter past six. It was already dusk.

'We drove back to camp, first the ranger vehicle, then my Land-Rover and then the Suzuki. Hamisi helped me out; he was crying. He took my arm and I saw that they had lifted out George's body and carried it into his hut, and I also saw there were two other bodies. I found out for the first time that George had those two with him, Kiya and Ongesa. They put them in the first hut. Hamisi took my arm and led me over to the mess hut and said, "Look, Inge, at the eggs, the monkeys were here." They had got all the eggs out of the fridge. There's a long table there. I always sit at the top with George when I'm serving the food. Everything was covered in [broken] eggs. Then he made me sit down and asked me if I wanted something to eat and at that moment, outside [Inge began to cry], all the lions arrived, all, all the lions, right beside the fence. It was nearly dark but I could see them and I told Hamisi, "We must feed the lions," and someone brought the box. There wasn't much meat in it and Hamisi and I fed the lions. When I had finished doing that, the rangers wanted to use the radio, and I told them, "You can't use it until half past seven" [when the Laikipia security network came on the air]. I think they were hungry. In any case Mohammed said I should give some food for the rangers. I had the key. They wanted salt and milk, and I can't remember, everything out of the store, it was all the same to me. So I gave the key to Hamisi. Then I went to have a shower. I was so dirty and itchy. The rangers split up. I don't know how many there were, twelve or fifteen; their boss told me that they would stay there all night. I needn't be afraid, the bandits certainly wouldn't come to the camp. I told one of the rangers he should stand outside the shower. I was still afraid.

'After my shower, when I was in my hut changing, Mohammed suddenly came in. He had under his sweater George's big red purse, in which he kept all the money to pay the staff. It was usually [supposed to be] kept in the safe. But there were so many people there that he kept it in his hut because he always needed money to buy meat and pay bills. Mohammed gave me the money and said I should hide it; it was better if I had it. I didn't ask, how did Mohammed have the money. I think that George must have taken all his money with him so that he could give it to the bandits to release me. Perhaps he guessed that they wanted money. Otherwise, why should Mohammed have had the money?

'They were still trying to get through on the radio, and I said, "It's no good; there's no vehicle outside with a battery [to power it]." You know, it wasn't connected up. In any case, I can't remember what the [head] ranger did, but he was able to get through at half past seven. You have to wait your turn. When it was ours, he said, "SOS, we've been attacked. George Adamson and two others are dead." I can't remember the rest. I sat at the table; the lions were still all there, outside. They didn't make a sound. When they came, they just looked; they didn't roar; it was completely calm.

'When the ranger had finished radioing, he said, "Tomorrow morning, at six, help is coming." I should be ready; they were coming to pick me up. I told him that my air ticket and passport and everything else was in the safe and George had the key in his trouser pocket. He said I should go with him to George and get the key, but I said I wouldn't, so Hamisi and Mohammed went with the ranger and came back with the key and we opened the safe and got my things. There were cigarettes there too which I gave to the ranger and some batteries which we'd bought at Mwingi and left inside. Then we locked the safe again and the ranger kept the key. I went to my hut and packed my case. Hamisi helped me. I packed a few things; others I didn't want, so I gave them to Hamisi, my shoes, trousers. Hamisi took them to his hut and came back with my camera. He said he had hidden it because I had left it in the mess hut at lunchtime. I finished packing and looked over to where Bitacha was; he was lying outside his hut. Hamisi asked me where I wanted to sleep, and I said not outside, inside the hut, and I asked Mohammed to please sleep in my hut. There were two beds there. I was frightened and told him he should sleep in my hut. Then I went to bed. I had seen outside how the rangers were split up round the perimeter and a bit later Mohammed came back with the rifle and also lay down. And I asked myself, why, why did George have to die? What did they want? Mohammed had been nine years with George. What's going to happen to them all? Two were dead; they had no jobs. What was going to happen to Kora? I talked about it with Mohammed. We'd be silent for an hour and then Mohammed would say, "I just don't understand." We didn't talk a lot, just now and again. Then in the morning, at six, I heard vehicles. I don't know where they came from, more rangers and then a helicopter arrived, making a lot of noise; and then I saw that they had chopped down some bushes and suddenly a huge helicopter was there. At seven the head of the rangers came to me and said, "You can speak to Nairobi over the radio." I rang Franz Lang [a local pilot] and told him what had happened and asked him to come and fetch me straightaway. He said he would come immediately.

'I went over to see Bitacha. He had a headache and a stomach ache; everything was wrong with him. I gave him some tablets, I had lots of medicines with me, and made some camomile tea and then the big helicopter arrived with the press and photographers and Dr [Richard] Leakey [the Director of Kenya's Wildlife Services]. I didn't know who they were. Bitacha complained about his foot [in fact, it was his thigh that was broken]. I had an elastic bandage. I took the rag off his leg and we got some pieces of wood; he told us where it was sore, and I strapped his foot up nicely with the pieces of wood and the elastic bandage. The ranger held him from behind and Mohammed held his foot. Then I went back into my hut and lay down on the bed.

'I could see from my hut there were only two cubs in the compound so I went to find Mohammed and asked him, "Where is Rafiki?" – one of the female cubs. He said that yesterday, when the shooting started, all the cubs ran away and only Batian and Furaha came back later to their *boma* [compound]: Rafiki was out all night; she didn't come back. So I told him to get George's loud-hailer and call her, which he did and she did come and we tried to get her to go in with some meat, but she kept running away; she wouldn't go in. Then it all started, masses of helicopters, including a second big one, a lot of people, a real scrum, all going in to see George.

'The police came and asked for my passport and said they wanted to write everything up. I said Franz Lang, the pilot, must arrive at any moment and I would make a statement because he speaks English and Swahili; neither the ranger nor the police could speak English; nor can I. I had all my things ready but Franz Lang didn't come and at half past eleven Dr Leakey – they said they wanted my passport again – said I must fly back to Nairobi with them in the helicopter. Bitacha was on a stretcher and George – they'd put him in a plastic bag – he was lying on the floor of the helicopter. I sat beside him, and Bitacha was on a kind of couch and we took off for Nairobi. Leakey, the policeman and the reporters, they were all on board; there was room for about fifteen people.'

That night, Monday, 21 August, Inge Ledertheil boarded a Lufthansa flight for Frankfurt.

'For me, it's clear that they [the bandits] were no poachers, nor were they robbers, because they're not so stupid. They would have waited until I had been to the airstrip, [to collect] the people who'd arrived. They had money and jewellery. Not in the middle of the bush.' In other words, Inge believes George Adamson was deliberately murdered, the victim of a Somali vendetta. She is not alone in that belief. Someone as experienced as Jack Barrah agrees. First, he says, 'I believe that George was not hesitant and went in blazing away, into a typical Somali-style ambush.' Then he adds that 'Inge is correct that they [the Shifta] had every intention of murdering George, who was frustrating their efforts to have Kora de-gazetted as a Game Reserve, where they wished to graze their livestock in lieu.' It is also suggested that there was an added element of revenge for the shooting of Somali camels by security forces in Kora in 1988. Richard Leakey acknowledges the argument although he does not accept it. He thinks the killing was a mistake, and says:

'The situation as I reconstruct it is that the bandits were not after George *per se*, but took him on when he intercepted what was happening on the road, which was an attempted robbery. I think it was a miscalculation. They probably wanted to catch people coming from the airstrip to the camp, rather than people from the camp to the airstrip, or catch people going from the camp to the airstrip who were going out with money and possessions, not an empty car. I think it was a miscalculation. There are certainly reports that the Somali community in the area was angry at the periodic expulsions of their *manyattas* [camps] from Kora and held George responsible. There'd been an incident the year before when seven camels had been shot by the security forces in retribution for illegal grazing. The killing of a Somali's cattle is a very serious offence and will often carry a blood debt, and there are reports that a particular village (Mbalambala) vowed that George Adamson would pay with his life for the loss of their seven camels.'

But, Dr Leakey said, there was no evidence 'so far' [January 1990] to link the threat with the killing. The village said to have made the threat had been investigated and although an automatic weapon with ammunition had been found there, ballistic tests had shown that it was not one of the weapons used in the murders, despite the fact that it was alleged to have been one of the guns involved. 'So I think there's a certain amount of rumour and charge and counter-charge.'

Dr Andrew Meyerhold, who piloted his own plane into Kora more than 260 times in the thirteen years he was George's doctor, agrees with Dr Leakey that it was not a deliberate assassination. 'I quite frankly don't believe it. George was so easily killed. There was no problem. They could kill him with a rifle, just taking him out on his way from his hut to the loo in his camp, any time when he was walking with the cubs, any time when he was travelling. This was just a coincidence, that this woman [Inge] travelled on the road where these people were; it was sheer coincidence. The reserve is full of people walking for miles, for days, and particularly if they are bandits they walk from one place to another; they walk twenty, thirty miles a day carrying with them their ammunition. You see, at the same time, buses were being ambushed in the same area, many people shot, maybe by the same guy or at least the same kind of people, the same bandits, in broad daylight, because at night they never do anything; they never attack anyone at night. In broad daylight they used to stop a bus and kill everybody inside. This was happening every month, every six weeks; people were being attacked and shot and killed and for this reason: Kora was central to this area and all the bandits who were attacking anybody south of Kora would walk across Kora and cross the Tana River to go north. So it was a place where constantly bandits were crossing and for us it became increasingly dangerous to land there and visit George. We have been warning our passengers, "Please do not go out of the camp and do not travel around in Kora, because there is no security." For the past two years before George died the security was gone.

'We always said it is quite extraordinary that across the river people were being killed, to the east they were being killed, and south, yet nobody attacked the old man. All those bandits must have crossed, probably within hundreds of metres of his camp, and he was never attacked. I was increasingly worried. The local population really wanted to get rid of the old man – but they wouldn't kill him! – they just wanted him out. I thought that sooner or later one of his visitors would be shot, and if this happened the government would simply close down the camp and remove the old man and say it was not safe enough for anyone to be there. But I do not believe the attack was aimed at Adamson.'

Rick Matthews, a young professional hunter who helped Dougie Collins run the camp after George's death, would not venture an opinion as to whether it was deliberate assassination or random killing. But from his examination of the Land-Rovers, which he helped to tow back to Nairobi from Kora, he thought the attack was 'very well carried out', with 'a degree of professionalism, but also with a degree of nonchalance'. He told me, 'The evidence on the vehicle is that they fired in bursts of three, and I have it from people who know the G3s and other automatic weapons that to get controlled bursts of threes with accuracy, which is what they were doing, I believe, is very difficult. It takes a lot of training. I believe it was three bullets in each of the people with a doubt on Ongesa whether it was two or three.'

Rick Matthews confirms that while the bullet that killed George Adamson was fired from behind, he was also shot at from the side and the front. 'There was a bullet hole in the front differential of the Land-Rover, in the housing, which was just like someone taking a punch and whacking it in. There was a bullet hole just about where you crank it, and then one into the block. Then there were three from the side. There was one straight through George's door, which would have just missed his legs.

'I'm trying to think how much glass was left in the car. There was that one back window; it was almost as if he [the Shifta] had lifted his gun and shot it from quite high through the back of the car. There's one bullet through the back seat, which would explain the large exit hole in George. It was already rolling as it went in, incredible velocity those rifles have.'

Rick Matthews emphasised the cold-bloodedness of the killers. 'You've got to be pretty nonchalant after you've killed someone to stick your head in and pull the body back – which would have gone forwards – and lean over. He wore his watch on his left hand, so you've got to lean over and open the door, pull him over, pull off his watch. He had his mag light in the centre of the car; they took his mag light. They rummaged around a little bit; they took his gun, his knife. To be able to shoot somebody and then walk up to them and take things off them, you've got to be a cool customer. You've got to know what you're doing.

'I think he [George] was hoping that they would break and run. I think that's what he felt they would do.'

Not long after George's death, Sue Gardner, a British Airways hostess who had often visited him, made a last pilgrimage to Kampi ya Simba. 'I flew to Kora and drove with Moti, George's driver, down to the river to a spot where George and I went quite often, sometimes to swim, sometimes for a picnic or just for the drive. I could feel him all around. I remember I placed the flowers – roses, he said he'd like roses – not in any particular spot but in the waters of the Tana that gave Kora its life, so they could float away in a gesture of freedom. As I let the flowers go and watched them gently float away, I felt happy, so many memories. George may have gone but his spirit and memory live on.'

She remembers having a 'bizarre conversation' with George about death. 'We were walking the lion cubs round the back of Kora Rock and we came to a place known as Rhino Pass, where the path narrowed between a succession of large rocks, twisting this way and that and finally coming out at a small *lugga*. It's overgrown with foliage all along the rocks and we had to walk carefully in single file until we reached the *lugga*. It was a favourite place for the cubs; they would disappear into the bush and ambush you. On this particular day, they really had it in for George and by the time we reached the *lugga* they had made several successful attacks. George, who was laughing at their antics, said, "I've been attacked by bigger lions than you," and I said, "It would be strange if George Adamson should end his days being killed by a lion."

'He said he hoped he wouldn't be, although he hoped he'd die at Kora, not in some hospital bed with everyone waiting for him to die. He hated hospitals. He said he'd like to die in the bush and be left there so the animals could take something back: he could really go back to the earth and remain a free spirit in Kora. I said the chances of that were pretty remote as there was always someone with him. He asked me, if I was with him in the bush and he died, would I leave him if that was what he wanted? I said I wouldn't be able to. "Can you imagine me going back to camp and saying, 'Oh, George is dead. I've left him there because he wants to be eaten!' They would put me away, and besides," I said, "your friends and people in Nairobi would want to bury you properly: a full service, a grave where people could pay their respects."

'"God, how awful," was George's reply. "People could just come to Kora and remember me. They don't have to stand round a pile of rocks." "Well, that's the way it will be," I said. George said he hoped he would be buried at Kora with a few friends there; something quiet. He wanted them all to have a drink and remember the funny times. He also said he'd probably end up being shot defending Kora or the camp. He quite liked things to be dramatic. It's ironic he should die as he said, by the gun.'

Hamisi, the loyal retainer, for whom George was a friend as well as a master, breaks down at the funeral and is comforted by a fellow mourner (Chris Wood)

George Adamson's funeral took place at Kora on 2 September. Friends and admirers came from all over the world to pay their last respects to Baba ya Simba, the Father of the Lions, among them Dr Leakey, who gave the address. 'George Adamson,' he said, 'put Kenya on the map.

He was a man of incredible character and dedication who died fighting against people who would harm the wildlife he loved so much.' Virginia McKenna and Bill Travers were also there, as well as Tony Fitzjohn, George's extrovert assistant for sixteen years, Georgina [Doddie] Edmonds, the beautiful girl who helped to run Kora for seven years, Ken Smith, who was with George when they shot Elsa's mother, Monty Ruben and a host of other friends from George's various lives: from the Game Department, the *Born Free* days, and the last nineteen years at Kora. They all congregated a few hundred yards from the camp, on an open sandy space near Boy's Lugga, in the part shade of a big acacia tree. An honour guard of game rangers fired a volley of shots over the body and George Adamson was laid to rest under the wide African sky, beside his brother Terence and a lion called Supercub. There were unseemly scenes round the grave as cameramen and photographers fought for position, jostling and elbowing the mourners and one another. In a way, of course, it was an accolade.

Among the mourners was George's old friend, Major Dougie Collins. 'I do realise now,' he wrote to me describing his last stay at Kora, 'it was a mistake my ever going back. It was all so sad. I coped by day but the evenings were over long, for I missed our sundowners and storytelling under that stunted thorn tree as the moon came up, when we both reminisced of days long ago. [Dougie Collins stayed at Kora until early October 1989. He decided to leave when a gang of seven Shifta were seen on the opposite bank of the Tana. The staff threatened to walk out unless an armed guard was provided. None was forthcoming.]

'Incidentally, around the three graves [of Supercub, Terence and George] I planted a dozen desert rose trees. When I left they were in full bloom. Two days after the funeral I walked from camp to the graves (with an inadequate guard I must say), armed with a bucket of water to help the desert roses along. The previous night there had been a high wind and on my arrival the bunches of flowers and wreaths had been scattered, except for one wreath I remembered well, for it was professionally made with two long white ribbons. It had been brought up [to Kora] by George's godson, Jonny Baxendale, the son of George's old friend Nevil, from way back in the thirties when the two of them made their epic voyage across Lake Rudolf [Turkana].

'I noticed lots of lion spoor and saw where a whole pride had slept near the graves as though on guard. I then noticed a curious thing. The beautiful wreath in particular was now lying on George's grave in an entirely different position. Watching where I placed my feet, so as not to disturb the spoor marks clearly imprinted in the soft pink sand, I investigated. I picked up the wreath and clearly saw lion teeth marks on the ribbon and the wreath itself. From the cairn of quartz stones I carefully back-tracked the spoor of one large male lion to where it had evidently picked up the wind-blown wreath to replace it on the grave. There could be no other explanation.

'Now we all remember Karen Blixen's beautiful book *Out of Africa* in which the white hunter, Denys Finch Hatton, figured prominently. When he was killed in his aeroplane he was buried in the Ngong Hills. Shortly after the burial it was said that lion had been seen resting by his grave. This is as maybe. Finch Hatton was purely a hunter and had no empathy with lion – excellent fellow though he was. That I think was in the early thirties when lion were vermin – alas for the golden years – and I am sure that any lion seen near his grave [which was in a prominent position] would be there to look down the valley, prior to making an early evening approach to buffalo, eland or any other animal they fancied for supper.

'So please remember, these observations and remarks of mine are not made by some fanciful romantic but by a white hunter, professionally trained over the long years in bush lore. Back in camp that night, alone and in thoughtful mood under the same stunted thorn and moon, I saluted his memory with a few extra *wompos* [glasses of whisky], for the lions had not forgotten.'

George Adamson always maintained that lions had a telepathic sense which human beings had lost. If he had been away from Kora, even for weeks at a time, the lions always knew when he came back and would suddenly arrive at camp, materialising silently out of the warm dusk to greet their old friend. So he would not have been in the least surprised, although deeply moved, that his lions had turned up to pay their last respects, and he would have asked for no better send-off into the next world.

Although George's old camp has reverted to the bush and the birds and animals which used to come to his table have disappeared, I like to think his presence is still there, floating over Kora, as free as the Bateleur eagles that soar above the great pink Rock. He sleeps in a sand *lugga* next to his brother, Terence, where at the end he wanted to be buried. Boy's grave is only a stone's throw away and the lions which he returned to the wild and their offspring are all around him. At night, their roars reverberate majestically, an elemental voice which, he once said, he hoped would never be stilled. If he can hear them, perhaps a last ghostly chuckle will float down from some leonine Olympus where George and his heavenly pride, Boy, Girl, Ugas, Coretta, Suleiman and Sheba, Growe, One Eye, Maggie and Denis and all the others, including, of course, the incomparable Elsa, are finally, happily, gathered together.

PICTURE CREDITS

Black and white photographs

Matt Turner pp. 12, 14, 178, 179, 198
Elsa Conservation Trust pp. 24 (Collins Archive), 29 (Collins Archive), 57 (Collins Archive), 74 (Collins Archive), 76 (Willie Hale), 82 (Collins Archive), 90 (Collins Archive), 108 (Collins Archive), 165 (Collins Archive), 170 (Willie Hale)
Margot Henke pp. 70, 78, 89, 93, 97, 116, 122, 124, 129, 132
Michael Prynne pp. 71, 72, 92, 99
Dorothy Cooper pp. 54 (2 pictures), 55 (2 pictures), 58, 59, 60, 168, 190
Julian McKeand p. 80
Jonny Baxendale pp. 140, 143, 146, 149 (3 pictures), 151 (3 pictures), 152, 153, 154 (2 pictures), 155 (2 pictures), 158
Camerapix pp. 209, 230

Colour photographs

SECTION I

George and furry friend *Elsa Conservation Trust/Collins Archive*
Cubs from Haile Selassie's zoo (2 pictures) *Giles Remnant*
Boy and Girl *Giles Remnant*
Henrietta *Giles Remnant*
Boy with a bottle of White Horse *Giles Remnant*
George with one of the Kora prides *Zoocheck Charitable Trust*
Terence's grave *Sandy Gall*
Elsa's grave *Mike Shrimpton*
George and Abdi at foot of Kora Rock *Warwick Johnson*
Batian *Matt Turner*
George with Batian, Rafiki and Furaha *Matt Turner*
George with cubs in the heat of the day *Matt Turner*
George on early morning stroll *Matt Turner*

SECTION II

The Tana River *David Coulson*
Kora Rock *Sandy Gall*
Kora Tit *Matt Turner*
Main gate and guest huts *Matt Turner*
Somalis and camels *Matt Turner*
Carcase of an elephant *Matt Turner*
Prince Bernhard on the elephant-jaw loo *Ken Smith*
Marabou storks *Matt Turner*
Tony Fitzjohn with Komunyu *Tim Lapage*
Vervet monkey *Matt Turner*
George with dik-dik *Margot Henke*
George watching a hornbill *Sandy Gall*
Ground squirrel *Matt Turner*
Mohammed Maru *Matt Turner*
Ongesa *Matt Turner*
Bitacha *Matt Turner*
Hamisi *Matt Turner*

SECTION III

Georgina (Doddie) Edmonds with George *David Coulson*
Inge Ledertheil and George *Inge Ledertheil*
One of the cubs held by George *Warwick Johnson*
Carla Loeffelholz with a cub *Sandy Gall*
George on the Tana River (2 pictures) *Sandy Gall and Mike Shrimpton*
George setting off on safari *Sandy Gall*
Calling Growe *David Coulson*
George feeding Growe *David Coulson*
Lighting the Tilley lamps *Sandy Gall*
'Lord of the Lions' with eleven o'clock gin *Mike Shrimpton*
George celebrating his 83rd birthday *David Coulson*
The funeral *David Coulson*
Jonny Baxendale's wreath *David Coulson*
One of the cub's watching over George's grave *Jason Witney*

INDEX

Note: Arrangement is word-by-word, thus Elsa Trust precedes Elsamere. GA and JA are used as abbreviations for George Adamson and Joy Adamson respectively.

Page references in *italic* denote photographs.